FOREWORD

*B*ooks for the Journey is a guide especially for traveling the world between childhood and adulthood. This journey is rarely easy; happily, books can be sources of enlightenment, knowledge, comfort, understanding, and even wisdom along this often-tumultuous landscape.

Good reading is about expanding our capacities and understanding what it means to be human—whether fiction or history, poetry or biography, art or science. Through reading, we come to know the world in which we live. We learn about who we are and how we feel. Watching Hamlet struggle to come to terms with his destiny, we grow courageous about our own futures. Experiencing the hilarity of the offbeat Gully Jimson, a starving artist in London (*The Horse's Mouth*) we learn to laugh at ourselves. Poetry especially takes us inward to that mysterious world of metaphor where things are other than what they seem. At its best, reading can be a spiritual experience. Through reading we create rich imaginations which pull us beyond our own lives and into the fullness of Life itself.

A book is a ticket to another world. I discovered this early on, first in pouring over the pictures of my earliest children's books and later in creating the inner pictures that every good writer evokes. Besides the normal joys of swimming, hiking, and riding my pony, summer was a time to withdraw into other worlds. I had a book with a bookplate of a child reading in a tree. I took this to heart. Hauling my ever-patient beagle, Spot, along with me, I would climb into the cherry tree outside my house, position myself on a natural seat of branches, and read until someone called me back to my more mundane life and family chores.

By the time I was a teenager, reading took me into new worlds peopled by exotic colors and smells. I could be in India or Africa, inside the homes of the very rich and the very poor, inside the minds of saints and villains. But,

BOOKS FOR THE JOURNEY

A Guide to the World of Reading

Edited by Pamela J. Fenner
 Beyond the Rainbow Bridge: Nurturing our children from birth to seven
 Waldorf Education: A Family Guide
 Waldorf Student Reading List

Authored or edited by John H. Wulsin, Jr.
 Laws of the Living Language
 Proverbs of Purgatory
 Riddle of America

 Articles for:
 Renewal, A Journal for Waldorf Education
 Towards
 Independent School

Articles authored by Anne J. Greer for:
 Renewal, A Journal for Waldorf Education
 Orbit: A Commentary on the World of Education
 The Globe and Mail

BOOKS
FOR THE
JOURNEY

A Guide to the World of Reading

Compiled and Edited by
PAMELA J. FENNER
ANNE J. GREER
JOHN H. WULSIN, JR.

MICHAELMAS
PRESS
Amesbury, MA

Books for the Journey: A Guide to the World of Reading
© 2003 by Pamela J. Fenner

Published by Michaelmas Press

Attention corporations, schools, libraries, and book clubs: If you would like to use this book as a fundraiser or premium, please contact the publisher.

Michaelmas Press, PO Box 702, Amesbury, MA 01913-0016 USA.

Library of Congress Cataloging Data available on request

ISBN 0-9647832-4-X

10 9 8 7 6 5 4 3 2 1

Printed in the United States of America
Printed on recycled paper

The ideas, opinions, statements, and annotations expressed within this book are those of the editors. They assume no responsibility for inaccuracies, omissions and specifically disclaim any liability, loss, or risk, whether personal, financial, or otherwise, that is incurred as a consequence, directly or indirectly, from the use and or application of any of the contents of this book. The editors request that any corrections be sent to the publisher.

Illustrations: Getty Images, Inc. / Susan LeVan
Illustration adjustments by Z deZigns
Text design and production by Bookwrights Design
Cover design by Dale Hushbeck

In Memoriam

Christy MacKaye Barnes
1909–2002

Her love of literature and language lives on through
the teachers and students she taught and inspired

CONTENTS

most of all, especially as a teenager, reading allowed me to glimpse new possibilities and to explore the mystery of what it means to be a human being in all its myriad shapes and forms.

Here, then, in *Books for the Journey* are hundreds of opportunities to explore wonders, exotic and ordinary. It is a long-needed compendium of some of the richest literature available for young people and their elders. Its pithy descriptions of each book and easy-to-use categories will help readers, educators and librarians find rich and rewarding reading material of almost any description. It can serve as a guide for a lifetime of reading.

May the journey be rich – and, as the Irish say, "May the road rise to meet you!"

—Meg Gorman, Humanities Faculty
San Francisco Waldorf High School
San Francisco, California

READING FROM THE BOOKS OF LIFE

Reading is a quintessential human activity. One way or another, we spend our lives learning to read. As newborns, we discover human experience by learning to read the sounds, intonations, and rhythms of speech, especially our mother's and father's; we decipher their gestures and decode their expressions. We read the tastes, smells, and textures of the world. As toddlers, we begin to read the ever-changing terrain of the earth on which we walk. We carry this further throughout childhood, as our skipping, running, hiking, bicycle riding, snow skiing and more quicken our understanding of the surface of the earth. We read the water by swimming, the air by sailing.

We learn to read "The Books of Life" in the shapes, colors, scents, and life cycles of the plant world, as well as in the gestures, movement, habits, and sounds of animals. As we learn to read the weather, we discover the rhythms of the seasons.

We can carry the skills we acquire in the natural world into the realm of culture: we can learn to read art. Drawing, painting, film, sculpture, music, dance, architecture all write in strokes large and small.

In our modern world, beginning around age six, we also begin to learn to read the abstract markings of our alphabet. We learn the relationship of form to sound. Whether the moment arrives effortlessly, as a gift, or comes only after years of struggle, almost everyone remembers the exhilarating joy when these symbols magically transformed into language—language written, written language understood.

"There it is! Aha! Now I can read!" The mystery of the written word, unveiled. Now we are readers in full—readers of experience; readers of speech, of nature, of art; and, through the act of imagination, we are readers of the written word. We can read the thoughts, the stores of knowledge, and the hearts of others in and beyond our time and place—the inheritance of humanity.

Books for the Journey celebrates every kind of reading there is, expressed through writing. Each book is a trustworthy guide helping us read into life.

READER'S ROAD MAP

One of the gifts of a good education is a love of reading, and those who love reading can't help inviting others to share their favorite books. Teachers, especially those in the English department, are certainly among those who love and often prepare a yearly list of titles for their students' use, whether for course work or outside reading.

HOW WE BEGAN

We invited teachers and graduating students to submit their lists—the replies poured in, numerous and enthusiastic. As the lists came together and were shared, many other favorites sprang to mind, too good not to add. *Books for the Journey* came to include almost 1500 tempting titles. In the end, although our list has never stopped growing, we simply declared that it was time to go to press—but with a promise to ourselves that there will be future editions that will include even more books.

We have annotated these books with short descriptions intended as invitations that help you decide where to begin your exploration, where to go next.

FINDING YOUR WAY

In each of the five sections you will find titles listed alphabetically, followed by author, editor, and in some cases translator. All entries include the year of earliest publication and suggested grade levels.

We begin with *Drama, Mythology, Poetry, and Sacred Writing* because that is how literature itself began. All entries in this section include country of origin or the birth country of the author. *Fiction* also includes the birthplace of the author.

Titles in *Biography and History* do not include countries of origin but sometimes have additional category information. *Nonfiction* is categorized according to type, such as *Exploration*, *Philosophy*, or *Ecology*. *Seniors Look Back* is a gathering of well-loved books, chosen by Grade 12 students, not teachers, and includes a little something for everyone.

We like to think that our list will entice you into unexplored terrain. Although it was originally intended for high school students, we have come to recognize that it is a reference list that can be carried through life. Many adults who have had a chance to be part of the list's development have commented that they'd like to start reading or read again some of the books they left behind, the ones they didn't finish because they were so busy writing papers and studying in high school or college. Now that they have a little more leisure time, they'd like to pick up some of them again, often with the plaintive cry, "How many years do I have left to read all these?"

As author Edith Wharton reminds us, "Books have souls, like people". *Books for the Journey* invites you to meet many new ones, some to simply nod to as you pass, some to spend a little time with, and some to remain cherished lifelong companions. Happy Traveling!

LEGEND

= part of the curriculum of one or more of the schools that responded

= an "easier-to-read" book

DEAR READER

Baudelaire considers you his brother,
and Fielding calls out to you every few paragraphs
as if to make sure you have not closed the book,
and now I am summoning you up again,
attentive ghost, dark silent figure standing
in the doorway of these words.

Pope welcomes you into the glow of his study,
takes down a leather-bound Ovid to show you.
Tennyson lifts the latch to a moated garden,
and with Yeats you lean against a broken pear tree,
the day hooded by low clouds.

But now you are here with me,
composed in the open field of this page,
no room or manicured garden to enclose us,
no Zeitgeist marching in the background,
no heavy ethos thrown over us like a cloak.

Instead, our meeting is so brief and accidental,
unnoticed by the monocled eye of History,
you could be the man I held the door for
this morning at the bank or post office
or the one who wrapped my speckled fish.
You could be someone I passed on the street
or the face behind the wheel of an oncoming car.

The sunlight flashes off your windshield,
and when I look up into the small, posted mirror,
I watch you diminish—my echo, my twin—
and vanish around a curve in this whip
of a road we can't help traveling together.

—Billy Collins, *U.S. Poet Laureate*

Drama, Mythology, Poetry and Sacred Writing

Reader's Road Map

The earliest literature was born from a desire to speak to the gods through song, dance, and drama. These expressions crystallized into wise and beautiful stories of spiritual striving dating back thousands of years. Reading them today gives us comfort in our individual quest by helping us to understand the many upward paths upon the sacred mountain. We can also begin to see how human history carries echoes of these archetypal tales.

Drama emerged directly from the celebration of festivals to the gods. Forms and conventions from Ancient Greece, Medieval Europe, and Ancient China continue to influence the modern stage. While understanding that background is interesting, it is not necessary to enjoy reading plays.

Getting together with a few friends to read aloud is one way to read a play. Another is to be all the characters yourself, perhaps reading the lines for each character in a different voice, or hearing the differences in one's own head while imagining how the actions would be carried out on stage. A good play often demands to be read more than once.

This is also true of most poems. Some poems become lifelong friends from the first reading because they seem to share our most intimate moments. We want to keep them beside us, so we learn them by heart. Others require more time to get to know. Poets savor sounds and often readers need to do the same to get the most from a poem. Reading a poem out loud once or twice before looking up unfamiliar words is a good way to begin.

Sometimes it's just one or two lines or an image that stay with us to lend light to our path for years to come. Often poems seem to improve with age: we read the same poet year after year and marvel at what we haven't noticed ever before, like finding a small treasure in the most familiar of places.

Aeneid, The

Virgil   Robert Fitzgerald, trans.   Epic / Ancient Rome   📖 10, 11

Aeneas, son of the Goddess Venus, escapes the fall of Troy. Carrying his father on his back, he undertakes a long and arduous journey and, fulfilling a prophecy, founds a new empire for his people with the city he names Rome. (ca. 40 B.C.E.). Fitzgerald's 1990 verse translation is widely considered to be the best in English. (ca. 19 B.C.E.)

All My Sons

Arthur Miller   Drama / U.S.   📖   11, 12

Joe Keller, an airplane manufacturer who turns a blind eye to defective parts, loses one of his two sons in World War II, During the course of a single day, family secrets emerge that shatter the family's fragile attempt to return to a peaceful life. This play established Miller's reputation as a major dramatist. (1947)

All's Well That Ends Well

William Shakespeare   Drama / Britain   📖   10, 11, 12

Helena loves Bertram, a young count, and names him as her husband. He imposes an impossible set of conditions on her that she manages to accomplish by cunning; in the end, he realizes the depth of her love and returns it. (1623)

Amadeus

Peter Shaffer   Drama / Britain   📖   12

Shaffer's powerful drama explores a fictitious account of the relationship between the composers Mozart and Salieri. Antonio Salieri is the most famous composer in 18th-century Vienna until the young genius Mozart arrives. Salieri's ambition pushes him to desperate measures and the unexpected results haunt him for life. (1980)

📖 = part of the curriculum of one or more of the schools that responded

〜 = an "easier-to-read" book

American Indian Myths and Legends
Richard Erdoes and Alphonso Ortiz
Mythology / Native American   11, 12

One hundred and sixty-six well-researched myths reflect the diversity of Native Americans and the organic nature of their everyday lives. They are interesting in themselves and fascinating in comparison to classic Greek and Roman myths and legends. (1984)

American Indian Voices
Karen Harvey   Anthology   11, 12

A sampling of stories, poetry, songs, and speeches introduces younger readers to the thoughts and feelings of Native American peoples. (1995)

Androcles and the Lion
George Bernard Shaw   Drama / Britain   📖   11

Shaw's delightfully witty retelling of Aesop's fable portrays Androcles as a gentle Greek tailor who removes the thorn from the lion's paw. Later, Androcles reluctantly joins a group of Christians on their way to the Roman Coliseum where a surprise awaits. (1913)

Antigone
Sophocles   Drama / Ancient Greece   📖   9, 10

The third play in the Theban tragedy of Oedipus revolves around the theme of earthly law versus heavenly duty. Antigone challenges her uncle Creon, now king, in an attempt to give proper burial to her fallen brother. (ca. 490 B.C.E.)

Antony and Cleopatra
William Shakespeare   Drama / Britain   📖   10, 11, 12

Shakespeare's tragedy tells the story of the ill-fated love of Roman prince and soldier Marc Antony and Cleopatra, the beautiful Queen of Egypt. (1623)

Arcadia

Tom Stoppard   Drama / Britain   📖   12

Stoppard's brilliant play crosses several centuries and many fields of knowledge: literature, botany, landscape architecture, and chaos mathematics, as well as the tension between the romantic and the classical. He weaves all this magically together with several love stories and a profound mystery. (1993)

Arms and the Man

George Bernard Shaw   Drama / Britain   📖   9, 10

This comic look at the idea of the romantic idealist brings together a professional soldier, a lying heroine, and a romantic buffoon. (1898)

As You Like It

William Shakespeare   Drama / Britain   📖   10, 11, 12

The forest of Arden is the setting for this delightful comedy of exiled maidens, mistaken identities, court jesters, and true love rewarded, all with more songs than any other of Shakespeare's plays. (1623)

Ballads and Other Poems

Henry Wadsworth Longfellow   Poetry / U.S.   📖   9, 10

Longfellow was the most popular poet of his dayThis collection includes the "Wreck of the Hesperus" and "The Village Blacksmith." (1841)

Beowulf

Epic / Old English   📖   10, 11

The oldest long work of literature in English dates from as early as the eighth century and tells the epic tale of the hero Beowulf who slays the monster Grendel and Grendel's mother and is, in turn, slain by a dragon. There are several excellent translations. Burton Raffel's translation is often recommended for its powerful images and poetic strength. (1963) Frederick Rebsame's translation is commonly used in classroom teaching. (1971) Seamus Heaney's translation has a parallel Old English text. (2000)

Best Loved Folktales of the World

Joanna Cole, ed.   Mythology / World   9, 10, 11, 12

Cole has brought together 200 of her favorite folk and fairy tales from the oral cultures of Europe, Asia, the Americas, the Caribbean, and Africa. The excellent thematic index makes this an essential sourcebook for storytelling. (1982)

Bhagavad-Gita

Sacred Writing   📖   10, 11, 12

In this central Hindu sacred writing Krishna counsels Arjuna before battle. During this counsel, Arjuna is given answers to life's existential questions. Believers say that Arjuna represents every man, and the answers Krishna gives provide the basis for much of what Hindus believe. (2–5 B.C.E.) See *Mahabharata*.

Bible, The

Sacred Writing

The Bible contains the sacred texts of Judaism and Christianity. The Jewish Bible (or *Tanakh*) is also known as the *Old Testament*. See *Old Testament, New Testament, New Testament and Other Christian Writings,* and *Tanakh.*

Biederman and the Firebugs

Max Frisch   Drama / Switzerland   📖   12

Frisch's satire on complacency, misplaced guilt, and self-deception takes place in an upper-middle-class suburb where homes are being burned by unknown arsonists. Biedermann invites two strangers into his house, gives them rooms, and feeds them. Despite warnings from a farcical fire department, Biedermann refuses to see the truth. (1958)

Birds, The

Aristophanes   Drama / Ancient Greece   📖   11

The comedies of Aristophanes are the only surviving examples of the Old Comedy of classical Greece. *The Birds* is a satire of idealism gone wild and is frequently translated and performed. (ca. 400 B.C.E.)

Blood Knot

Athol Fugard   Drama / South Africa   📖   10, 11, 12

Set in South Africa in the early 1960s, this play tells of two brothers, one light-skinned, one dark-skinned, who experience the racial conflicts of their country coming between them. (1963)

Blues for Mister Charley

James Baldwin   Drama / U.S.   📖   11, 12

In a small Southern town, a white man murders an African American, then throws his body in the weeds. This act of violence, loosely based on a real event, allows Baldwin to present an unsparing analysis of the tensions and sufferings of centuries of contempt, brutality, and fear as truth prevails. (1964)

Bonds of Interest

Jacinto Benavente Y Martinez   Drama / Spain   📖   12

Benavente's masterpiece is a farce based on *commedia dell'arte*. In it, he asserts the necessity of evil. (1907)

Camino Real

Tennessee Williams   Drama / U.S.   📖   12

The dream-like setting is a walled community, from which the characters ceaselessly and unsuccessfully try to escape. Kilroy, the central figure, an ex-boxer, never quits hoping for something better in life than what he has so far been given. His story is woven together with that of the romance between the aging Camille and the fading Casanova. (1953)

Canterbury Tales, The

Geoffrey Chaucer   Neville Coghill, trans.
Poetry / England   📖   10, 11, 12

Chaucer's humorous, moral tales depict 14th-century English society through a frame story of a pilgrimage to Becket's tomb in Canterbury. Coghill's translation is the most often used. (ca.1380)

Canto General

Pablo Neruda   Poetry / Chile 📖   12

This epic narrative by the Chilean Nobel laureate encompasses the destiny of Latin American peoples through the history, geography and politics of the South American continent. Although its central theme is the struggle for social justice, it is nevertheless a deeply personal work. (1950)

Cheery Soul, A

Patrick White   Drama / Australia 📖   11, 12

This exploration of goodness, grace, and redemption is set in a suburban house, a seniors' home, and a church on the brink of collapse for want of a congregation. Miss Docker, the cheery soul of the title, represents the relentlessly blunt, practical survivor, who knows what is good for others, but in fact dispenses guilt and inspires rejection. (2001)

Cherry Orchard, The

Anton Chekhov   Drama / Russia 📖   10, 11, 12

A Russian family struggles to hold on to outmoded aristocratic values in a changing world. (1904)

Collected Poems, 1942–1970

Judith Wright   Poetry / Australia 📖   12

Judith Wright is one of Australia's finest post-war poets. Her work is marked by a compassionate activism that explores a broad range of contemporary issues. She writes of aboriginal rights, feminism, conservation, and the environmental challenges facing Australia. (1975)

Collected Poems of Langston Hughes, The

Rambersad and Roessel, eds.   Poetry / U.S. 📖   10, 11, 12

Langston Hughes (1902–1967) remains one of America's best-loved poets. Natural folk and jazz rhythms blend humor and sarcasm in his sardonic poems. This is the first complete collection of his poetry. (1994)

Collected Poems of Wallace Stevens, The

Wallace Stevens   Poetry / U.S.   📖   12

Stevens (1878–1955) is one of the most widely respected of 20th-century U.S. poets. His sparse, elegant poems include "Thirteen Ways of Looking at a Blackbird" and "The Man with the Blue Guitar." (1954)

Comedy of Errors, The

William Shakespeare   Drama / Britain   📖   10, 11, 12

Egeon, a merchant, finds himself in enemy territory and is given until sundown to find the necessary ransom. His two identical sons with the same name and their two identical servants with the same name have been lost to him, as has his wife. Much comedy results before they are all reunited. (1623)

Complete Poems: Edgar Allen Poe

Edgar Allen Poe   T. O. Mabbott, ed.   Anthology / U.S.   📖   9, 10, 11, 12

While recognized for his short stories, Poe wished to be lauded as a poet. Thomas O. Mabbott, eminent Poe scholar, assembled an exhaustive collection of Poe's poetry, fragments, and poems attributed to him along with annotations and explanations for the general reader or scholars. (1969)

Complete Poems of Emily Dickinson, The

Emily Dickinson   Thomas H. Johnson, ed.   Poetry / U.S.   📖   9, 10, 11, 12

When the remarkable modern visionary Dickinson died in 1886, only 11 of her 2000 poems had been published. Some 70 years later, all her poetry was finally brought together in this collection. (1955)

Complete Poems of John Keats, The

John Keats   Poetry / Britain   📖   10, 11, 12

John Keats (1795–1821) was one of the most important of the Romantic poets and made the pursuit of beauty the goal of his poetry. (1817)

Complete Works of Shakespeare

William Shakespeare   Drama / Britain   📖   10, 11, 12

Love poems and tragic and comic plays of Shakespeare (1564–1616) reflect the politics, morals, and conventions of Elizabethan England while offering contemporary readers much wisdom and humor. *The Norton Shakespeare*, edited by Greenblatt *et al* (1997) is one of several excellent editions of his complete works.

Conference of the Birds, The

Farid-Ud-Din Attar   Drama / Persia   📖   12

Attar's 12th-century Sufi poem was adapted for the theatre by Jean-Claude Carriere and Peter Brook. The Hoopoe challenges the birds of the world to set out on a pilgrimage to find their King. In times of doubt and despair, the Hoopoe tells them parables to spur them forward. (1982)

Coriolanus

William Shakespeare   Drama / Britain   📖   12

Probably Shakespeare's final tragedy, this is the story of a Roman general who is received as a hero and almost becomes consul until his arrogance and contempt for the people lead to his banishment. In turn, he seeks revenge. (1623)

Crucible, The

Arthur Miller   Drama / U.S.   📖   11, 12

The Salem witch trials at the end of the 17th century are used as a parable for McCarthyism in America in the 1950s. (1952)

Curious Savage, The

John Patrick   Drama / U.S.   📖

The widowed Mrs. Savage has been left a large amount of money. When she decides to give it to those in need, her children have her committed to a sanatorium where she meets fellow eccentrics very much in need. (1950)

Cymbeline

William Shakespeare   Drama / Britain   📖   12

King Cymbeline's daughter, Imogen, secretly marries; when this is discovered, her husband is banished to Rome. While in Rome, he is convinced of her infidelity and orders her killed. Imogen, however, disguises herself as the page, Fidele, and when the Roman army invades Britain, she is united with her husband. (1623)

Cyrano de Bergerac

Edmond Rostand   Drama / France   📖   9, 10, 11, 12

The romantic, dashing Cyrano with the grotesque nose never relinquishes his love for Roxanne in this play about unrequited love and sacrifice. (1897)

Death of a Salesman

Arthur Miller   Drama / U.S.   📖   11, 12

In this tragedy, the glad-handing, backslapping Willy Loman must confront failure when the truths of his life shatter his illusions. (1949)

Divine Comedy, The

Dante Alighieri   Poetry / Italy   📖   11, 12

Dante's epic poem is a vision of his spiritual journey to *Inferno, Purgatorio,* and *Paradisio* and is considered the most important poetic masterpiece of the Middle Ages. (ca. 1309–1320)

Doll's House, The

Henrik Ibsen   Drama / Norway   📖   11, 12

In Ibsen's classic play, a Norwegian woman finally breaks free of a domineering husband and her own oppressive subservient role. (1879)

Dr. Faustus

Christopher Marlowe Drama / Britain 📖   11, 12

This is Marlowe's version of a scientist whose desire for absolute power drives him to conjure up the devil and sell his soul. The devil fulfills his every demand but cannot ease his anguish of mind as he faces his final surrender. (1604)

Duino Elegies

Rainer Maria Rilke Poetry / Germany 📖   11, 12

These poems reflect Rilke's search for a spiritual path amid the horrors of Europe during and after World War I. (1920)

Elephant Man

Bernard Pomerance Drama / U.S. 📖   9, 10, 11, 12

The deeply moving true story of John Merrick, the victim of a hideous disease that distorts his face and body, is a powerful yet contemplative play. He is discovered in virtual slavery in a circus and rescued by a doctor. (1979)

Emperor Jones, The

Eugene O'Neill Drama / U.S. 📖   12

Brutus Jones is a Pullman porter who commits murder, spends time on a chain gang, and becomes the megalomaniac dictator of a Caribbean island, revealing O'Neill's theme of self-denial and redemption. (1921)

Enchanted, The

Jean Giraudoux Drama / France 📖   12

A comic love story about truth and illusion, a young teacher in a provincial French town is obsessed by the supernatural and falls in love with a ghost. The government inspector regards her as a threat to order and security and attempts to rid her of her obsession. (1950)

Enemy of the People

Henrik Ibsen Drama / Norway 📖 11, 12

An idealistic doctor discovers that the town's water supply is causing people to become sick. He is subsequently labeled an enemy of the people and forced to leave. The play rings as true today as when it was first produced well over 100 years ago. (1882)

Equus

Peter Shaffer Drama / Britain 📖 12

This powerful play focuses on an analyst's relationship with his horse-obsessed patient. (1973)

Every Shut Eye Ain't Asleep

Michael S. Harper and Anthony Walton, eds. Poetry / U.S. 📖 12

Subtitled *Anthology of Poetry by African American Poets Since 1945,* it includes works by Derek Walcott, Amiri Baraka, Ishmael Reed, Gwendolyn Brooks, and Rita Dove. (1994)

Faust

Johann Wolfgang von Goethe Drama / Germany 📖 12

Goethe's masterpiece introduces the devil Mephistopheles as "the spirit that denies," thus pitting cynicism against the search for goodness. In "Part I" (1808), Mephistopheles tempts Faust by offering to satisfy him with the pleasures of the earth, leading to the seduction and eventual death of Gretchen. "Part II" (1832) blends somewhat obscure symbolism into a prophetic realization of the need to unify the classical and the romantic in the pursuit of Truth, Beauty, and Goodness.

Fences

August Wilson Drama / U.S. 📖 11, 12

This powerful play by one of America's best playwrights is a slice-of-life drama set in a black tenement in the late 1950s through 1965. It tells the story of a garbage collector who takes great pride in his role as provider but builds fences between himself and others as he deals with his struggles. (1988)

Final Harvest

Emily Dickinson   Thomas H. Johnson, ed.   Poetry / U.S.   📖   12

Dickinson was one of America's most original poets; Thomas, a Dickinson scholar, presents the definitive selection of her poems. (1962) See *The Complete Poems of Emily Dickinson.*

Fires in the Mirror

Anna de Vere Smith   Drama / U.S.   📖   11, 12

Part drama, part documentary, part community theater, *Fires in the Mirror* tells the story of a tragic 1991 accident that set off a conflict between African Americans and Hasidic Jews in the Crown Heights neighborhood of Brooklyn, N.Y. (1993)

Four Quartets, The

T. S. Eliot   Poetry / Britain   📖   12

The four poems "Burnt Norton" (1936), "East Coker" (1940), "The Dry Salvages" (1941), and "Little Gidding" (1942) were published together as *The Four Quartets.* The four poems represent the four seasons and the four elements and blend together a fascination with time and the experience of modern Christianity. (1943)

Gilgamesh

H. Mason, trans.   Epic / Mesopotamia   📖   11

In this retelling of one of the oldest recorded stories in the world, Gilgamesh, the King of Urak in Southern Mesopotamia, seeks immortality. (1970)

Glass Menagerie, The

Tennessee Williams   Drama / U.S.   📖   11,12

Williams' sad story of Amanda and her working son and disabled daughter is semi-autobiographical. Tom is both narrator and character as he tells of his mother's overbearing attempts to prepare Laura for a "gentleman caller." This drama won the New York Drama Critics' Circle Award as well as the Pulitzer Prize for Drama. (1944)

Golden Ass, The

Apuleius   Mythology / Ancient Rome   **11, 12**

In this classic work, also known as *Metamorphoses*, the hero, Lucius, eager to experience the sensations of a bird, is changed by witchcraft into an ass instead. He retells many of the stories he hears including Psyche and Eros. (ca. 150 C.E.)

Grandchild of Kings

Harold Prince   Drama / U.S.   📖   **12**

Prince adapted this play about the life of Irish playwright Sean O'Casey from O'Casey's autobiographies. (1992)

Hamlet

William Shakespeare   Drama / Britain   📖   **11, 12**

Hamlet, Prince of Denmark, seeks revenge for his father's murder against his uncle but becomes immobilized by doubt. This classic tragedy continues to resonate with modern audiences. (1605)

Harvard Book of Contemporary American Poetry, The

Helen Vendler, ed.   Poetry / U.S.   📖   **12**

Vendler is a well-respected critic and professor at Harvard. Her anthology includes works over the past 50 years by 35 poets as well as their biographies. (1985)

Hedda Gabler

Henrik Ibsen   Drama / Norway   📖   **12**

Hedda, a newly-wed, beautiful, cold, and pathologically destructive woman, finds herself bored by her upper middle class life; a fire within her begins to burn out of control from the fuel of longing, entrapment and scandal. (1890)

Henry IV: Part I

William Shakespeare   Drama / Britain   📖   12

Based on a historical event that occurred in 1403, this play describes Henry IV and Prince Hal as they successfully quell the rebellion of the Percys at Shrewsbury. The enormously popular character Falstaff appears for the first time. (1598)

Henry IV: Part II

William Shakespeare   Drama / Britain   📖   12

The comic sub-plot involving Falstaff and his cronies balances the historic content of the rebellion of Archbishop Scroop, Mowbray, and Hastings against Henry IV. The king dies at the close of the play and is succeeded by Prince Hal, Henry V. (1600)

Henry V

William Shakespeare   Drama / Britain   📖   12

Henry V wins the Battle of Agincourt and woos Katherine of France in this patriotic play. The misadventures of Falstaff continue. (1600)

Iceman Cometh, The

Eugene O'Neill   Drama / U.S.   📖   12

In a skid row bar/hotel in 1912 a drunken collection of society's failures, drifters, pimps, police informers, former anarchists, failed con-artists, ex-soldiers, and prostitutes await the annual arrival of the big-spending, happy-go-lucky Hickey. This year, though, things will be different. (1946)

Iliad, The

Homer   Epic / Ancient Greece   📖   10, 11, 12

The epic depicts the last year of the Trojan War and includes tales of Achilles, Helen of Troy, the trick of the Trojan Horse, and the last battle of the Trojans against the Greeks. (8th c. B.C.E.)

Importance of Being Ernest, The

Oscar Wilde   Drama / Britain   📖   9, 10, 11, 12

Two young men seek the hands of two young ladies despite conventional obstacles. This delightful English comedy has become a classic of Wildean wit. (1895)

Inherit the Wind

Jerome Lawrence and R. E. Lee   Drama / U.S.   📖   10, 11, 12

Darwin's theory of evolution is debated in this courtroom drama of the famous monkey trials of the 1920s. (1955)

Inspector General

Nikolai Gogol   Drama / Russia   📖   12

Gogol's brilliant satire of bureaucracy and its impact on a small provincial town still rings true. (1936)

J. B.

Archibald MacLeish   Drama / U.S.   📖   10, 11, 12

This modern re-telling of the *Old Testament* story of Job takes place in a circus ring; God and the Devil struggle for Job's soul. (1958)

Jabberwock

Jerome Lawrence and Robert E. Lee   Drama / U.S.   📖   11, 12

The play is a fictionalized account of a young James Thurber growing up in Columbus, Ohio. It was written by the noted playwrights for the opening of the Thurber Theatre at Ohio State University. (1972)

Julius Caesar

William Shakespeare   Drama / Britain   📖   9

The tragedy of Caesar's assassination and its aftermath contains some of the most powerful of Shakespeare's speeches. (1623)

Juno and the Paycock

Sean O'Casey   Drama / Ireland   📖   12

In Ireland during the time of the Troubles, Juno Boyle discovers her family's impending inheritance and watches in dismay as the prospect of great wealth destroys those she loves. (1924)

King and the Corpse, The: Tales of the Soul's Conquest of Evil

Heinrich Zimmer   Joseph Campbell, ed.   Mythology   📖   9

These stories of our eternal conflict with the forces of evil include "Tales from the Arabian Nights," Irish paganism, medieval Christianity, the Arthurian cycle, and early Hinduism. (1971)

King Lear

William Shakespeare   Drama / Britain   11, 12

Shakespeare's classic tragedy tells the story of an aging king who disowns one daughter while giving his property to her two evil sisters. (1608)

Kings, Gods & Spirits From African Mythology

Jan Knappert, ed.   Mythology / Africa   9, 10, 11, 12

Maps, illustrations, and a guide to symbols support these 35 traditional tales from the oral tradition of the Zulu, Swahili, Ashanti, Bantu, and other African tribes. (1993)

Koran, The

Muhammad   Sacred Writing   📖   12

The prophet Muhammad is believed to have received divine inspiration between about 610 and his death in 632 from the angel Gabriel. This holy book of Islam is the prime source of all Islamic ethical and legal doctrines.

Leaves of Grass

Walt Whitman   Poetry / U.S.   12

Leaves of Grass went through nine editions in Whitman's lifetime between 1855 and 1890. The free verse poems, including "I Sing the

Body Electric" and "Songs of Myself", celebrate democracy, sexuality, the individual, kinship with nature, and the liberated American spirit.

Lesson from Aloes

Athol Fugard   Drama / South Africa   📖   10

The memories of three characters — a Dutch Afrikaner, his English wife, and an African American friend — are sharp reminders that the apartheid policies in South Africa affected the entire population. (1980)

Life of Galileo, The

Bertold Brecht   Drama / Germany   📖   9, 10, 11, 12

This play explores the conflict between the search for truth and religious authority that occurred when Galileo, under threat by the Catholic Inquisition, publicly recanted his acceptance of the Copernican universe. (1943)

Long Day's Journey into Night, A

Eugene O'Neill   Drama / U.S.   📖   11, 12

Written in 1940–1941 but not produced until after O'Neill's death, this play is considered his masterpiece and is the semi-autobiographical account of a highly dysfunctional family. (1956)

Love's Labours Lost

William Shakespeare   Drama / Britain   📖   10, 11, 12

The King of Navarre and three of his lords take a vow to study and fast and look not on women for a period of three years. However, the arrival of the princess of France and her attendant ladies causes complications. (1598)

Macbeth

William Shakespeare   Drama / Britain   📖   9

In this Shakespearean masterpiece, a Scottish king attains power through greed and murder with the help of his wife. (1606)

Madwoman of Chaillot, The

Jean Giraudoux   Drama / France   📖   12

Vendors, rag pickers, musicians and other street people gather in a cafe in Paris. The reigning queen is the countess, the "madwoman," humored in her claim to nobility. When prospectors, presidents and press agents, representing capitalism and materialism, threaten with a development project, the little people set out to foil them. (1945)

Mahabharata

Sacred Writing   📖   11, 12

One of the two great Sanskrit epics and probably the longest poem in the world, it tells the story of a civil war waged between the five Pandava brothers and their one hundred step-brothers. It includes the *Bhagavad-Gita*. (ca. 400 C. E.)

Major Barbara

George Bernard Shaw   Drama / Britain   📖   11, 12

Young Barbara, the daughter of a millionaire armaments manufacturer, turns against capitalism and becomes a Salvation Army worker; a series of revelations causes her to re-examine her hastily drawn conclusions. (1907)

Man for All Seasons

Robert Bolt   Drama / Britain   📖   10, 11, 12

Bolt's play depicts the struggle for absolute power by Henry VIII against the conscience and faith of Sir Thomas More. (1960)

Master Builder, The

Henrik Ibsen   Drama / Norway   📖   11, 12

A master builder of family homes in 19th-century Norway is coming to the end of his life, despairing of his work and caught in a loveless marriage. When a young woman from the mountains visits him, he finds a new vision of himself and his future. (1892)

Matchmaker, The

Thornton Wilder   Drama / U.S.   📖   12

In New York and Yonkers of the 1890s, the scheming Dolly Gallagher Levi is determined to find love for a cranky, middle-aged merchant and his overworked and underpaid clerks. In the end, Dolly unexpectedly finds love herself. (1955)

Member of the Wedding, The

Carson McCullers   Drama / U.S.   📖   9

A 12-year-old motherless girl imagines she will join her brother and his wife on their honeymoon and in their future life. Her loneliness and insecurity is poured out during kitchen conversations with the family's African American cook and with her dying six-year-old cousin. (1946)

Merchant of Venice, The

William Shakespeare   Drama / Britain   📖   10, 11, 12

Antonio borrows money from the moneylender, Shylock, on the condition that he will forfeit a "pound of his flesh" if the money is not repaid on time. (1600)

Merry Wives of Windsor

William Shakespeare   Drama / Britain   📖   10, 11, 12

Falstaff woos the wives of two rich gentlemen but, foolishly, sends the same love letter to both resulting in delicious comedy. (1623)

Midsummer Night's Dream, A

William Shakespeare   Drama / Britain   📖   9, 12

Young lovers and a band of guildsmen are led on a merry chase by the fairy world as they prepare a play for a noble wedding. (1600)

Misanthrope, The

Molière   Drama / France   📖   11

A wonderful comedy; Alceste has become so bitter toward the superficiality and hypocrisy of society that he declares an extravagant personal war with the world, under the banner of truthfulness. (1666)

Morte d' Arthur, Le

Thomas Mallory   Poetry / England   📖   11

Mallory's classic poem combines many tales of Arthurian legend, and shows the end of Arthur's reign, the Round Table, and the quest for the Holy Grail by Lancelot and Galahad. (1485)

Mother Courage

Bertold Brecht   Drama / Germany   📖   11

Written in response to the outbreak of World War II, Brecht tells the story of a stubborn old woman who travels back and forth across Europe selling provisions to the soldiers from her wagon. One by one, her children are devoured by war, but she will not give up her livelihood. (1941)

Mourning Becomes Electra

Eugene O'Neill   Drama / U.S.   📖   11, 12

O'Neill adapts the mythological story of Clytemnestra, Agamemnon, and their children to the aftermath of the American Civil War. (1931)

Mouse that Roared, The

Leonard Wibberley   Drama / Ireland   📖   12

A small European country finds itself facing financial ruin and decides that the only way to rescue itself is to declare war on the United States and lose. Hilarious consequences follow. (1955)

Mousetrap, The

Agatha Christie   Drama / Britain   📖   10, 11, 12

Probably the longest-running play of the 20th century, this murder mystery, set in an English country house, is Christie at her best. (1952)

Much Ado About Nothing

William Shakespeare   Drama / Britain   📖   10, 11, 12

Beatrice and the sworn bachelor Benedick mock each other. When their friends contrive to make them each think the other is truly in love, the mocking fades to sincerity. (1600)

Murder in the Cathedral

T. S. Eliot   Drama / Britain   📖   10, 11, 12

This is a powerful and poetic retelling of the story of the life and assassination of the 12th-century archbishop Thomas à Becket who dared to defy King Henry II. (1935)

Mythology: Timeless Tales of Gods and Heroes

Edith Hamilton   Mythology   10, 11, 12

This collection of Greek, Roman, and Norse tales bring the glory of their ancient gods to life. (1942)

Myths of the World

Padraic Colum   Mythology   📖   9

Originally titled *Orpheus: Myths of the World*, this selection of powerful myths with background notes includes tales from Egypt, Mesopotamia, Greece, Rome, and Celtic Europe told in Collum's poetic language. (1930)

New and Selected Poems

Mary Oliver   Poetry / U.S.   📖   10, 11, 12

Oliver has become one of the best-loved modern poets for her deceptively simple meditations on nature and self-exploration. This volume, spanning three decades, won the National Book Award for Poetry. (1992)

New Testament, The

Sacred Writing   📖   11

The *New Testament* gathers together stories of Jesus from his birth, ministry and death: the story of the conversion and works of St. Paul; the acts of early disciples; St. Peter's vision for the early church; and the description of the apocalyptic vision of St. John. Paul's writings (minus those attributed to him but considered to be written by others) date as a whole from ca. 40–70 C.E. The other books date from ca. 130–200 C.E.

New Testament and Other Christian Writings

Bart D. Ehrman, ed.   Sacred Writing   📖   11

This reader in early Christianity presents all the texts of known Christian authors written during the first two centuries of the church. It includes the *New Testament* itself as well as other significant early Christian writings in new translations with excellent introductions to each text. (1997)

Nibelungenlied

A. T. Hatto, trans.   Poetry / Germany   📖   11

The story of Siegfried and Kriemhild as told in the translation of a 13th-century version of the tale differs significantly from the original Icelandic saga. Here, the romantic love of Kriemhild for Siegfried turns her against her blood family. Rather than Kriemhild avenging her brothers, she kills them to avenge Siegfried. This shift is clear evidence of the change from Epic to Romance in European literature in 12th and 13th-century Europe. (1965)

Nicholas Nickleby

Tim Kelly   Drama / U.S.   9, 10, 11, 12

An upright and independent young man cares for his mother and sister after his father's death in this adaptation of Dickens' novel. (1982)

Night Thoreau Spent in Jail, The

Jerome Lawrence and Robert E. Lee   Drama / U.S.   📖   12

Thoreau chooses to go to jail rather than pay taxes to a government that is conducting what he feels is an unjust war in Mexico. The play incorporates flashbacks from his earlier life. When Emerson visits him on the other side of the bars, Thoreau engages his former hero in a timeless debate about the role of the citizen in a democratic country. (1975)

Odyssey, The

Homer   Epic / Ancient Greece   📖   10, 11, 12

After the fall of Troy, Odysseus journeys for 20 years, facing adventures stirred up by angry gods as he seeks to return and reclaim his kingdom and his wife. This ancient epic remains exciting reading. (8th c. B.C.E.)

Oedipus Rex

Sophocles   Drama / Ancient Greece   📖   11, 12

Sophocles depicts the fate of Oedipus who is unable to avoid the curse cast upon the house of Thebes and unknowingly fulfills dire prophecies. (ca. 490 B.C.E.)

Old Possum's Book of Practical Cats

T. S. Eliot   Poetry / Britain   📖   9, 10

T. S. Eliot adored the nonsense poetry of Edward Lear and originally wrote these poems to delight children. They have since gained wide popularity and the musical adaptation, *Cats,* achieved remarkable success. (1939)

Old Testament

Sacred Writing   📖   10, 11, 12

This is the name Christians give to the Bible of the Jewish people. Written in Hebrew and called the *Tanakh* it consists of 39 books, which include the Five Books of Moses (the *Torah*), the Prophets (Joshua through Malachi as arranged in the Hebrew Bible — called *Nevi'im* in Judaism), and the Writings (Psalms through 2 Chronicles as arranged in the Hebrew Bible — called *Kethuvim* in Judaism). The *Torah* is thought to have been codified ca. 550–400 B.C.E; the Prophets — ca. 300–200 B.C.E; and the Writings — 90–200 C.E.

Once in a Lifetime

George Kaufman   Drama / U.S.   📖   12

The play centers on three vaudevillians that go to Hollywood at the dawn of sound films to start a school of elocution. Two of the vaudevillians fall in love. (1937)

Othello
William Shakespeare   Drama / Britain   📖   11, 12

Misguided jealousy undermines Othello's love for Desdemona and results in murder. This tragedy of betrayal and deception is set in Venice and Cyprus. (1622)

Our Town
Thornton Wilder   Drama / U.S.   📖   9, 10

Wilder's moving play reveals archetypal patterns in its story about the youth, courtship, marriage, and separation by death of Emily and George in the small village of Grover's Corners, New Hampshire. The drama earned a Pulitzer Prize and quickly became a classic. (1938)

Parsival
Wolfram von Eschenbach   Poetry / Germany   📖   11

This 13th-century Grail Romance is the first European story of the quest for meaning. Considered by Joseph Campbell to be the most important myth for our time, it is essential reading for Grade 11 students in Waldorf schools worldwide.

Peer Gynt
Henrik Ibsen   Drama / Norway   📖   12

Ibsen moves through Scandinavian oral folk traditions, the Moroccan coast, the Sahara Desert, and the absurd images of a Cairo madhouse in this portrayal of one of modern drama's first anti-heroes. A highly imaginative, irresponsible youth, Peer grows into a self-seeking opportunist who, finally, is forced to confront the choices he has made. (1867)

Pisan Cantos LXXIV –LXXXIV, The
Ezra Pound   Poetry / U.S.   📖   12

Currently published as part of *The Cantos of Ezra Pound*, *The Pisan Cantos* are inspired by the landscape, events, and experiences Pound witnessed in his adopted homeland of Italy and reflect his love for that land's history and culture. Pound was the most influential of early 20th-century poets. He edited much of T. S. Eliot's work, was secretary to W. B. Yeats, and was a founder of Imagism. (1948)

Poems of Dylan Thomas, The

Dylan Thomas   Poetry / Britain / Wales   📖   11, 12

Thomas was one of the best-loved poets of the 20th century. Published after his death, this collection includes "Fern Hill" and "Do Not Go Gentle into That Good Night." (1971)

Poetry Handbook, A

Mary Oliver   Poetics   📖   12

Oliver's small handbook gives indispensable advice on sound, line (length, meter, breaks), poetic forms, tone, imagery, and revision, well illustrated by a small number of her favorite poems. (1994) See *Rules for the Dance: A Handbook for Writing and Reading Metrical Verse.* (1998)

Poetry of Black America: Anthology of the 20th Century

Arnold Adoff, ed.   Poetry / U.S.   📖   12

Adoff includes more than 600 poems by over 140 African American writers with an introduction by Gwendolyn Brooks. (1973)

Poetry of John Greenleaf Whittier, The: A Readers' Edition

John Greenleaf Whittier   William Jolliff, ed.   9, 10, 11, 12

Joliff has organized the 19th-century poet's selections in four thematic groupings: the crusading abolitionist political prophet, the nostalgic recorder of a vanished rural past, the hardy balladeer of New England history, and the contemplative Quaker mystic. Includes 56 of his finest works along with sensitive introductions. (2000)

Poetry of Robert Frost, The

Robert Frost   Poetry / U.S.   📖   9, 10, 11, 12

One of America's best-loved poets describes life in New England in a remarkable combination of the down-to-earth and the transcendent. A Pulitzer Prize-winner. (1930)

Portable Romantic Poets

W. H. Auden and N. H. Pearson, eds.   Poetry / Britain and U.S.   📖   10

Poems of 27 British and American poets from 1750 to 1850 are arranged in chronological order with a clear introduction to their historical context. It includes a time line of contemporary publications, art exhibits, music, and events, such as "Watt's Steam Engine Patented" and "Lewis and Clark Expedition." (1977)

Primal Myths

Barbara C. Sproul   Mythology   📖   9

This anthology of creation myths from around the world includes accounts of the beginning of life, the earth, and people from every continent, from the familiar Genesis story to tales from dozens of indigenous cultures. (1979)

Prufrock and Other Observations

T. S. Eliot   Poetry / Britain   📖   12

Eliot's first volume of verse earned him the reputation of one of the best of 20th-century poets. It includes "The Love Song of J. Alfred Prufrock." (1917)

Pygmalion

George Bernard Shaw   Drama / Britain   📖   11, 12

On a bet, a linguistics expert in London transforms a cockney flower girl into an elegant lady and passes her off as a Duchess. It was later adapted into the Broadway musical, *My Fair Lady.* (1913)

Questions About Angels

Billy Collins   Poetry / U.S.   📖   9, 10, 11, 12

Collins was appointed U.S. Poet Laureate in 2001, a post that offers a unique opportunity to bring more exposure of this form of literary artistry to the general public. His work has been lauded for its imagery, reverence, humor, and accessibility. This collection has been described as "a book for the body and soul." (1991)

Raisin in the Sun, A

Lorraine Hansberry   Drama / U.S.   📖   11, 12

An African American family, led by a strong matriarch, moves up to a middle-class Chicago neighborhood but wonder what they have given up in exchange in this groundbreaking, realistic drama. (1959)

Ramayana, The

Epic / Sanskrit   📖   10, 11

One of the two great Sanskrit epics (the other is *the Mahabharata*), tells the story of Rama, cast out of his kingdom, needing the help of the monkey-king to rescue his beloved wife Sita. (ca. 300 B.C.E.)

Riding the Earthboy

James Welch   Poetry / Native American   11, 12

Welch offers a collection of 40 poems about Native American life. (1998)

Rivals, The

Richard Sheridan   Drama / Britain   📖   11, 12

Sheridan's delightful farce introduced to the world the much beloved Mrs. Malaprop who is proud of her large vocabulary although she doesn't know what most of the words mean. The love story of Captain Absolute and Lydia Languish is full of disguises, mistaken identities, and close calls. (1775)

Robert Browning: Selected Poems

Robert Browning   Daniel Karlin, ed.   Poetry / Britain   📖 10, 11, 12

Robert Browning (1812–1889) is considered one of the most important of British Victorian poets. His dramatic monologues portray complex psychological characters and blend rhythm with form. Originally published in 1896. (2001)

Romeo and Juliet

William Shakespeare   Drama / Britain   📖   9, 10

Considered one of the greatest love stories of all time, star-crossed lovers find and lose each other amid a family feud. (1597)

Rosencrantz and Guildenstern are Dead

Tom Stoppard   Drama / Britain   📖   11, 12

Rosencrantz and Guildenstern are minor characters in Shakespeare's *Hamlet*. Stoppard gives them an entire play of their own in which Hamlet is the bit player. Stoppard's wit and humor delight, but the metaphysical questions that are raised throughout outlast the laughter. This is an excellent companion to *Hamlet*. (1967)

Royal Hunt of the Sun, The

Peter Shaffer   Drama / Britain   📖   11, 12

Shaffer's epic about the conquest of Peru by the Spanish is powerfully written and brilliantly theatrical. (1965)

Rules for the Dance: A Handbook for Writing and Reading Metrical Verse

Mary Oliver   Poetics   📖   10

Oliver offers a useful tool for the practicing poet. "Part One" is twelve brief chapters on technique such as Breath, Line Length, and Meter in Non-Metric Verse. "Part Two" is a single chapter on Style. "Part Three" explores scansion for both reader and writer. "Part Four" is a succinct statement on the timelessness of poetry. "Part Five" is a short illustrative anthology. (1998)

Russian Fairy Tales

Aleksandr Afanasyev   Mythology   📖   12

This collection of nearly 200 traditional folk and fairy tales is the most comprehensive text available in English. (1945)

Saga of Burnt Njal

M. Magnusson, trans.   Epic / Norse   📖   10, 11

The best-known of the Norse family sagas tells the story of Gunnarr and his wife, Hallgeror. (ca. 12th c.)

Saint Joan

George Bernard Shaw   Drama / Britain   📖   11, 12

Although probably not historically accurate, Shaw's portrayal of Joan of Arc as a spirited rebel against convention is considered one of his finest plays. (1924)

School for Scandal, The

Richard B. Sheridan   Drama / Britain   📖   11, 12

The making and undoing of the fortunes of two very different brothers provides the framework for this delightful comedy of manners. One of the best of English dramas. (1777)

Seagull, The

Anton Chekhov   Drama / Russia   📖   12

Chekhov's story of the fragility of young and innocent love and its inevitable destruction remains a classic. (1896)

Secrets from the Center of the World

Joy Harjo   Poetry / Native American   📖   10, 11, 12

This moving collection of prose poems is paired with photographs of complementary landscapes from Arizona, New Mexico, and Utah. (1989)

Selected Poetry of Robinson Jeffers, The

Robinson Jeffers   Poetry / U.S.   📖   12

Jeffers (1887–1962) is one of the great 20th-century poets. His poetry resonates with what he termed "Inhumanism," the insignificance of individual human life in the enduring processes of nature. (1941)

Shaking the Pumpkin

Jerome Rothenberg   Poetry / US   📖   11, 12

This collection of Native American poetry in which traditional elements of dance, vowel changes, ethnography, and movement are made evident. (1972)

She Stoops to Conquer

Oliver Goldsmith   Drama / Britain 📖   10, 11, 12

A delightful romp results when two young gentlemen, intending to pay a visit to a prospective marriage partner, mistake her family home for an inn. This is one of the best known of English plays. (1773)

Shelley's Poetry and Prose

Reiman and Fraistat, eds.   Poetry / Britain 📖   11, 12

Percy Bysshe Shelley lived from 1792 to 1822. He was a prolific poet and is considered one of the most important of the British Romantics. This 2nd edition of the Norton Critical Editon reflects the increased interest in Shelley in the past five years by scholars and the public. (2002)

Sir Gawain and the Green Knight

Burton Raffel, trans.   Poetry / England 📖   10

Sir Gawain, in his loyalty to King Arthur, accepts the challenge to behead the enormous Green Knight even though it means that he himself will in turn be beheaded one year hence. This tale is considered to be one of the greatest poems in Middle English. (ca. 1375)

Skin of our Teeth, The

Thornton Wilder   Drama / U.S. 📖   12

With wit and wisdom and a great deal of fun, Wilder brings the Antrobus family to the stage. They hang on through the eons although plagued by the Ice Age, the Great Flood, and the wars of the 20th century. What will come next? (1942)

Song of Hiawatha, The

Henry Wadsworth Longfellow   Poetry / U. S. 📖   9, 10, 12

This classic poem tells of the legendary Native American, Hiawatha, as he grows up in the early days of European settlers. (1858)

Songs of Innocence and Songs of Experience

William Blake   Poetry / Britain   📖   11

Blake (1757–1827) brought these two volumes together to "Shew…the Two Contrary States of the Human Soul." His deceptively simple poems present his profound vision of the necessary interdependence of good and evil. This volume contains such well known poems as" Little Lamb Who Made Thee" and "Tyger! Tyger! Burning Bright." (1795)

Sonnets to Orpheus

Rainer Maria Rilke   Poetry / Germany   📖   12

Rilke wrote these spiritually passionate poems seemingly spontaneously in an exuberance of joy. (1923)

Spring Awakening

Frank Wedekind   Drama / Germany   📖   12

Wedekind's portrait of budding sexuality, adolescent confusion, and the pressures to conform through the forces of society is as disturbing today as when it was first produced. (1891)

State of Siege

Albert Camus   Drama / France   📖   12

"The Plague" and his secretary appear in a small walled town and usurp the governor's post. They put into effect an insidious bureaucratic program in which all sentiment and emotion are replaced by organization. Death becomes a matter of logic and efficiency, and certificates of existence are prerequisites for living. (1948)

Stolen

Jane Harrison   Drama / Australia   📖   10, 11, 12

This tender and moving play tells of five young aboriginal children forcibly removed from their parents, brought up in a repressive children's home, and trained for domestic service and other menial jobs. (1998)

Taming of the Shrew
William Shakespeare   Drama / Britain   📖   10, 11, 12

A Paduan gentleman has two daughters, shrewish Katherina, and her much sought after younger sister, Bianca. Bianca cannot marry until a husband is found for Katherina. From Verona comes Petruchio who undertakes to tame Katherina and help his friend win Bianca. (1623)

Tanakh
Sacred Writing   📖   10

The Jewish name for the Hebrew scriptures is derived from the Hebrew letters of its three components: "Torah" (the Five Books of Moses), "Nevi'im" (Prophets), and "Ketuvim" (Writings). Christians know it as the *Old Testament. See Old Testament* and *The Bible.*

Tao Te Ching
Lao-Tzu   Sacred Writing   📖   12

The sage Lao-Tzu reputedly wrote down the most influential and best known of Taoist texts in one night as he left China for the West. This collection of 81 sections of oracular sayings and proverbs is ascribed to Lao Zi (the Old Master). (5th c. B.C.E.)

Tartuffe
Molière   Drama / France   📖   11

The hypocritical Tartuffe ingratiates himself into the family of a French gentleman who tries to marry him to his daughter, very much against her wishes. (1664)

Tempest, The
William Shakespeare   Drama / Britain   📖   11, 12

Probably Shakespeare's last play, this is the tale of Prospero, Duke of Milan, who is a magician. When he and his daughter Miranda are banished to an isolated island, he assumes command over the lively sprite Ariel and the misshapen monster Caliban. A shipwreck brings others to the island, including Ferdinand with whom Miranda falls in love. (1623)

Temptation

Vaclav Havel   Drama   📖   12

Czechoslovakian dissident and later president, Havel gives a contemporary twist to the Faust story. Dr. Foustka becomes involved in mysticism and takes the risk of attacking the limitations of scientific knowledge. (1986)

Ten Principal Upanishads, The

Sri Purohit and W. B. Yeats, eds., trans.   Sacred Writing   📖   12

The Upanishads are based on the earlier Vedas and mark a transition from ritual sacrifice to a mystical inquiry into the nature of reality, equate the atman (self) with the Brahman (supreme spirit), and develop the principle of reincarnation. This is perhaps the most beautiful English translation of these sacred Hindu books. (800–200 B.C.E.)

Theban Plays

Sophocles   Drama / Ancient Greece   📖   9, 10

The story of Oedipus the King and the tragic events that follow the revelation of his horrifying crime are told in this classic Greek trilogy. (ca. 490 B.C.E.)

Three Sisters

Anton Chekhov   Drama / Russia   📖   12

Three sisters of the petty aristocracy in pre-Revolutionary Russia, although talented and full of promise, contemplate their unsatisfactory lives and seem unable to make decisions; Chekhov called this play a comedy. (1901)

Tiger at the Gates

Jean Giraudoux   Drama / France   📖   10

Giraudoux borrows the basic setting of the Trojan war, but gives events a modern interpretation as he explores the ability of human beings to struggle against destiny. The translator Christopher Frye, gives this title to the play. (1955)

Timon of Athens

William Shakespeare   Drama / Britain   📖   12

A rich Athenian becomes poor through excessive hospitality to friends who desert him in his time of need. He leaves the city and lives in a cave with exiles and thieves and dies a misanthrope. (1623)

Titus Andronicus

William Shakespeare   Drama / Britain   📖   12

Titus Andronicus returns to Rome after his conquest of the Gauls and becomes involved in increasing treachery and revenge including rape, dismemberment, and serving his enemy a stew made from the flesh of her own sons. Probably Shakespeare's earliest tragedy. (1594)

Twelfth Night

William Shakespeare   Drama / Britain   📖   9, 10

One of Shakespeare's most popular comedies tells the tale of two twins separated by a shipwreck; Viola, the sister, disguised as a man, serves Orsino who is in love with Olivia; Olivia, in turn, falls in love with the disguised Viola. A raucous sub-plot among the servants adds a second level of hilarity. (1623)

Two Gentlemen of Verona

William Shakespeare   Drama / Britain   📖   9, 10

Set in Italy, this comedy follows two friends and their servants through an intricate web of courtship, betrayal, mistaken identity and discovery. (1623)

Uncle Vanya

Anton Chekhov   Drama / Russia   📖   12

Sonya, the plain 19-year-old daughter of a famous professor, is stranded in a rural estate with her Uncle Vanya. They are raising money for her father who is traveling with his young wife. Sonya's hopes for liberation through marriage to a visiting doctor are thwarted when he doesn't return her affections. (1900)

Under Milkwood

Dylan Thomas   Drama / Britain   📖   12

Thomas' poetic play, originally written for radio, lovingly describes one day in the life of a small Welsh seaside town with a cast of unforgettable characters. (1954)

View from the Bridge, A

Arthur Miller   Drama / U.S.   📖   11, 12

Two illegal immigrants move into a longshoreman's apartment with tragic consequences. This is one of Miller's most powerful dramas. (1955)

Vintage Book of Contemporary American Poetry, The

J. D. McClatchy, ed.   Poetry / U.S.   📖   10

Sixty-five poets from World War II until the present, including Robert Lowell, Allen Ginsberg, Theodore Roethke, Anne Sexton, James Dickey, Denise Levertov and Gary Snyder, are included in this volume. For each, McClatchy gives a brief biography. (1996)

Volsunga Saga, The

Epic / Norse   📖   10, 11

Originally written in Icelandic (Old Norse) by an unknown hand, these tales date from a much earlier oral tradition and tell the story of the Volsungs, Gjukungs, and Budlungs, three families fated to destroy each other. (13th c.)

Waiting for Godot

Samuel Becket   Drama / Britain / Ireland   📖   10, 11, 12

Two tramps endlessly wait for the mysterious Godot while they debate the time and place of his coming. The play was written in French and translated into English three years later. (1952)

Wasteland, The

T. S. Eliot   Poetry / Britain   📖   **11**

One of the most influential and widely read poems of the 20th century is based in large part on the Grail legend. Heavily edited by Ezra Pound before its publication, it was immediately hailed as a powerful evocation of the post-war sense of desolation and futility enveloping Europe at that time. (1922)

Wild Duck, The

Henrik Ibsen   Drama / Norway   📖   **11, 12**

Blending the naturalism of Ibsen's middle dramas with the symbolism of his late period, this play explores the world of the Ekdals, a family whose peaceful existence is fragmented and destroyed in the name of truth. (1884)

Winged Serpent, The

Margot Astrov   Mythology   **11, 12**

This work is an anthology of Native American oral literature from more than fifty tribes. (1946)

Winter's Tale, The

William Shakespeare   Drama / England   📖   **12**

Leontes, King of Sicily, is deluded by his own jealousy into believing his wife and his best friend are lovers. His wife is imprisoned and gives birth to a daughter who is left to die by her father. The daughter is rescued and grows up to fall in love with the son of her father's exiled friend. (1623)

FICTION

Reader's Road Map

Novels and short stories give us a combination of entertainment and insight. Reading fiction helps us to relax, to dream, to experience something new, to have an emotional reaction that changes us, to escape to unfamiliar worlds where we can live through the impressions of characters just like us or strangely different. Most short stories are best enjoyed in a single sitting while novels can be our companions for days, weeks, or even months.

Sometimes the worlds we are invited into through fiction are so unusual that it takes an extra effort on our part to transport ourselves there. Then, we have to work hard at first to enter the world that the writer is describing. Great classics from the past might seem daunting for that reason. But, as millions of readers have discovered, they are classics because the extra effort is well worth it.

Perhaps some of us begin by flipping through the book and reading a few paragraphs out loud here and there to feel the rhythm of the language. Some of us might keep a dictionary handy to see how words have changed from past ages. Others might skip unfamiliar words and be carried along by the story itself as it becomes more and more interesting.

If you aren't hooked by the story or by the people in it after an hour or two, try another. There are many ways to read a book and many books to read. The brief descriptions in this section are meant to tempt you into new realms. Those of you who haven't done much reading yet or have been a little reluctant to voyage into the land of fiction might want to try one of the books with this symbol beside it ᐸᗐ.

Absalom, Absalom!

William Faulkner   Novel / U.S.   12

A young man and a dynasty begun in pre-Civil War Mississippi come to terms with the complexity of truth as he encounters the past. (1936)

Acorn People

Ron Jones   Novel / U.S.   📖   9, 10

A group of disabled boys at summer camp prove that they can do a whole lot more than they or others imagined. (1985)

Across Five Aprils

Irene Hunt   Novel / U.S.   ⌇   9

A coming-of-age novel authentically reflects the turbulence of the Civil War and the importance of family. (1964)

Across the River and Into The Trees

Ernest Hemingway   Novel / U.S.   📖   10, 11, 12

An American officer revisits Italy where he is haunted by his World War II experiences. He falls in love with a Countess who brings him renewed hope. (1950)

Acts of King Arthur and his Noble Knights, The

John Steinbeck   Novel / U.S.   11

Steinbeck was deeply influenced by the tales of King Arthur that he read as a child. This excellent modernization of Mallory's *Morte D'Arthur* was a life-long project. (1976)

Adam Bede

George Eliot   Novel / Britain   10, 11, 12

In Eliot's classic, a young woman in rural England leads a tormented life. She turns down the love of a good man, becomes pregnant with another who deserts her, and is imprisoned for killing her unwanted child. (1859)

Adventures of Augie March, The

Saul Bellow   Novel / U.S.   12

In this early Bellow novel, Augie describes his boyhood and coming-of-age in Chicago and his search for meaning in Mexico and Paris. (1953)

Adventures of Huckleberry Finn, The

Mark Twain   Novel / U.S.   11

The sequel to *Tom Sawyer*, this humorous masterpiece describes the adventures of Huck who journeys down the Mississippi on a raft with Jim, a runaway slave. (1885)

Adventures of Tom Sawyer, The

Mark Twain   Novel / U.S.   9

Twain's classic of the mischievous but good-hearted adventures of an orphan boy along the Mississippi depicts life in the pre-Civil War times with wit and humor. (1876)

African Child, The

Camara Laye   Novel / Guinea   ᴖ̑   9, 10

An autobiographical novel of childhood in a Malinka village in Guinea (formerly French West Africa) is set in colonial times in the early 20th century. (1953)

African Queen, The

C. S. Forester   Novel / Britain   9, 10

A mismatched English female missionary and a gin-swilling engineer take on the Germans in this World War I classic adventure. (1935)

Afro-American Folktales: Stories from Black Traditions in the New World

Collected by Roger D. Abraham   Short Stories / U.S.   📖   10, 11, 12

Included are 107 tales of wit and wisdom that range from creation myths to moral tales about kings and servants, masters and slaves. (1985)

Age of Innocence

Edith Wharton   Novel / U.S.   12

Conventions of late 19th-century New York society undermine happiness for three people bound by rules that test duty toward family, honor, and love. (1920)

Agony and the Ecstasy, The

Irving Stone   Novel / Historical / Renaissance   9

This popular fictionalized account of Michaelangelo's life, from the age of 13 until his death at 88, focuses primarily on the five years during which he painted the Sistine Chapel. (1961)

Alias Grace

Margaret Atwood   Novel / Canada   11, 12

An actual 1843 murder case in what is now Ontario was Atwood's starting point for this remarkable novel. Grace Marks, a servant, has served 16 years of a life sentence for a murder she does not remember committing. Dr. Simon Jordan is brought to Canada to determine whether Grace is innocent or guilty. (1996)

Alice's Adventures in Wonderland

Lewis Carroll   Novel / Britain   📖   9, 10, 11, 12

Originally written for children, Carroll's classic for all ages is full of delightful absurdities, word play, and such unforgettable characters as the White Rabbit, the Cheshire cat, the Mad Hatter and the March Hare. (1865)

All Creatures Great and Small

James Herriot   Novel / Britain   9, 10

The first of several wonderful books, this heartwarming and humorous account of the life of a veterinarian on the Yorkshire downs introduces James, his wife Helen, and a cast of characters, human and animal. (1975)

All Quiet on the Western Front

Erich Remarque   Novel / Germany   📖   12

One of the most powerful anti-war novels ever written, this is the wrenching story of a German platoon in the trenches and on leave during World War I. (1929)

All the King's Men

Robert Penn Warren   Novel / U.S.   10, 11, 12

This is a scathing account of a power-crazed, corrupt Southern politician. (1946)

All the Live Little Things

Wallace Stegner   Novel / U.S.   12

Set in the "hippy" 1960s, a grumpy old man and a young man with a different set of values meet. How they learn to live together and even love each other makes for compelling reading. (1967)

Almanac of the Dead

Leslie Marmon Silko   Novel / Native American   11, 12

Silko's epic uses the frame story of a secretary who is transcribing an ancient manuscript that foretells the second coming of Quetzalcoatl and the apocalyptic end of white rule in the Americas. It depicts heroin and cocaine use as weapons of the capitalist establishment. (1991)

Ambassadors, The

Henry James   Novel / U.S.   12

Set in Paris at the turn of the 20th century, a wealthy New England widow sends her fiancé to bring her son home. He finds himself entangled in the son's life, the seductions of Paris itself, and poignant questions of right and wrong. (1903)

Amber Spyglass, The

Phillip Pullman   Novel / Britain   9, 10, 11, 12

The final, and most powerful book in Pullman's *His Dark Materials* trilogy finds Lyra and Will involved in an all-out war in Heaven. (2000) See *The Golden Compass* and *The Subtle Knife*.

American, The

Henry James   Novel / U.S.   11, 12

James' novel contrasts European and American social codes in the 19th century. On a trip to Paris a naïve and goodhearted wealthy American falls in love with a deceitful French widow with unfortunate results. (1877)

American Tragedy, An

Theodore Dreiser   Novel / U.S.   12

The son of evangelist parents leaves home for the excitement of city life. When his girlfriend becomes pregnant his life takes a dramatic and tragic turn. (1925)

Ancient Child, The

N. Scott Momaday   Novel / Native American   10, 11, 12

The search for identity of a young adopted Kiowa boy who returns to the reservation for his grandmother's funeral is the focus of Momaday's classic Native American novel. Momaday weaves the Indian legend of the boy who turned into a bear into this tale of Set finding his tribal roots. (1989) See *House Made of Dawn* and *The Way to Rainy Mountain*.

And Then There Were None

Agatha Christie   Novel / Britain   9, 10, 11, 12

Christie is the best-known mystery writer in the world, with 80 novels and short story collections and 14 plays to her credit. In this tale, ten strangers are invited to a private island off the coast of Devon. Strangely, their host fails to show up. Stranger still, one by one, they begin to die. (1939)

Andromeda Strain, The

Michael Crichton   Science Fiction   11

Scientist turned novelist, Crichton creates a spellbinding tale of the first space age biological disaster and five days of suspense during which all life on earth is threatened. (1969)

Angel Landing

Alice Hoffman   Novel / U.S.   10, 11, 12

Aunt Minnie, a 74-year-old vegetarian and political activist, gives wise and hilarious counsel to her social worker niece who finds herself caught up in anti-nuclear protests and in love with a man known as "the bomber." (1999)

Anil's Ghost

Michael Ondaatje   Novel / Canada   11, 12

A young forensic anthropologist, educated in North America, returns to Sri Lanka to discover the source of murder campaigns that are fueling the Civil War; what she discovers in this powerful novel is a deeper mystery of love, loss, and redemption. (2000)

Animal Dreams

Barbara Kingsolver   Novel / U.S.   9, 10, 11, 12

The protagonist of this love story comes home to confront her past and finds her place as a heroine who averts an ecological disaster in her hometown. (1990)

Animal Farm

George Orwell   Novel / Britain   10, 11, 12

The allegorical story of the overthrow of a farm by the animals satirizes the Russian revolution. (1945)

Anna Karenina

Leo Tolstoy   Novel / Russia 📖   12

A married woman's passion for a young officer leads to a tragic end. (1877)

Annie John

Jamaica Kincaid   Novel / U.S.   9

An adolescent girl living in Antigua faces her changing relationship with her mother as she finds her own truth. (1985)

Anti-Christ

Vladimir Soloviev   Novel / Russia   📖   12

Soloviev foresaw much that came to be in the 20th century including a "United States of Europe." The Anti-Christ is a spiritualist, an admirable philanthropist, a committed pacifist, a practicing vegetarian, and a determined defender of animal rights; he is, of course, welcomed. (1900)

April Morning

Howard Fast   Novel / Historical / U.S.   9, 10

A boy witnesses the first fateful moments of the American Revolution and steps into adulthood. (1961). See *Freedom Road, The Immigrants, The Last Frontier,* and *Spartacus.*

Around the World in Eighty Days

Jules Verne   Novel / France   9

A best seller for over a century, the story of Phineas Fogg's race against time in his five weeks in a balloon remains a fast-paced and delightful adventure. (1873)

Arrow of God

Chinua Achebe   Novel / Nigeria   12

Achebe gives a vivid and disturbing portrayal of the traditional Ibo people in what is now Nigeria at the time of the first confrontation with European settlers. It can be considered the first of a series in which he recreates Africa's journey from traditional to modern times. (1964) See *A Man of the People, No Longer at Ease,* and *Things Fall Apart.*

Arrowsmith

Sinclair Lewis   Novel / U.S.   9, 10

A doctor with high ideals is tempted to relinquish these for comfort and prestige. (1925)

As For Me and My House

Sinclair Ross   Novel / Canada   11, 12

A frustrated artist earns a meager living as a minister in a bleak wind-swept prairie town. The compelling story is told through his wife's diary. (1941)

As I Lay Dying

William Faulkner   Novel / U.S.   11, 12

Faulkner's tragicomic novel is about the death of Addie Bundren and her children's attempts to fulfill her wish to be buried in Jefferson. (1930)

Assistant, The

Bernard Malamud   Novel / U.S.   9

Malamud explores the humble lives of a New York Jewish family who own a grocery store. Their assistant, an Italian American, reexamines his values and beliefs when he finds love and faith in the Jewish community. (1957)

At Play in the Fields of the Lord

Peter Matthiessen   Novel / U.S.   11, 12

Two cultures in contemporary South America collide: the Niaruna, an indigenous tribe virtually untouched by modern life, and the Christian missionaries who attempt to convert them. (1965)

At Risk

Alice Hoffman   Novel / U.S.   10

A family is shattered by tragedy when 11-year-old Amanda is diagnosed with AIDS, the result of a blood transfusion several years earlier. (1988)

Aunt's Story, The

Patrick White   Novel / Australia   12

The account of the travels of an independent Australian spinster is wonderfully sympathetic and often humorous. (1948)

Autobiography of Miss Jane Pittman

Ernest Gaines   Novel / U.S.   9

Gaines looks at the history of the black race in America from the 1860s to the 1960s through the eyes of a fictional narrator and deals with issues of compassion, sacrifice, tolerance, and risk-taking. (1974)

Awakening, The

Kate Chopin   Novel / U.S.   11, 12

A shocking novel in 1899, Chopin's story depicts the pressures of Victorian society against a woman who seeks love outside of a loveless marriage. (1899)

Away

Jane Urquhart   Novel / Canada   11, 12

A poetic and passionate tale of Irish immigrants to Canada in the 1800s weaves together myth, magic and history. (1993)

Babbitt

Sinclair Lewis   Novel / U.S.   10, 11, 12

George Babbitt, a prosperous and self-satisfied member of the middle class in the American Midwest, begins to doubt the conventions of the life he is leading. (1922)

Balzac and the Little Chinese Seamstress

Dai Sijie   Novel / China   10, 11, 12

In the 1960s and '70s, the Chinese Cultural Revolution of Chairman Mao Zedong "re-educated" thousands of Chinese intellectuals by sending them to remote peasant villages. This is the story of two 17-year-olds who survive by telling stories to the villagers from stolen and forbidden Western books. (2001)

Barchester Towers

Anthony Trollope   Novel / Britain   12

This is the second, and best known, of a series of novels set in a fictional town in England's west country in the early Victorian age; it is full of wonderful characters and political intrigues. (1857)

Barnaby Rudge

Charles Dickens   Novel / Britain   11, 12

In 1780 fierce anti-Catholic riots terrorized London. Dickens brings these to life as he weaves together love, murder, and redemption. (1841)

Barren Ground

Ellen Glasgow   Novel / U.S.   11, 12

A gifted woman attempts to overcome the Southern tradition of domesticity and dependence on men. (1925)

Bean Trees, The

Barbara Kingsolver   Novel / U.S.   10, 11

The female protagonist of this coming-of-age novel faces issues of motherhood, friendship, and questions of identity and belonging. (1988) See *Pigs in Heaven.*

Beet Queen, The

Louise Erdrich   Novel / Native American   11, 12

The second novel in Erdrich's four-part series is the story of Mary Adare, an 11-year-old orphan who travels by boxcar to live with her aunt and uncle in North Dakota. It covers a 40-year period of intertwining lives, relationships, and unforgettable characters who search for happiness. (1986)

Beginners, The

Dan Jacobson   Novel / South Africa   12

Three Jewish children in strife-torn South Africa search for a new set of values to begin a peaceful world. (1966)

Bell for Adano, A

John Hersey   Novel / U.S.   9, 10

A feisty Sicilian village is taken captive during World War II. This Pulitzer Prize-winning novel is written in the style of a documentary. (1945)

Beloved

Toni Morrison   Novel / U.S.   11

A ghost lives at the heart of this story of slavery and freedom experienced through the souls of African-Americans at the time of the Civil War. (1987)

Bend in the River, A

V. S. Naipaul   Novel / Trinidad   11

Naipaul is a master at writing realistic stories of ordinary people caught in a changing world. This novel tells the story of a Muslim storekeeper in a French-speaking Central African state in a time of revolution and counter-revolution. (1979)

Ben-Hur

Lewis Wallace   Novel / U.S.   9

Widely translated, *Ben-Hur* depicts the oppressive Roman occupation of ancient Palestine and the origins of Christianity through the story of Jewish-born Judah Ben-Hur. (1880)

Best of Simple, The

Langston Hughes   Short Stories / U.S.   📖   12

Narrated by Jesse B. Semple, "Simple" ran in the *Chicago Defender* for 23 years beginning in 1943. The format allowed Hughes the opportunity to write about life and politics in Harlem.

Big Sky, The

Alfred B. Guthrie   Novel / U.S.   9, 10

The first of Guthrie's epic adventure novels of America's vast frontier during the 1830s describes a legendary hero and his love for the beautiful daughter of a Blackfoot chief. (1947)

Big Sleep, The

Raymond Chandler   Novel / U.S.   9, 10, 11, 12

Cool, wisecracking detective Philip Marlowe, solves the first of Chandler's classic mysteries. (1939)

Billy Budd

Herman Melville   Novel / U.S.   📖   **12**

Adapted by Benjamin Britten into an opera in 1951, "Billy Budd" is the innocent hero whose guilt is a matter of perspective. Humanity and justice are radically scrutinized. Written in 1891 and published in 1924.

Bingo Palace, The

Louise Erdich   Novel / Native American   📖   **12**

Lipsha Morrisey struggles with his love for Shawnee Ray Toose in these alternately heartbreaking and hilarious adventures.(1994)

Black Beauty: The Autobiography of a Horse

Anna Sewell   Novel / Britain   🐎   **9**

A heartwarming horse story told from the animal's point of view was intended to raise awareness of the mishandling and abuse of animals. (1877)

Bleak House

Charles Dickens   Novel / Britain   **11, 12**

Set in London, England, *Bleak House* is full of fascinating characters whose lives serve as examples of the injustice of the Victorian legal system and the inequalities between rich and poor. (1852)

Bless Me Ultima

Anaya Rudolfo   Novel / U.S.   **11, 12**

A Chicano boy in New Mexico in the 1940s tries to balance Catholic beliefs against the "old ways" of his grandmother in this fascinating and mystical novel. (1973)

Bless the Beasts and Children

Glendon Swarthout   Novel / U.S.   **9**

Misfits at a summer camp discover their courage by freeing a herd of buffalo in this heartwarming tale. (1970)

Blue Diary

Alice Hoffman   Novel / U.S.   10, 11, 12

A man's past finally catches up with him after 13 peaceful years, shattering the protective bubble of ordinary life. (2001)

Bluest Eye, The

Toni Morrison   Novel / U.S.   11, 12

A young African American girl is driven mad trying to attain beauty as defined by white and unattainable standards. (1970)

Bonfire of the Vanities

Tom Woolf   Novel / U.S.   12

Woolf's satirical attack on the materialism of the 1980s follows Sherman McCoy, a wildly successful investment banker in New York, through his fall and eventual redemption. (1987)

Border Trilogy, The

Cormac McCarthy   Novel / U.S.   12

Storyteller McCarthy follows the relationships, adventures, loves, and losses of two young men growing up along the Mexican-U.S. border in the 1930s. They are as much the stories of the change in the American West. The separate titles are: *All the Pretty Horses* (1992 National Book Award-winner), *The Crossing (1994), and Cities of the Plain (1998)*.

Bostonians, The

Henry James   Novel / U.S.   12

A young woman is caught between emerging feminism and the love of a man who considers that a woman's role is to be agreeable to the opposite sex. (1886)

Brave New World

Aldous Huxley   Novel / Britain   11, 12

This chilling classic is set in the 7th century AF (after Ford), peopled by individuals and clones hatched from test tubes. The pleasures of the tranquilizing drug, Soma, and the multi-sensory movies, the "feelies," are promoted over the search for meaning, art, and individuality. (1932)

Brian's Winter
Gary Paulsen   Novel / Britain   9, 10

Readers who read Paulsen's *The Hatchet* could not help but speculate on what might have happened to Brian had he not been rescued at the end of his solitary summer. This novel begins with that alternate possibility. Brian's winter survival skills are put to the test. Readers who enjoy these Paulsen novels might also enjoy *Brian's Return* and *The River.* (1998)

Brideshead Revisited
Evelyn Waugh   Novel / Britain   11, 12

An English soldier in World War II is co-incidentally billeted at a country estate where as a college student he had visited his close friend, a handsome and whimsical alcoholic. He remembers his intimacy with his friend's family with mixed emotions. (1945)

Bridge of San Luis Rey, The
Thornton Wilder   Novel / U.S.   9, 10, 11, 12

Brother Juniper witnesses a bridge collapse in Peru in the 18th century that kills five people. In his shock, the monk begins to explore the lives of those who died to discover whether it was an accident or divine intervention. (1927)

Brighton Rock
Graham Greene   Novel / Britain   11, 12

Seventeen-year-old Pinkie, known to his fellow gang members as "The Boy," is led to murder and deceit; Greene's understanding of the complexity of motive and the final triumph of good is fully evident. (1938)

Brothers Karamazov, The
Fyodor Dostoevsky   Novel / Russia   📖   12

The Russian classic is at once a mystery of the murder of a father by one of his sons and a brilliant metaphysical exploration of human freedom; it includes the famous story of "The Grand Inquisitor." (1880)

Buddenbrooks: The Decline of a Family

Thomas Mann   Novel / Germany   10, 11, 12

Four generations of a North German family are realistically explored through the lives of three young people who inherit the legacy of their wealthy businessman father in the last half of the 19th century. (1901)

Bull From the Sea

Mary Renault   Novel / Historical / Ancient Greece   ∽   10

Continuing from *The King Must Die,* this extraordinary retelling of the legend of Theseus begins with his triumphant return from Crete after slaying the Minotaur. An engrossing saga. (1962)

Burger's Daughter

Nadine Gordimer   Novel / South Africa   12

Written by Nobel Prize-winner Gordimer, this is a young woman's account of the personal and political heritage of having an Afrikaner father, a Communist, who dies in prison. Gordimer's stories often address the conflicts and tensions of her native South Africa. (1979)

Caine Mutiny, The

Herman Wouk   Novel / U.S.   9, 10

The neurotic behavior of Captain Queeg brings about a mutiny aboard the *U.S.S. Caine.* Wouk's story won a Pulitzer Prize. (1951)

Call it Sleep

Henry Roth   Novel / U.S.   11, 12

A classic of Jewish American literature published in 1934, this stream of consciousness novel centers on the perceptions of a young boy, the son of Yiddish speaking Jewish immigrants in a squalid ghetto in New York City. (1934)

Call of the Wild, The

Jack London   Novel / U.S.   ∽   9, 10

Set in the Canadian north, this is the classic story of Buck, a dog who returns to the wild and becomes a leader of a wolf pack after his master's death. (1903)

Cancer Ward, The

Aleksandr Solzhenitsyn   Novel / Russia   📖   12

A psychologically tough novel, about a group of men in a Soviet cancer ward in the 1950s, serves as a metaphor for hope in post-Stalin Russia. (1968)

Candide

Voltaire   Novel / France   11, 12

Voltaire describes the outrageous adventures of a gentle young man who, in the face of all evidence to the contrary, continues to believe that he lives in the "best of all possible worlds." (1759)

Cane

Jean Toomer   Novel / U.S.   9, 10

This classic chronicles the lives of poor African Americans in Georgia through stories, character sketches, and poems. (1923)

Cannery Row

John Steinbeck   Novel / U.S.   ∿   11, 12

This is a wonderful novel about the interwoven lives of an exuberant cast of characters who live along a stretch of the Monterey Coast in California. (1945)

Captain Horatio Hornblower Series

C. S. Forester   Novel / Britain   9, 10

Eleven enthralling tales of naval warfare in the Napoleonic Wars of the late 1700s and early 1800s tell of the adventures of Horatio Hornblower from the time he is a midshipman until he becomes Lord Admiral. It is claimed that this hero inspired the creation of Star Trek Captain Kirk. (1937–1967)

Captains Courageous

Rudyard Kipling   Novel / Britain   9

Set on the wild waters of the Grand Banks, this novel tells the story of a shipwrecked millionaire's son who is rescued by the crew of a fishing schooner and taught much needed-lessons about life at sea. (1897)

Captain's Daughter, The

Aleksandr Pushkin   Novel / Russia   12

A tale of integrity, loyalty, and love is set against a backdrop of rebellion on the Russian steppes. (1836)

Castle, The

Franz Kafka   Novel / Czechoslovakia (German)   11, 12

Kafka's bleak and absurdist tale tells of the futile efforts of the protagonist to gain recognition from the rulers of a village where he wants to establish himself. (1926)

Castle of Ostranto, The

Horace Walpole   Novel / Britain   10, 11

This first Gothic novel blends wild imagination with probable characters and settings to create a new type of novel. Pretending to be a translation of an Italian story of the time of the Crusades, this tale of exciting situations, mistaken identities, and ghostly interventions still holds the reader's attention over 200 years later. (1764)

Catch-22

Joseph Heller   Novel / U.S.   11, 12

The strange and sprawling account of American soldiers in Italy during World War II has become a modern classic. The phrase "Catch-22" has entered the language to describe an impossible situation where the only solution to a problem is denied by a circumstance implicit within the situation itself. (1961)

Catcher in the Rye

J. D. Salinger   Novel / U.S.   📖   9, 10

This coming-of-age novel is told by young Holden Caulfield as a series of flashbacks. He suffers a breakdown, revealing the confusion and disillusionment of adolescence that led up to his collapse. (1951)

Cat's Cradle

Kurt Vonnegut   Novel / U.S.   ∽   12

One of Vonnegut's best-loved novels, this apocalyptic tale is peopled with wacky characters who, among other things, practice an illicit religion called Bokonism in a Caribbean banana republic. (1963) See *Player Piano* and *Slaughterhouse Five.*

Cat's Eye

Margaret Atwood   Novel / Canada   📖   11

When middle-aged painter Elaine Risley returns to Toronto where she grew up, she finds herself confronting her memories of adolescent betrayals and cruelties. (1988)

Cay, The

Theodore Taylor   Novel / U.S.   9

Love and the need for survival overcome prejudice in this powerful World War II classic. An adolescent white boy, blinded by a blow to the head, is stranded on a tiny Caribbean island with an old black West Indian sailor. A German submarine torpedoes the freighter on which they were traveling. (1969)

Celebrated Jumping Frog of Calaveras County, The

Mark Twain   Short Stories / U.S.   📖   9

Twain's first collection of humorous sketches established his reputation as a storyteller. (1867)

Ceremony   98

Leslie Marmon Silko   Novel / Native American   📖   11, 12

A young Native American, imprisoned by the Japanese during World War II, returns to his reservation and seeks healing in the tribal traditions and stories of the past rather than in alcohol and despair. (1977)

Chant of Jimmy Blacksmith, The

Thomas Keneally   Novel / Australia   10, 11, 12

Thomas Keneally studies those who are caught irreconcilably between the two worlds of aboriginal and white Australia, unable to fit into either. His book remains as powerful, confronting and topical as when it first appeared. (1978)

Chesapeake

James Michener   Novel / Historical / U.S.   9

The history of the North American East Coast, from the late 16th century to the present is told in Michener's highly readable style. (1978)

Childhood's End

Arthur Clarke   Novel / U.S.   9

Seemingly benevolent Overlords appear over the earth bringing a golden age of peace but at a great cost: the loss of creativity and ingenuity. (1953)

Children of Violence,

Doris Lessing   Novel / Britain   12

This five-volume series is part realistic and part futuristic. Drawing on her own childhood in Africa, Lessing's central character is Martha Quest, born and raised in Rhodesia, who moves to post-war Britain and experiences the apocalypse at the turn of the 21st century. The order of the series is: Martha Quest, A Proper Marriage, Ripple from the Storm, Landlocked, and The Four-Gated City (1952–1959)

Child's Christmas in Wales, A

Dylan Thomas   Novel / Britain   9, 10, 11, 12

Loosely autobiographical, this delightful classic describes Christmas Day in a small Welsh seaside village from the viewpoint of remembered childhood. (1952)

China Men

Maxine H. Kingston   Novel / U.S.   12

A companion to *The Woman Warrior,* the Chinese American experience is explored through the eyes of several generations of men.(1980)

Chocolate War, The

Robert Cormier   Novel / U.S.   9

A freshman at a private high school declares his individuality by refusing to participate in the annual fundraiser and faces the wrath of the school's bullies. (1974)

Chosen, The

Chaim Potok   Novel / U.S.   9, 10, 11

A special friendship between two Jewish boys in Brooklyn, one from a Hasidic sect and the other from an Orthodox sect, builds a bridge of understanding across religious boundaries and difficult times. (1967) See *The Promise.*

Christmas Carol, A

Charles Dickens   Novel / Britain   9, 10, 11, 12

The ghosts of Christmas Past, Present, and Future bring about the spiritual conversion of the miserly Ebenezer Scrooge in this classic tale. (1843)

Chrysalids, The

John Wyndham   Novel / Britain   9, 10, 11, 12

In a future world, long after a nuclear holocaust has made parts of the planet uninhabitable, young David Strom hides his abnormality, his telepathy, from his rigid father. Gradually he realizes that he and a few others who have abnormalities must escape the society they have been born into. (1955)

Clockwork Orange, A

Anthony Burgess   Novel / Britain   11, 12

This terrifying futuristic novel depicts a society where violent gangs rule in a technological urban jungle and raises issues of free will, good and evil, and the role of art and language. (1962)

Cold Mountain

Charles Frazier   Novel / U.S.   11, 12

A young soldier deserts the Confederate army to return to his sweetheart in North Carolina; his story and hers are delicately and poetically interwoven in this unforgettable story. (1997)

Cold Sassy Tree

Olive A. Burns   Novel / U.S.   9

Both hilarious and deeply touching, this novel tells of the trials of 14-year-old Will when his grandfather, a widower of three weeks, falls passionately in love with a young feminist in a Southern town in the early part of the 20th century. (1984)

Collected Stories

Gabriel Garcia Marquez   Novel / Columbia   📖   12

Twenty-six stories published in chronological order not only give the reader the delight of reading Marquez, who was awarded the Nobel Prize in Literature in 1982, but also offer an understanding of his development as an author. (1999)

Collected Works of Edgar Allan Poe

Edgar Allen Poe   Anthology / U.S.   📖   9, 10, 11, 12

Edited by T. O. Mabbott *et al.*, this is a three-volume collection of the tales and poetry of "the Master of Macabre." (1969)

Collector, The

John Fowles   Novel / Britain   10, 11

A young man moves on from collecting butterflies to kidnapping a female art student with whom he is obsessively in love. This haunting novel explores the nature of good and evil. (1963)

Color Purple, The

Alice Walker   Novel / U.S.   📖   10, 11, 12

An abused and uneducated southern African American woman struggles for empowerment and freedom from her oppressive husband. Praised for its character development and use of dialect, it won both a Pulitzer Prize and American Book Award. (1982)

Complete Sherlock Holmes

Sir Arthur Conan Doyle   Novel / Short Stories / Britain   📖   10

In this great collection of mysteries, Doctor Watson recollects the famous cases solved by Sherlock Holmes, known for his infallible deductive reasoning. (1897–1902)

Complete Short Stories of D. H. Lawrence, The

D. H. Lawrence   Short Stories / Britain   12

This three-volume collection contains all the published stories of Lawrence (1885–1930) whose reputation as a short story writer remains strong. The favorite "The Rocking Horse Winner" with Lawrence's life-long theme of the relationship between a son and his mother is included.

Complete Short Stories of Ernest Hemingway, The

Ernest Hemingway   Short Stories / U.S.   10, 11, 12

This definitive collection contains 60 of Hemingway's small masterpieces, some of which were later expanded into novels. Hemingway was noted for his clean, terse prose; many of his subjects drawn from his experiences as a journalist. This volume includes "The Short Happy Life of Francis Macomber", "The Snows of Kilimanjaro", "A Clean, Well Lighted Place". (1987)

Complete Stories, The

Bernard Malamud   Short Stories / U.S.   📖   12

Perhaps more known for his novels, Malamud creates compelling characters in ordinary settings. These 55 short stories published from 1940 to 1984, edited and introduced by Robert Giroux, cover the full range of this great writer's work. (1994)

Complete Stories, The

Flannery O'Connor   Short Stories / U.S.   11, 12

Raised in the deep South, O'Conner struggles with religious and moral questions, especially in connection with racial prejudice. Redemption can arise, however, even in the brutal world she portrays. (1971)

Confederacy of Dunces, A

John Kennedy Toole   Novel / U.S.   📖   12

Ignatius J. Reilly a 30-year-old medievalist is very much at a loss in the 20th century. Published by his mother after Toole's suicide, and winner of the Pulitzer Prize in 1981, this tragicomedy became a bestseller and remains an underground favorite. (1980)

Connecticut Yankee in King Arthur's Court, A

Mark Twain   Novel / U.S.   9

Classic humor abounds when a mechanically inventive blacksmith travels back to medieval Camelot and finds that all isn't quite as perfect as he has been led to expect. (1889)

Cossacks, The: A Tale of the Caucasus

Leo Tolstoy   Novel / Russia   12

Tolstoy's early novel was called the masterpiece of Russian fiction by Turgenev; it is based on the author's youthful experiences fighting mountain tribes as a volunteer attached to the regular Russian army and raises profound questions of religion and morality. (1852)

Count of Monte Cristo, The

Alexandre Dumas   Novel / France   9

Edmond Dantes plots an elaborate vengeance after being falsely accused and imprisoned as a Bonapartiste conspirator. (1845)

Country of the Pointed Firs, The

Sarah Orne Jewett   Novel / U.S.   9, 10

These realistic stories of ordinary people and their daily lives in a Maine seaport town continue to charm readers. Jewett's prominence in literary circles extended beyond New England. (1986)

Coup, The

John Updike   Novel / U.S.   11, 12

A fictional first-person narration by an ex-dictator describes violent events in the imaginary African nation of Kush. (1978)

Crime and Punishment

Fyodor Dostoevsky   Novel / Russia   12

A poor student explores the question of whether great people can live above or outside the law and puts his life and the lives of others on the line. (1866)

Crossing to Safety

Wallace Stegner   Novel / U.S.   10, 11, 12

Set in Wisconsin and Vermont, this is the story of two young couples who meet during the Depression and form an instant friendship that lasts 34 years. (1987)

Cruel Sea, The

Nicholas Monsarrat   Novel / Britain   11, 12

A classic war story about the Battle of the Atlantic in World War II documents the struggle between the German U-boats and the British merchant fleet and the battles both navies fought with the cruel sea. (1951)

Cry the Beloved Country

Alan Paton   Novel / South Africa   9, 10, 11, 12

This powerful and moving portrait deals with the struggle of conscience and the clash of two ways of life that dominated South Africa before the end of apartheid. Paton's novel is considered "the greatest novel to emerge out of the tragedy of South Africa." (1948)

Daisy Miller

Henry James   Novel / U.S.   11, 12

Daisy Miller, an innocent young American, travels to Europe with her mother and unwittingly offends European convention. (1879)

Dance of the Happy Shades

Alice Munroe   Short Stories / Canada   9, 10

Munroe's first collection of intricately woven short stories is set in the semi-rural towns of southwestern Ontario. (1968)

Dance of the Tiger: A Novel of the Ice Age

Bjorn Kurten   Novel / Finland   9, 10, 11, 12

This is a scientifically well-informed novel about contact between Cro-Magnon and Neanderthal man in prehistoric Scandinavia. (1980)

Dandelion Wine

Ray Bradbury   Novel / U.S.   9

A twelve-year-old boy's magical summer in small town Illinois in 1928 has a bittersweet edge in this semi-autobiographical Bradbury classic. (1979)

Daniel Deronda

George Eliot   Novel / Britain   11, 12

The last novel written by George Eliot is in many ways her finest. A young woman abandons her dreams of becoming a singer and marries for money. In her subsequent despair, she turns to Daniel Deronda, the illegitimate son of an internationally known Jew. (1874-1876)

Daniel Martin

John Fowles   Novel / Britain   11, 12

A disillusioned Hollywood scriptwriter returns to Britain to visit a dying old friend and faces the most important of all questions: how to live. (1977)

Darkness at Noon

Arthur Koestler   Novel / Germany   11, 12

A thinly veiled attack on Stalinism, this novel tells of the arrest, imprisonment, and trial of a man in an unnamed dictatorship ruled by No.1. (1940)

Daughter of Fortune, The

Isabel Allende   Novel / Chile   10, 11, 12

Allende's powerful story begins in mid-19th-century Valparaíso, Chile, then a thriving British port. A British couple raises a foundling girl who grows up poised between European and Chilean values. (1999)

Daughter of Time, The

Josephine Tey   Novel / Britain   9, 11

A hospital-bound Scotland Yard detective, with the help of a historical researcher, becomes engrossed with solving the old mystery of who really killed the Princes in the Tower in the 15th century. The reader is left with a new understanding of the nature of truth and the rewriting of history. (1951)

David Copperfield

Charles Dickens   Novel / Britain   9, 10

The novel Dickens liked best is the heartwarming story of the life of a young boy who grows into manhood in England in the early 1800s. (1850)

Davita's Harp

Chaim Potok   Novel / U.S.   9, 10

A Jewish girl grows up in New York in the 1930s and '40s amid the tensions and yearning for a better world. She has to overcome losing her father and the prejudice against women in parochial education, but finds liberation in her freedom to recognize "the decent music in humanity." (1985)

Dead Souls

Nikolai Gogol   Novel / Russia   12

This is an ingenious story of a clever Russian who generates power and respect based on dead souls. (1842)

Death Comes for the Archbishop

Willa Cather   Novel / U.S.   📖   10, 11, 12

This historical novel tells of the mission of the French Father Latour and his work among the peasants in New Mexico. (1927)

Death in the Afternoon

Ernest Hemingway Novel / U.S. 11, 12

Hemingway describes "the emotional and spiritual intensity" of bull-fighting, an activity he considered far more than "mere sport." As with many of his writings, he offers commentary on life and literature.(1932)

Death in the Family, A

James Agee Novel / U.S. 10, 11, 12

This semi-autobiographical Pulitzer Prize-winning novel about courage and love in the face of tragic loss is told through the eyes of two young children. (1957)

Death of Ivan Ilych, The

Leo Tolstoy Novel / Russia 📖 12

Ivan Ilych begins to feel ill and eventually realizes, as we all must, that death awaits him. (1886)

Death of the Heart, The

Elizabeth Bowen Novel / Britain 12

Orphaned 16-year-old Portia moves in with her half-brother and his wife and, through her innocence, unwittingly causes great pain. (1938)

Deerslayer, The

James Fenimore Cooper Novel / U.S. 📖 9, 10

Cooper's great American wilderness saga tells the adventures of a noble pioneer woodsman, Natty Bumppo and his companion, Chingchgook. This is the last written of the *Leatherstocking Tales,* but the first chrono-logically in the series. (1841)

Demian

Hermann Hesse Novel / Germany 11, 12

Hesse's first novel tells of the growing individuality of young Emil Sinclair. He is greatly influenced by his friendship with Max Demian, who intro-duces him to the idea that good and evil co-exist and that each must receive its due. (1919)

Diedrich Knickerbocker's History of New York

Washington Irving   Novel / U.S.   📖   9

This is an amusing and witty semi-fictional description of the settlement of New York. (1809)

Dinner at the Homesick Restaurant

Anne Tyler   Novel / U.S.   9

An ordinary family experiences conflict as they search for meaning in their own lives. Their realistic struggles are sympathetically portrayed.(1982)

Disappearances

Howard Mosher   Novel / U.S.   11, 12

Set on the Vermont-Canadian border in 1932, Mosher's story is part mystery, part adventure, and part rite of passage. This is the story of a young boy and his memorable father as the boy discovers his family roots. (1977)

Disraeli: A Picture of the Victorian Age

Andre Maurois   Novel / Britain   12

Maurois gives a vivid picture of the life of Benjamin Disraeli, Prime Minister under Queen Victoria at the height of the British Empire, and of the Victorian Age. (1927)

Doctor Zhivago

Boris Pasternak   Novel / Russia   📖   12

Zhivago, poet and physician, struggles with life and love during the chaos of the Russian Revolution. Pasternak's semi-autobiographical novel achieved worldwide fame although it was not published in the U.S.S.R. until 1987. (1957)

Doll's House and Other Stories, The

Katherine Mansfield   Short Stories / New Zealand   11, 12

This collection, published 18 years after Mansfield's death, brings together several of her remarkable stories based on the years of growing up in Wellington and observations of her later life in England. (1951)

Dombey and Son

Charles Dickens   Novel / Britain   11, 12

Dombey is a cold and heartless owner of a shipping house. A series of tragedies befalls him, including the death of his wife and son, before he is able at last to accept the love of his patient daughter. (1848)

Don Quixote

Miguel Cervantes   Novel / Spain   10, 11, 12

Don Quixote roams the world in search of chivalrous adventures with his rustic squire, Sancho Panza. This remains a delightful satire almost 400 years after it was written. (1615)

Double, The

Fyodor Dostoevsky   Novel / Russia   12

A civil servant suffers from the delusion that a demonic double is persecuting him and ruining his career. (1846)

Double Hook, The

Sheila Watson   Novel / Canada   11, 12

Well-respected for its inventive style, this novel enters the world of characters in an isolated Rocky Mountain Plateau who are intertwined by love, lust, need, and most of all, a sense of community. (1959)

Dr. Jekyll and Mr. Hyde

Robert Louis Stevenson   Novel / Britain   ⟿   9, 10

Dr. Jekyll discovers a way to isolate all his evil tendencies in a separate personality, his double, who gradually gains full power. (1886)

Dragonwings

Laurence Yep   Novel / U.S.   9

Eight-year-old Moon Shadow leaves China to join his father, a famous kite-maker in San Francisco. He learns that his father dreams of building and flying his own airplane. Together they experience the 1906 San Francisco earthquake. (1973)

Dream Stuff

David Malouf Short Stories / Australia   11, 12

Malouf's most recent collection of 12 stories, each of a distinctly different time and place, are set in the multi-faceted landscape of Australia
and threaded together by the motif of dream, daydream, nightmare, fantasies, echoes and imaginings. (2000)

Drowning Season, The

Alice Hoffman Novel / U.S.   10, 11, 12

Esther the White has brought up her granddaughter, Esther the Black,
away from the world. At 18, Esther the Black escapes and discovers that
the world outside can be mysterious and frightening, but also full of
love. (1979)

Dubliners

James Joyce Novel / Britain / Ireland 📖   11, 12

Each of the seemingly real stories in Joyce's first important work revolves around an epiphany, a somewhat ordinary experience which resonates with profound meaning. A good first book to discover this great
20th-century writer. (1914)

East of Eden

John Steinbeck Novel / U.S.   10

A California family's life depicts the struggle of good over evil, and shows
the power of free will to change one's destiny in this biblical allegory.
(1952)

Edible Woman, The

Margaret Atwood Novel / Canada   11, 12

A young woman becomes increasingly aware that her identity is being
consumed by her fiancé, her job, and the insistence on conformity by
the urban world around her. Atwood's first novel, set in Toronto in the
1960s, is a comic account. (1969)

Education of Little Tree, The

Forrest Carter & Rennard Strickland
Novel / Native American ⌒⌒   9

The sentimental story of a young half-Cherokee orphan who is raised by his Cherokee grandparents is set in the 1930s in Appalachian Tennessee. It exposes the cruelty and prejudice of the whites in a boarding school. (1979)

Eighth Day, The

Thornton Wilder   Novel / U.S.   11, 12

On the surface, this story set during the American age of innocence, from 1880 to 1905, can be read as a murder mystery, full of surprises. Beneath the exterior radiates Wilder's great hope in the future of humanity. (1967)

Emma

Jane Austen   Novel / Britain   10, 11, 12

Emma, a clever, pretty, and self-satisfied young woman, finds her matchmaking schemes eventually deepen and humble her. (1816)

English Creek

Ivan Doig   Novel / U.S.   11, 12

This first novel of Doig's three-part saga of life in Montana's Two Medicine country tells of the coming-of-age of 14-year-old Jick McCaskill during the summer of 1939. (1984)

English Patient, The

Michael Ondaatje   Novel / Canada   12

A Canadian nurse, her long lost family friend, and a Sikh bomb-disposal expert form a bond of love around a dying man whose identity they can only guess at. Co-winner of the Booker Prize, this highly acclaimed novel is set in Italy during the final days of World War II. (1992)

Equations of Love, The

Ethel Wilson   Novel / Canada   9, 10

Wilson's two novellas enter into the complexities below the surface of ordinary lives. The first is about two days in the lives of an ordinary couple, and the second deals with an unmarried mother's struggles to bring up her child independently. (1952)

Essential Tales of Chekhov, The

Anton Chekhov   Richard Ford, ed.   C. Garnett, trans.
Anthology / Russia 📖   12

This collection includes 20 of the best of Chekhov's 200 short fiction written between 1886 and 1889. Chekov's stories feel "of our own time and mind." (1998)

Ethan Frome

Edith Wharton   Novel / U.S.   12

The bleakness of the landscape matches the hopelessness of the relationships in Wharton's masterpiece. Narrated by a visitor to the village, this heart-rending novel tells of the struggles of a New England farmer torn between love and duty. (1911)

Eugenie Grandet

Honoré de Balzac   Novel / France   11, 12

One of Balzac's greatest works, this is the story of a miser and his formative influence on his daughter. (1833)

Excellent Women

Barbara Pym   Novel / Britain   10, 11, 12

With gentle irony and detachment, Pym offers a comic description of daily life in a London Anglican parish shortly after World War II when a handsome naval officer and his feckless, unprincipled wife cause havoc among the flower-arranging ladies and the local vicar. (1952)

Ex-colored Man, The

James Johnson Novel / U.S. 10

Although called an autobiography, this is really a novel that explores the questions and issues about passing for white in American society in the early part of the 20th century. (1912)

Fahrenheit 451

Ray Bradbury Novel / U.S. 10, 11, 12

Guy Montag defies a powerful government that controls imaginative thinking by providing technological comforts while banning books. What was considered a futuristic novel is timely today. (1953)

Falconer

John Cheever Novel / U.S. 10

This is a powerful novel about the inner suffering and salvation of an imprisoned professor who has become a drug addict and murderer. (1977)

Fall of the House of Usher and Other Stories, The

Edgar Allen Poe Short Stories / U.S. 9, 10

Originally titled *Tales of the Grotesque and Arabesque*, these haunting tales of mystery and horror have remained classics since they were first published. (1840) See *Short Stories: Poe* and *Collected Works of Edgar Allen Poe*

Far Off Place, A

Laurens van der Post Novel / South Africa 9, 11

In the gripping conclusion of *A Story Like the Wind*, the heroes must trek across the Kalahari Desert to safety. Van der Post drew on his childhood experiences in Africa for these novels of courage and survival. (1974)

Far From the Madding Crowd

Thomas Hardy   Novel / Britain   11, 12

A young shepherd patiently loves the spirited young woman who owns
the farm he works on. The young woman, in turn, falls in love with an
unscrupulous soldier. (1874)

Farewell to Arms, A

Ernest Hemingway   Novel / U.S.   📖   9, 10, 11, 12

A love affair between an ambulance driver and the nurse who works
beside him in the turmoil of World War I asks the deepest questions
about trust and meaning. (1929)

Farming of Bones: A Novel

Edwidge Danticat   Novel / U.S.   12

In 1937, the head of the Dominican Republic ordered the slaughter of
all Haitians on Dominican land. This is the historical backdrop for a
story of love, survival, and the treachery of language. (1998)

Farthest Shore, The

Ursula Le Guin   Novel / U.S.   9, 10

In the third volume of *The Earthsea Trilogy*, Ged has grown older and is
now Archmage. With a young companion, he sets off to cure Earthsea of
the woes afflicting it and meets an old foe. (1972) See *A Wizard of Earthsea*
and *The Tombs of Atuan*.

Fathers and Sons

Ivan Turgenev   Novel / Russia   12

Turgenev introduces Nihilism and its first hero, Bazarov, who acts against
social institutions such as parental authority and marriage. (1862)

Fellowship of the Ring

J. R. R. Tolkien   Novel / Britain   9, 10

This is the first of the three-volume masterpiece, *The Lord of the Rings*.
After inheriting a magic ring from Bilbo, young Frodo finds himself forced
to gather a group of stouthearted companions and battle Sauron, Middle

Earth's ultimate evil warlord. (1954) See *The Two Towers* and *The Return of the King*.

Few Green Leaves, A

Barbara Pym   Novel / Britain   **10**

A gently ironic picture of a middle-aged anthropologist who retires to an English village and gets to know the local residents is written with a Jane Austen flavor. (1981)

Fields, The

Conrad Richter   Novel / U.S.   **9, 10**

The second volume of *The Awakening Land* trilogy describes the growing settlement in southeastern Ohio, home of the Luckett family, becoming a town. (1946) See *The Trees* and *The Town*.

Fifth Business

Robertson Davies   Novel / Canada 📖   **12**

In the first in *The Deptford Trilogy*, Dunstan Ramsey writes his life story to be read after his death. In a boyhood tussle, a snowball with a stone in it, intended for him, hits a pregnant woman by mistake and sets Dunstan off on a life quest into the nature of good and evil. See *The Manticore* and *World of Wonders*. (1970)

Fine Balance, A

Rohinton Mistry   Novel / Canada   **11, 12**

Winner of the Giller Prize in 1995, Mistry's novel is an extraordinary account of real people in the confusing world of late 20th century India. (1995)

Fire from Heaven

Mary Renault   Novel / Historical / Ancient Greece   **9, 10**

The first of a trilogy about the life of Alexander the Great follows him until the age of 20. (1969) See *The Persian Boy* and *Funeral Games*.

First Circle, The

Aleksandr Solzhenitsyn   Novel / Russia   12

Solzhenitsyn's novel gives readers the day-to-day account of life on a tiny island in Stalin's vast Gulag Archipelago, where a few imprisoned scientists are allowed to do research possibly useful to the state. The title refers to Dante's first circle of hell. (1968)

Fixer, The

Bernard Malamud   Novel / U.S.   11, 12

The victim of a vicious anti-Semitic conspiracy, Yakov Bok is in a Russian prison, with only his indomitable will to sustain him; this novel was a Pulitzer Prize-winner upon publication. (1967)

Flamingo Feather

Lauren van der Post   Novel / South Africa   9, 10

Dedicated to the "fast vanishing Africa of his boyhood," this is a story of the adventure undertaken by two hunters, one old and one young, to save Africa from an unknown but vast evil. (1955)

Flatland: A Romance of Many Dimensions

Edwin Abbott   Novel / Mathematics   10, 11, 12

An average square in a two-dimensional world has a mystical encounter with a sphere in this highly entertaining parable combining dimensional theory and social satire. (1894)

Flowers for Algernon

Daniel Keyes   Novel / U.S.   9, 10

A mentally challenged man, temporarily becomes a genius through scientific means. (1959)

Flush

Virginia Woolf   Novel / Britain   9, 10, 11

Woolf discovered Flush, a companion spaniel, in the letters exchanged between Elizabeth Barrett and her lover Robert Browning. This is a dog's eye view of the famous relationship and elopement of the two Victorian poets. (1933)

Flying Home and Other Stories

Ralph Ellison   Short Stories / U.S.   📖   12

Ralph Ellison (1914–1994) is best known for his autobiography, *Invisible Man*. This is a posthumous collection of 13 of his best short stories about the reality of being black in America. (1996).

Fool's Crow

James Welch   Novel / Native American   11

Fool's Crow struggles to maintain his own culture in the mystical world of the Pikunis, a Blackfoot tribe, as white civilization seeks to destroy it. A coming-of age-novel set in 1890s Montana. (1986)

For the Term of His Natural Life

Marcus Clarke   Novel / Australia   12

Clarke's classic novel gives a powerful portrayal of life as experienced by colonial Australians through the experience of a transported convict. (1874)

For Whom the Bell Tolls

Earnest Hemingway   Novel / U.S.   📖   10, 11, 12

Following his reporting on the Spanish Civil War, Hemingway penned one of the most powerful love stories of all times in which an American joins in a doomed but heroic resistance to enemy forces. (1940)

Forsyte Saga, The

John Galsworthy   Novel / Britain   10, 11, 12

Three novels, published in one volume, of the ebbing social power of the commercial upper middle-class Forsyte family between 1886 and 1920 give an excellent picture of the wider developments within society, particularly the changing position of women. (1922)

Fortune's Daughter

Alice Hoffman   Novel / U.S.   11, 12

The story of two women, a young single mother, and a Russian fortune-teller, are woven together with the usual Hoffman magic. (1989)

Fourteenth of October, The
Winifred Bryher   Novel / Historical / Ancient Britain   **11, 12**

Wulf, a Saxon boy, stands guard against the Danes on the British coast.
(1959)

Frankenstein
Mary Shelley   Novel / Britain   📖   **10, 11**

Frankenstein, an idealistic student of natural philosophy in Geneva at
the dawn of the 19th century creates a creature of supernatural strength
and size and brings it to life. (1818)

Franny and Zooey
J. D. Salinger   Novel / U.S.   **11, 12**

The author of *Catcher in the Rye* offers two stories about the spiritual
crisis of college student Franny Glass. (1961)

Freedom Road
Howard Fast   Novel / U.S.   **10, 11, 12**

Gideon Jackson, an ex-slave, is elected to the South Carolina Constitutional Convention assembled in Charleston in 1868. He then begins an
agrarian integrated community and goes on to Congress. Regrettably,
Gideon's attempts at equality run parallel to the formation and growth
of the Ku Klux Klan. (1944)

French Lieutenant's Woman, The
John Fowles   Novel / U.S.   **11, 12**

An amateur paleontologist falls in love with a young woman who is
attempting to redefine what it is to be female in mid-1800s England.
(1969)

Fringe of Leaves, A
Patrick White   Novel / Australia   **11, 12**

The early life of Ellen Gluyas, her marriage, brief stay in Tasmania and a
disastrous shipwreck in 1836 leave her abandoned on the Queensland
Coast among the aborigines. The story explores a character's growth
towards understanding. (1976)

Fruits of the Earth

Frederick Grove   Novel / Canada   10, 11, 12

A tragic heroic figure works all his life to expand his Manitoba farm but has no time, until too late, for human relationships. (1933)

Fugitive Pieces

Anne Michaels   Novel / Canada   11, 12

Seven-year-old Jakob Beer is rescued from the Nazis in Poland by a Greek archaeologist and brought to Canada. As an adult, he becomes a renowned poet who inspires Ben, a young Canadian professor. Ben's parents have survived the death camps but their memories have left a deep scar. (1996)

Funeral Games

Mary Renault   Novel / Historical / Ancient Greece   9, 10

The last of the *Alexander Trilogy* focuses on the 15 years following the great king's death. (1981) See *Fire from Heaven* and *The Persian Boy.*

Garden Party and Other Stories, The

Katherine Mansfield   Short Stories / New Zealand   11, 12

This is the third and final volume of short stories published by Mansfield in her lifetime (1888–1923). The 15 stories are small masterpieces of the nuances and subtle undertones that make up everyday life. (1922)

Giants in the Earth: A Saga of the Prairie

O. E. Rolvaag   Novel / U.S.   10, 11, 12

A Norwegian pioneer family struggles with the land and elements in the Dakota Territory as it tries to make a new life in America in the mid-1800s. (1955; originally published in Norwegian in 1927)

Girl With a Pearl Earring

Tracy Chevalier   Novel / U.S.   10, 11, 12

Taking a painting by the Dutch painter Johannes Vermeer as her starting point, Chevalier has created a moving fictional account of the master's intimate relationship with the novel's narrator, a 16-year-old servant. (2001)

Giver, The
Lois Lowry   Novel / U.S.   ⌐◡   9

Twelve-year-old Jonas is caught in a futuristic world governed by the principle of "Sameness." When he is made "giver" for the community, he begins to experience all the joys and sorrows of the past. (1993)

Giving Birth to Thunder, Sleeping With His Daughter
Barry Lopez   Short Stories / Native American   9, 10, 11, 12

Coyote is the legendary Native American trickster hero. Lopez gathers oral history from 40 tribes across America to write these 68 tales that are various incarnations of coyote mythology. (1977)

Glass Bead Game, The
Hermann Hesse   Novel / Germany   12

Josef Knecht lives in Castalia, a remote place society has provided for the intellectual elite in the 23rd century. Knecht's passion is to master the Glass Bead Game, which demands knowledge of all aesthetic and scientific arts. The German title has also been translated as *Magister Ludi*. (1943)

Go Tell It On The Mountain
James Baldwin   Novel / U.S.   10, 11, 12

Hailed as one of the best books of the 20th century, the novel begins with the religious awakening of a 14-year-old boy in a Harlem storefront church. Through the explorations that follow, Baldwin dramatizes the story of the great black migration from the rural U.S. south to the urban north. (1953)

God of Small Things, The
Arundhati Roy   Novel / India   10

The lives of inseparable twins in rural India change forever in this beautifully told story filled with mystery, humor, horror, and poetic insight. (1996)

Golden Bowl, The
Henry James   Novel / U.S.   12

In Henry James's last completed novel, a young American woman marries an impoverished Italian prince. The Golden Bowl, found in a London second hand shop, is really gilded crystal; it serves as a symbol for the relationship between the characters. (1904)

Golden Compass, The
Philip Pullman Novel / Britain   11, 12

In the first book of the highly popular three-part *His Dark Materials*, Lyra, who lives in Oxford in a universe parallel to our own, discovers a plot to experiment on stolen children that involves her own mother and father. (1995) See *The Amber Spyglass* and *The Subtle Knife*.

Golden Notebook, The
Doris Lessing Novel / Britain   12

Anna Wulf experiences a crisis in her life and works through it to a tenuous freedom in this feminist classic. (1962)

Good Earth, The
Pearl Buck Novel / U.S.   9

This poignant portrayal of a poor farmer's life and his bond with the land in early 20th-century China won a Pulitzer Prize and became a widely read best seller. (1931)

Grain of Wheat, A
(James) Ngugi wa Thiong'o Novel / Kenya   9, 10, 12

An exciting string of events takes place five days before Kenyan independence and focuses on the Mau Mau freedom struggle and the changing face of an African country. (1967)

Grand Avenue
Greg Sarris Short Stories / U.S.   11, 12

This first collection of short stories about a Native American community is set in a northern California landscape of tumbledown shacks. It portrays its inhabitants as caught between the bleak realities of everyday life and the magical lore of their ancestors. (1994)

Grapes of Wrath, The

John Steinbeck   Novel / U.S.   10, 11, 12

Oklahoma farmers desperately seek the promised land of California after drought and the banks take their farms. Their plight and poverty do not crush their indomitable spirit and dignity. A Pulitzer Prize-winning novel. (1939)

Grass is Singing, The

Doris Lessing   Novel / Britain   12

Lessing's first novel tells the story of the complex relationship between a white farmer's wife and her black servant. (1950)

Great Expectations

Charles Dickens   Novel / Britain   9, 10

Young Pip's fate is entwined with the convict Magwitch, the eccentric Miss Havisham, and the beautiful Estella in one of Dicken's best-loved novels. (1862)

Great Gatsby, The

F. Scott Fitzgerald   Novel / U.S. 📖   11, 12

Jay Gatsby lives his own distorted vision of the American dream as he pursues his destructive passion for Daisy Buchanan in New York and Long Island in the 1920s. (1925)

Great Ponds, The

Elechi Amadi   Novel / Nigeria   10

A ruinous and near-epic battle takes place between two tribes in eastern Nigeria who fight with both physical and spiritual weapons. (1969)

Green Mansions

W. H. Hudson   Novel / U.S.   9

Set in the Amazonian jungles of South America, this is the story of young Abel's love for Rima, a child of nature who can imitate the birds so well that she can cast a spell over the natives. (1904)

Grendel

John Gardner Novel / U.S. 11, 12

The first and most terrifying monster in English literature, from the great early epic *Beowulf*, tells his side of the story. (1971)

Gulliver's Travels

Jonathan Swift Novel / Britain 11

This classic story depicts the fantasy-rich travels of a shipwrecked surgeon, Lemuel Gulliver, and satirizes humans and the governing institutions they have created. (1726)

Handful of Dust, A

Evelyn Waugh Novel / Britain 10, 11, 12

An aristocratic wife leaves her husband after the death of their only son. He seeks consolation on the Amazon where he spends the rest of his life reading Dickens to a mad recluse. This comic novel satirizes the empty morality of Britain in the 1930s. (1934)

Handmaid's Tale, The

Margaret Atwood Novel / Canada 12

Atwood's suspenseful novel is a shocking view of contemporary society's issues of prejudice and misogyny set in a futuristic, repressive society. (1986)

Hard Times

Charles Dickens Novel / Britain 9, 10, 11, 12

Dickens' classic presents the picture of the harsh Utilitarian Gradgrind's misguided attempts at raising his children, and his realization of what he has done once they have grown. (1854)

Hawthorne's Short Stories

Nathaniel Hawthorne Newton Arvin, ed. Short Stories / U.S. 📖 12

This collection of 24 of Hawthorne's stories includes the best known of his tales such as "Young Goodman Brown" and "Wakefield" as well as those lesser known but equally powerful. (1980)

Heart is a Lonely Hunter, The

Carson McCullers   Novel / U.S.   10, 11

A female protagonist's adolescence in a 1930s Georgia mill town is bittersweet; her interactions with some unique neighbors help her to face who she is. (1940)

Heart of Darkness

Joseph Conrad   Novel / Britain   📖   12

This archetypal story of a mission upriver into the African jungle to rescue a man mad with power reveals the abyss of the human soul. (1902)

Heart of the Matter, The

Graham Greene   Novel / Britain   10, 11, 12

Set in Africa during World War II, this novel traces the slow moral decay of Scobie, the deputy commissioner of police. (1948)

Heat of the Day, The

Elizabeth Bowen   Novel / Britain   12

Bowen's subtle treatment of wartime love and espionage condenses a full range of human emotion. (1949)

Henderson the Rain King

Saul Bellow   Novel / U.S.   11, 12

At times touching and at times hilarious, this is the story of a wealthy American pig farmer in a mid-life crisis who goes to deepest Africa in a quest for meaning. (1959)

Henry Lawson: Selected Stories

Henry Lawson   Short Stories / Australia   9, 10, 11, 12

Lawson's stories popularized the notion of mateship and present extraordinary impressions of rural life in Australia at the end of the 18th century. These accessible and immensely enjoyable tales have been recently republished. (2002)

Her-Bak, The Living Face of Ancient Egypt

Isha Schwaller De Lubicz   Novel / Ancient Egypt   9, 10

This two volume account of Her-Bak's initiation into the Inner Temple and his progressive penetration of the esoteric aspects of the Egyptian Mystery teachings takes place between the XX and XXI dynasties in the temple of Karnak. (1980)

Here On Earth

Alice Hoffman   Novel / U.S.   10, 11, 12

After 20 years away, March Murray returns to her hometown with her daughter, Gwen, to attend a funeral. Both find themselves caught up in relationships that change their lives. (1997)

Hero in our Time, A

Mikhail Lermontov   Novel / Russia   📖   11

Lermontov's protagonist is based on the Byronic ideal of the Romantic hero dedicated to freedom at whatever cost. (1841)

High Wind in Jamaica, A

Richard Hughes   Novel / Britain   9

Pirates abduct the Bas-Thornton children, sent home to England after a hurricane in Jamaica, with strange results. The story explores innocence and experience. (1929)

History of Tom Jones, The

Henry Fielding   Novel / Britain   10, 11, 12

One of the earliest of English novels, this is the delightful story of Tom, thought to be the illegitimate son of a servant, who, in fact, turns out to be the illegitimate son of the sister of the squire. (1749)

Hobbit, The

J. R. R. Tolkien   Novel / Britain   〰   9

Bilbo Baggins, a Hobbit, reluctantly leaves his comfortable life to undertake a very hazardous journey in search of a magical ring and encounters many adventures. A prelude to *The Lord of the Rings*. (1937)

Honorary Consul, The

Graham Greene   Novel / Britain   12

Master storyteller Greene explores moral issues within a political framework in this hostage drama set in Paraguay. (1973)

Horse's Mouth, The

Joyce Cary   Novel / Britain   11, 12

An inimitable iconoclastic artist, Gulley Jimson, insists upon living, speaking, and acting in freedom. These are his adventures. (1944)

Hot Water

P. G. Wodehouse   Novel / Britain   9, 10, 11, 12

Delightful and brilliantly written, the misadventures of Bertie Wooster, a young English gentleman in the 1920s and 30s and his wise butler and rescuer Jeeves, remain classic humor. This is one of many books Wodehouse wrote. Most are equally delightful. (1981)

Hound of the Baskervilles, The

Sir Arthur Conan Doyle   Novel / Britain   9, 10

Science and superstition meet on the English moors in this famous Sherlock Holmes mystery. (1902)

House for Mr. Biswas, A

V. S. Naipaul   Novel / Trinidad   10, 12

Mr. Biswas longs for a house of his own with some independence and dignity. Set in post-Colonial Trinidad with a central character inspired by the author's father, this novel traces the life of Biswas from birth to death as traditional island society changes radically. (1961)

House in Paris, The

Elizabeth Bowen   Novel / Britain   11, 12

Bowen weaves a masterpiece of nuance and atmosphere as two children wait, full of apprehension in a house in Paris, while upstairs an old woman is dying. (1935)

House Made of Dawn

N. Scott Momaday   Novel / Native American   10, 11, 12

Jemez, a Pueblo Indian, runs from his traditional roots, gets caught in the ways of white culture after returning from the war in Europe, and ultimately finds hope in reconnecting with his own traditions. This Pulitzer Prize-winning story is based on the lives of Momaday's ancestors. (1977)

House of the Seven Gables, The

Nathaniel Hawthorne   Novel / U.S.   📖   10, 11, 12

The Pyncheon family of New England suffers, generation after generation, from a curse placed on it by "old wizard Maule." (1851)

House of the Spirits, The

Isabel Allende   Novel / Chile   11

A powerful mix of passion and politics follows the Trueba family through four generations. It integrates the magical and real to reflect a contemporary view of Latin American people. (1982)

House on Mango Street, The

Sandra Cisneros   Novel / U.S.   11, 12

This series of powerful and poetic vignettes describes the childhood and coming-of-age of Esperanza Cordero who lives on Mango Street in a poor, Latino neighborhood in Chicago. (1984)

How Green Was My Valley

Richard Llewellyn   Novel / Britain   10, 11, 12

Set in a Welsh coal-mining village in the last quarter of the 19th century, this heartwarming story of young Huw Morgan allows an honest look into the physical and spiritual trials of Huw, his family, and his village. (1939)

How I Spent My Summer Vacation

W. O. Mitchell   Novel / Canada   9, 10, 11, 12

Both hilarious and deeply moving, this is a novel about loss of innocence and facing hypocrisy. (1981)

How the Garcia Girls Lost Their Accents

Julia Alvarez   Novel / U.S.   9, 10, 11, 12

This delightful story shows four adult sisters looking back at the privileged life they led growing up in a wealthy Dominican family, and the prejudice they faced as immigrants in America. (1990)

Howard's End

E. M. Forster   Novel / Britain   11, 12

The Schlegel family, people of culture and imagination, become drawn to the Wilcox family, business people who distrust emotion; the tension between relationships and conflicting values in Edwardian England is profoundly explored. (1910)

Human Comedy, The

William Saroyan   Novel / U.S.   9, 10

Homer and his brother Ulysses grow up without a father during World War II in California, where Homer is a telegraph boy delivering messages of war casualties to the townspeople. Although this is a time of suffering, Saroyan's message is clear: "There will always be pain in things, but this does not mean that a man shall despair." (1943)

Humboldt's Gift

Saul Bellow   Novel / U.S.   11, 12

This is a rowdy, funny, exuberant novel of a literary man and his complicated destiny, which becomes even more trying when he is introduced to the works of Rudolf Steiner. (1974)

Hunchback of Notre Dame, The
Victor Hugo   Novel / France   11

Although centered on the Gothic splendor of the famous Cathedral in medieval Paris, this is a timeless story of the doomed love of the hunch-backed bell-ringer, Quasimodo, for the gypsy Esmerelda. (1831)

I Am One of You Forever
Fred Chappell   Novel / U.S.   11, 12

An Appalachian coming-of-age story emerges as fictional poet Jess Kirkman reflects on his childhood and on a host of relatives who influence his development. (1985)

I Capture the Castle
Dodie Smith   Novel / Britain   9, 10, 11, 12

Seventeen-year-old Cassandra Mortmain longs to be a famous writer like her father once was. Her life in a crumbling English castle with him, her sister, and their somewhat strange step-mother, Topaz, is wonderfully described in a charming blend of romance and reality in this timeless novel. (1948)

I Heard the Owl Call My Name
Margaret Craven   Novel / Native Canadian   9, 10

A young vicar is sent to a Pacific Northwest village in remote Canada; gradually he gains the trust of the village people, as the old culture of totems and potlatch evolves into modern housing and alcoholism. (1973)

I Never Promised You a Rose Garden
Hannah Green   Novel / U.S.   9, 10

A mentally ill young girl battles her own "demons" to find health. (1977)

I, Claudius
Robert Graves   Novel / Britain   10, 11

Graves presents an imaginative but unforgettable character in Claudius, Emperor of Rome from 10 B.C.E. to 54 C.E. (1934)

Idiot, The
Fyodor Dostoevsky   Novel / Russia   12

Upon his return to Russia from an asylum in Switzerland in the pre-Soviet era, Prince Myshkin's honesty, goodness and integrity prove unequal to the moral emptiness of the world created by the ruling class. (1868)

Illumination Night
Alice Hoffman   Novel / U.S.   10, 11, 12

A disturbed and angry high school girl comes to Martha's Vineyard and, through her actions, reveals the fragility of the placid lives of the people who live there. (1987)

Immigrants, The
Howard Fast   Novel / U.S.   10, 11, 12

Master storyteller Fast spans his epic of three Californian families over the course of the 20th century. (1977) The other novels in the series are *Second Generation* (1978), *The Establishment* (1979), *The Legacy* (1981), *The Immigrant's Daughter* (1985), and the conclusion, *An Independent Woman.* (1997).

Impact: Fifty Short Stories
Fannie Safier, ed.   Anthology / U.S.   📖   9

This collection of 50 classic and modern short stories is popular as a text in high schools, colleges, and introductory university classes. (1993)

In Country
Bobbie Ann Mason   Novel / U.S.   10

A young woman comes to know more of her own dead father while she helps her uncle face the post-traumatic stress of Vietnam. (1982)

In Love and Trouble: Stories of Black Women
Alice Walker   Short Stories / U.S.   📖   12

Walker's first collection of short stories reveals her power to depict black women of varying backgrounds who are linked by their vulnerability. (1973)

In Our Time

Ernest Hemingway   Short Stories / U.S.   11, 12

Hemingway's second collection of short stories reflects his life in Paris in the 1920s. (1925)

In the Beginning

Chaim Potok   Novel / U.S.   10, 11

A Jewish Biblical scholar looks back to his own beginnings and coming-of-age in the Bronx through the golden years of the 1920s and into the terrifying rise to power of Hitler and the Nazis in Europe. (1975)

In the Castle of My Skin

George Lamming   Novel / West India   12

Lamming presents a fictional account of his early years growing up in Barbados and Trinidad where the white landlords hire black overseers to control the villagers, fostering hatred and mistrust. (1970)

In the Lake in the Woods

Tim O'Brien   Novel / U.S.   12

When Kathy Wade attempts to comfort her husband John after a political defeat, it becomes increasingly clear that secrets from the past, including John's time in Vietnam, stand between them. (1994)

In the Skin of the Lion

Michael Ondaatje   Novel / Canada   11, 12

This semi-historical novel about Toronto in the 1920s introduces two characters that later appear in *The English Patient*. It is a remarkable intermingling of various layers of society as well as elements of mystery, love, and social commentary. (1987)

In the Time of the Butterflies

Julia Alvarez   Novel / U.S.   11, 12

This blend of fact and fiction is inspired by the true story of the three Mirabal sisters who, in 1960, were murdered for their part in an underground plot to overthrow the corrupt government in the Dominican Republic. (1994)

Indian Tales

Jaime De Angulo   Anthology / Native American   11, 12

De Angulo collected tales, jokes, myths, and folklore from his 40 years of working with the Pit River tribe of California. As a linguist and anthropologist, he used the tales to entertain his children. They are not intended to be anthropologically correct, but rather to capture the spirit of an Indian family's life. (1953)

Indians of New Jersey: Dickon Among the Lenapes

Jan L. and M. R. Harrington   Novel / Native American   9, 10

A young English boy is saved from drowning by a Lenape family. He adapts to Lenape life and is eventually adopted. The book includes details about tanning leather, growing crops, religious ceremonies, and the sacred ways of the Lenape. Although this is rated as juvenile fiction it is an excellent detailed account of Lenape life and living without technology. (1963)

Innocents Abroad, The

Mark Twain   Novel / U.S.   📖   9

In an account of a voyage through Europe and the Holy Land, Twain describes how the "New Barbarians," Americans, meet the Old World. (1869)

Intruder in the Dust

William Faulkner   Novel / U.S.   11, 12

Set in Faulkner's fictional Yoknapatawpha County, this novel combines the solution of a murder mystery with an exploration of race relations in the South. (1948)

Invisible Man

Ralph Ellison   Novel / U.S.   9, 10

In this powerful coming-of-age story, a young black man tries to find his place in a world where he feels invisible. It became a classic as soon as it appeared and won the National Book Award for Fiction. (1952)

Ironweed

William Kennedy   Novel / U.S.   9, 10, 11, 12

An ex-ballplayer who has hit rock bottom returns to Albany in 1938 to try to make peace with the mistakes of his past; a Pulitzer Prize-winner. (1983)

Island of Dr. Moreau, The

H. G. Wells   Novel / Britain   *6∿*   9, 11, 12

This science fiction fantasy tells of a shipwrecked scientist who decides to humanize animals through surgery. (1896) See *The Time Machine*.

Ivanhoe

Sir Walter Scott   Novel / Historical / Britain   9, 10, 11

This is the exciting story of a knight and lady in the days of King Richard the Lion-hearted and Robin Hood. (1819)

Jane Eyre

Charlotte Bronte   Novel / Britain   9, 10, 11, 12

This is a classic novel of Jane, a penniless orphan, who becomes governess to the illegitimate daughter of Mr. Rochester; he and Jane fall in love but cannot marry because of Mr. Rochester's mad Creole wife. (1847)

Jesse

Gary Soto   Novel / U.S.   9, 10

Growing up in the shadow of the Vietnam War, two Mexican American brothers work hard to attend junior college which they hope will help them escape their heritage of tedious physical labor. (1994)

Journal of the Plague Year, A

Daniel Defoe   Novel / Britain   11, 12

Defoe presents a highly realistic account through the eyes of a London resident in the years 1664–65 as the city attempts to deal with the spread of the Plague and its aftermath. (1722)

Joy in the Morning

Betty Smith   Novel / U.S.   10, 11, 12

In this beautifully written story by the author of *A Tree Grows in Brooklyn*, newly married Annie must leave her family and friends and follow her husband as he enters law school in the 1920s. (1963)

Joy Luck Club, The

Amy Tan   Novel / U.S.   11

Tan portrays the lives of Chinese American women through mother-daughter relationships while reflecting issues of assimilation and acculturation. (1989)

Jude the Obscure

Thomas Hardy   Novel / Britain   10, 11, 12

A dark novel of tragic love relationships depicts the struggle of human passion and social values that result in ill-fated destinies. (1895)

Jungle, The

Upton Sinclair   Novel / U.S.   9, 10

Upton's most famous work is an exposé of the Chicago meatpacking industry at the beginning of the 20th century. (1906)

Keep the Aspidistra Flying

George Orwell   Novel / Britain   11, 12

Gordon Comstock is battling to remain a poet as he approaches thirty. But the world of the ordinary, with its compelling need to earn money, keeps drawing him away from his loftier intentions. Orwell's understanding and humor contribute to this book's lasting popularity. (1936)

Keepers of the Earth

Michael Caduto and Joseph Bruchac   Anthology / Native American
11, 12

This collection of 25 Native American tales and activities is co-authored by Bruchac, an Abenaki poet and novelist. The tales impart environmental awareness and a respect and love for the land and all the creatures that inhabit it. (1988)

Key to Rebecca, The

Ken Follett   Novel / Britain   9, 10, 11, 12

Set during World War II in North Africa, this is the story of master spy, Alex Woolf, who searches against time and the Nazis for a deadly code buried in the pages of Daphne du Maurier's novel, *Rebecca*. (1980)

Kidnapped

Robert Louis Stevenson   Novel / Britain   9

Young David Balfour's uncle has him kidnapped to prevent his claim on his inherited estate; David meets the Alan Breck and together they witness a murder and are forced to flee into the Scottish Highlands. As exciting an adventure today as when it was written. (1886)

Killer Angels, The

Michael Shaara   Novel / Historical / Civil War   9, 10, 11, 12

The Battle of Gettysburg is recreated through the thoughts and memories of each of the generals: Lee, Longstreet, and Chamberlain. (1974)

Kim

Rudyard Kipling   Novel / Britain 🔊   9

Considered by some to be Kipling's masterpiece, this is the exciting story of the orphaned Kim O'Hara who travels through India and the Himalayas with an old lama from Tibet. (1901)

Kinfolk: A Novel of China

Pearl S. Buck   Novel / U.S.   10

Louise Liang falls in love with an American in New York City and her father sends her back to China. (1949)

King Arthur and His Knights of the Round Table

Roger Lancelyn Green   Novel / Britain 🔊   11

This easy-to-read retelling of the legends of King Arthur is true to the Mallory original. (1953)

King Must Die, The

Mary Renault   Novel / Historical / Ancient Greece   9, 10

This novel is based on the adventures of the Greek hero Theseus, his encounter with the minotaur, and his trip home. (1948) His adventures continue in *The Bull from the Sea*.

King Solomon's Mines

H. Rider Haggard   Novel / Britain   9

African adventurer, Allan Quatermain, discovers an ancient map that leads to a lost tribe, a hidden country, and the secrets of Solomon's mines. (1886)

Kitchen God's Wife, The

Amy Tan   Novel / U.S.   9

A mother's stories of a troubled past in China before and after the Communist Revolution bring her closer to her daughter. (1991)

Krik? Krak

Edwidge Danticat   Short Stories / Haiti   12

This collection of short stories gives testimony to the strength of the human spirit in spite of overwhelming hardship. (1995)

Kristin Lavransdatter

Sigrid Undset   Tiina Nunnaly, trans.   Novel / Norway   11, 12

Undset's epic trilogy portrays a woman's life from childhood through old age, culminating with the plague in 14th-century Norway and offers an ultimately positive view of life. The separate stories are: *The Bridal Wreath*, *The Mistress of Husaby* and *The Cross*. It won the Nobel Prize for Literature (1928).

Lady Oracle

Margaret Atwood   Novel / Canada   11, 12

In this comic tale, a writer of melodramatic romance novels begins to invent her own existence, including a simulation of her death.(1976)

Lake Wobegon Days

Garrison Keillor   Novel / U.S.   9

Keillor's dry humor captures the essence of mid-western America; it chronicles the origins of Keillor's mythical but very real town and its inhabitants. (1985)

Last Frontier, The

Howard Fast   Novel / U.S.   10, 11, 12

Fast's offers a semi-fictionalized account of the move of 300 Cheyenne Indians in 1878 from their Oklahoma reservation back to their beloved Wyoming and Montana, 1000 miles away. They were persecuted all the way by the U.S. Cavalry. (1941)

Last Gentleman, The

Walker Percy   Novel / U.S.   11, 12

A dreamy and dislocated young man comes to himself in the midst of a Mississippi family in crisis during the period of the Civil Rights movement. (1977)

Last of the Mohicans, The

James Fenimore Cooper   Novel / U.S.   📖   9, 10

The second in the series of *Leatherstocking Tales* tells about the adventures of pioneer scout Natty Bumppo. (1826)

Last of the Wine, The

Mary Renault   Novel / Historical / Ancient Greece   9, 10, 11

Set in classical Athens, this is the story of a young follower of Socrates who becomes a friend, and lover, of an older follower. Together they participate in the Peloponnesian War and struggle with their sorrow as Socrates is put to death. (1981)

Last Report on the Miracles at Little No Horse, The

Louise Erdrich   Novel / Native American   11, 12

This novel by one of America's best and most popular writers follows the story of Agnes DeWitt, a rural Wisconsin girl turned nun, turned musical prodigy, turned farm wife, turned priest. (2001)

Last Unicorn, The

Peter Beagle   Novel / U.S.   9

An imaginative and touching tale of a unicorn's quest for her lost fellows, assisted by a mediocre magician and the ever-practical Molly. (1968)

Late Bourgeois World, The

Nadine Gordimer   Novel / South Africa   11, 12

Banned in South Africa for 12 years, this novel is about an activist in the struggle against apartheid who betrays his friends to save himself. (1966)

Laughing Boy

Oliver Lafarge   Novel / Native American   9, 10

A young Navajo couple fall in love and experience the dangers of life for them in a white town. It won a Pulitzer Prize in 1930. (1929)

Les Miserables

Victor Hugo   Novel / France   10, 11, 12

The classic story of the poor in post-Revolutionary France is seen through the life of Jean Valjean, an ex-convict who befriends a dying prostitute and cares for her orphaned daughter. (1862)

Lesson Before Dying, A

Ernest J. Gaines   Novel / U.S.   9, 10, 11, 12

An innocent young black man in a small Cajun community in 1940s Louisiana is about to go to the electric chair for murder when a black teacher befriends him. What they learn from each other transforms them both. (1993)

Life and Times of Michael K

J. M. Coetzee   Novel / South Africa   10

Michael K leaves his job as a municipal gardener to help his sick mother return to her birthplace in the country, but when she dies his life becomes a nightmare of war, roving gangs, and imprisonment. The novel is ultimately life affirming and won the Booker Prize. (1983)

Light in the Forest

Conrad Richter   Novel / U.S   9

A young man, born into a frontier family but captured and raised by the Lenape tribe, is returned after a treaty demands it. Strongly identified with the Lenapes and a stranger to white society, he struggles to find his place between the two cultures. (1951)

Lilac and Flag

John Berger   Novel / Britain   **11, 12**

Berger's final story in the *Into Their Labours* trilogy traces the lives of a young urban couple, descendents from peasants. (1990) See *Pig Earth* and *Once in Europa*.

Little Men

Louisa May Alcott   Novel / U.S.   9

The sequel to *Little Women* tells the story of the school Jo sets up with her beloved Mr. Bhaer. (1871)

Little Prince, The

Antoine de Saint-Exupéry   Novel / France   9

This is an allegorical tale of a pilot who lands in the Sahara Desert and meets a tiny prince from another planet who shares his stories about the meaning of life and the beauty of nature. (1944)

Little Women

Louisa May Alcott   Novel / U.S.   **9, 10, 11, 12**

A classic since its publication, this well-loved book tells the story of four sisters growing up in New England during the Civil War. Amy, Jo, Beth, and Meg are as real now as they were 150 years ago. (1868)

Little World of Don Camillo, The

Giovanni Guareschi   Novel / Italy   9

A delightfully humorous novel set in an Italian village tells of the vigorous ideological debates and entertaining adventures of Don Camillo, the local priest, and Peppone, the Communist mayor. (1951)

Lives of Girls and Women

Alice Munroe   Novel / Canada   9, 10

Munro's only novel reads like a series of short stories and gives a sensitive, funny, and realistic account of a girl growing up in a small Ontario town in the 1950s. (1971)

Local Girls

Alice Hoffman   Novel / U.S.   9, 10, 11, 12

Greta Samuelson is the central character in this series of stories told in alternating voices; Greta grows up with the help of three strong women as she experiences confusing relationships. (1999)

Loneliness of the Long Distance Runner

Alan Sillitoe   Novel / Britain   9, 10

An English reform-school adolescent rebels against the establishment by refusing to cross the finish line in a race he is winning. (1959)

Look Homeward, Angel

Thomas Wolfe   Novel / U.S.   11, 12

Wolfe's classic semi-autobiographical coming-of-age story set in North Carolina during the first quarter of the 20th century has inspired many authors, including the young Jack Kerouac. (1929)

Lord Jim

Joseph Conrad   Novel / Britain   📖   9, 10, 11, 12

Jim, a highly idealistic chief mate, involuntarily saves his own life over the lives of his passengers and is haunted for the rest of his life. This remarkable novel focuses on the values of honor, courage, and loyalty. (1900)

Lord of the Flies

William Golding   Novel / Britain   10

This modern parable reflects the human condition as a group of British school children survive a plane crash on an island but devolve into tribes engaged in a brutal and vicious struggle for power. (1954)

Lord of the Plains

Alfred Silver   Novel / Native Canadian   9, 10, 11, 12

Silver creates an engrossing fictionalized account of the Canadian Great Northwest Rebellion of the 1880s led by the settlers and Indians who occupied land that was being sold by the government. (1990)

Lord of the Rings, The

J. R. R. Tolkien   Novel / Britain   9, 11, 12

The three-volume masterpiece continues the story of *The Hobbit* as Frodo and the Fellowship engage in a classic battle of good and evil to save Middle-Earth. (1968) See *The Fellowship of the Ring, The Two Towers,* and *The Return of the King.*

Love In The Time of Cholera

Gabriel Garcia Marquez   Novel / Columbia   11, 12

This classic and hugely popular novel is about a woman who rejects her poet lover to marry a doctor; after her husband dies 51 years later, the poet returns. (1988)

Love Medicine

Louise Erdrich   Novel / Native American   11, 12

Erdrich's first novel in a four-part series tells the story of two extended families, the Kashpaws and the Lamartines. Several narrative voices reveal powerful contemporary issues of Native American life including the poverty of reservation life, government policies, alcoholism, and Christianity's effects on a culture that somehow survives. (1984)

Loved One, The

Evelyn Waugh   Novel / Britain   📖   11

Waugh's hilarious satire of the funeral industry and the California lifestyle in the 1940s remains a classic. (1948)

Lowenskold Ring, The
Selma Lagerlof   Novel / Sweden   9

This spellbinding ghost story of revenge for a ring stolen from a tomb in 18th-century Sweden focuses on the role of women and important questions of motive and power. (1925)

Luck of Ginger Coffy
Brian Moore   Novel / Canada   9, 10

A funny yet sad story tells of an Irish immigrant to Montreal who has difficulty adjusting to weather, work, family, and culture. (1960)

Lucky Jim
Kingsley Amis   Novel / Britain   📖   12

Amis's radical university lecturer, Jim Dixon, seems to be anti-everything in this amusing satire on English university life in the mid-20th century. (1954)

Lust for Life
Irving Stone   Novel / Biography / U.S.   10, 12

This highly readable fictionalized biography of the Dutch painter Vincent van Gogh is based on Van Gogh's three volumes of letters to his brother, Theo. (1961)

Madame Bovary
Gustave Flaubert   Novel / France   10, 11, 12

This masterpiece of French Fiction tells the story of the adulteries and suicide of a doctor's wife in Normandy. (1857)

Maggie: A Girl of the Streets
Stephen Crane   Novel / U.S.   📖   10, 11, 12

Crane's sympathetic study of an innocent and abused slum girl's descent into prostitution and her eventual suicide was so shocking at the time that he published it under a pseudonym at his own expense. (1893)

Magic Mountain, The

Thomas Mann   Novel / Germany   11, 12

Mann's classic novel, set in Europe just before and during World War I, details a young tuberculosis patient's quest for enlightenment in the face of disease and death. (1924)

Magus, The

John Fowles   Novel / Britain   10

A British schoolmaster is a guest on a Greek Island and experiences strange mythological appearances. (1966)

Main Street

Sinclair Lewis   Novel / U.S.   10, 11

Lewis describes with satirical realism the repetitive boredom of daily life in his fictional small mid-western town of Gopher Prairie. (1920)

Mama Day

Gloria Naylor   Novel / U.S.   11, 12

The magic of folk-healer Mama Day, part of an all-black community on an island off the coast of Georgia, meets and conquers the New York rationality of her niece and her husband. (1988)

Man in Full, A

Tom Woolf   Novel / U.S.   11, 12

In his second novel Woolf turns his satirical eye on Atlanta, Georgia, and the empire of Charlie Croker, "a man in full," in his prime and married to a much younger second wife. As Croker's world begins to crumble, he is forced to ask himself pressing questions. (1998)

Man of the People, A

Chinua Achebe   Novel / Nigeria   9

Written by one of the most highly regarded of African writers, this novel is a satirical account of the underbelly of Nigerian politics in the 1960s. (1966)

Man Who Killed the Deer

Frank Waters   Novel / Native American   10, 11, 12

This poignant novel centers on the search for cultural and personal identity. Waters tells the story of the metaphysical power of the tribes of the Blue Lake near Taos. (1970)

Manchild in the Promised Land

Claude Brown   Novel / U.S.   9

This classic autobiographical novel gives a starkly honest account of a young man, the son of southern black sharecroppers who move to Harlem, his growing up in the 1940s and 50s, and his escape to become an artist. (1965)

Mandarins, The

Simone de Beauvoir   Novel / France   12

Set in Paris in the late 1940s, this is the semi-autobiographical novel of de Beauvoir's friends and lovers in a politically fragmented, exhausted Europe just after World War II. (1954)

Manticore, The

Robertson Davies   Novel / Canada   12

The second novel in *The Deptford Trilogy* follows the Jungian analysis of Davis Staunton, the son of the boy who threw the fateful snowball in the first of the three books. David's journals reveal much about his father's life and his own. (1972) See *Fifth Business* and *World of Wonders*.

Many Waters

Madeleine L' Engle   Novel / U.S.   9, 10

The final book in L' Engle's classic science fiction series features time travel, mythical beasts, and fascinating adventures. (1986) See *A Swiftly Tilting Planet, A Wind in the Door,* and *A Wrinkle in Time.*

Mapmaker's Dream: The Meditations of Fra Mauro, Cartographer to the Court of Venice

James Cowan   Novel / Australia   11, 12

A 16th-century monk in Venice attempts to create the perfect map of the world through the stories told him by travelers and discovers that the interior world of the tellers is as wondrous as the reported marvels of recent discoveries. (1996)

Martin Chuzzlewit

Charles Dickens   Novel / Britain   9, 10, 11, 12

Young Martin is a young man in love with his grandfather's orphan girl companion. He is sent to America where he has many adventures before he returns. Dickens' novel is noted for its satire of mid-19th-century American life. (1844)

Master and Margarita, The

Mikhail Bulgakov   Novel / Russia   📖   12

The devil comes to Moscow with his companions and buys the soul of a married woman who longs for her lover, a young writer who is working on a novel about Pontius Pilate. This complex, delightful, magical, and hilarious novel was written in Stalinist Russia during the 1930s. (1967)

Mayor of Casterbridge, The

Thomas Hardy   Novel / Britain   10, 11, 12

This is the tragic story of a drunken man in 19th-century England who sells his wife and child and then reforms to become a rich and respected mayor; when his wife returns after 18 years, his fortunes begin to reverse. (1866)

Mean Spirit

Linda Hogan   Novel / U.S.   9, 10, 11, 12

Chickasaw environmentalist Hogan has based this novel in part on the 1920s history of white men marrying Osage women and then murdering them to gain control of their oil leases. (1990)

Memoirs of a Survivor

Doris Lessing   Novel / Britain   11, 12

In the future when the structure of society has broken down, a woman discovers her humanity and balance in the midst of inhumanity. (1975)

Memoirs of Sherlock Holmes

Sir Arthur Conan Doyle   Short Stories / Britain   9

This is the second volume of classic Sherlock Holmes detective stories, originally printed in *The Strand* magazine. (1894)

Men Against the Sea

Charles Nordhoff and James N. Hall   Novel / Britain.   9, 10

Captain Bligh emerges as a hero in this sequel to *The Mutiny on the Bounty*. After being cast adrift in a small boat with 18 loyal men, he successfully navigates a 3500-mile journey in the South Pacific. (1933) See *Mutiny on the Bounty* and *Pitcairn's Island*.

Men Without Women

Ernest Hemingway   Short Stories / U.S.   11, 12

Hemingway is considered one of the finest short story writers; this is a notable collection of some of his best stories. (1927)

Merry Adventures of Robin Hood, The 484

Howard Pyle   Novel / U.S.   ᏻ   9

Pyle's delightful illustrations accompany these classic tales of Robin, Friar Tuck, Little John, and Will Scarlet as they fight the Sheriff of Nottingham. (1897)

Metamorphosis

Franz Kafka   Novel / Czechoslovakia (German)   11, 12

This famous parable tells the story of a young traveling salesman who lives with and financially supports his parents and younger sister. He wakes up one morning to discover that he has been transformed into a huge insect. (1915)

Middle Passage

Charles R. Johnson   Novel / U.S.   10, 11, 12

A recently freed slave leaves New Orleans in 1830 aboard a clipper ship only to discover it is a slave ship bound for Africa. Winner of a National Book Award. (1990)

Middlemarch

George Eliot   Novel / Britain   10, 11, 12

Eliot's masterpiece is set against the background of the social and political upheavals in Britain during the first half of the 19th century. An idealistic and intelligent young woman marries an elderly scholar and later falls in love with his young cousin. (1872)

Mill on the Floss

George Eliot   Novel / Britain   10, 11, 12

A brother and sister differ in temperament and values in this tragic story. Jealousy distances them and forgiveness reunites them before their untimely deaths. (1860)

Moby Dick

Herman Melville   Novel / U.S.   📖   9, 10, 11, 12

This classic battle between man and fate, between the brutal forces of nature and human thought, is embedded in a realistic adventure story of a hunt for the white whale. (1851)

Mocassin Telegraph

W. P. Kinsella   Novel / Canada   9, 10

Kinsella creates touching and humorous stories of the lives of people in a small native village in Alberta. (1983)

Moll Flanders

Daniel Defoe   Novel / Britain   11, 12

One of the earliest novels in English literature portrays the humorous and unfortunate adventures of a female protagonist who struggles with sin and poverty. (1722)

Montana 1948

Larry Watson   Novel / U.S.   11, 12

A young boy tells of the breakdown of his family when his brother, the sheriff, arrests a physician uncle, suspected of sexually abusing his Native American women patients. (1993)

Moon is Down, The

John Steinbeck   Novel / U.S.   ⌒   10

This novel depicts Norwegian resistance to the German occupation in World War II. (1942)

Moons of Jupiter

Alice Munroe   Short Stories / Canada   9, 10

As in most of her collections, these short stories center on women and on what Munroe calls "the pain of human contact." (1982)

Moonstone, The

Wilkie Collins   Novel / Britain   9, 10, 11, 12

With this book, Collins invented the "first modern English detective story." This gripping example of the genre unravels the mystery surrounding the theft of an enormous diamond. (1868)

More Die of Heartbreak

Saul Bellow   Novel / U.S.   11

Benn Crader, a world-famous botanist, is ill fated in his attempts to find love in the dysfunctional emotional society of Western civilization in the late 20th century. (1987)

Mother Tongue

Demetria Martinez   Novel / U.S.   9, 10, 11, 12

A young Chicano woman falls desperately in love with a refugee from El Salvador whom she is helping to shelter. (1994)

Mountain and the Valley, The

Ernest Buckler   Novel / Canada   9

Set in the Annapolis Valley of Nova Scotia, this extraordinary novel chronicles the life of a potential artist in a family of sturdy, earthy, and inarticulate people. (1952)

Move Makes the Man, The

Bruce Brooks   Novel / U.S.   9

This story of friendship and struggle between two troubled youths, one black and one white, is woven around the game of basketball in North Carolina. (1984)

Moviegoer, The

Walker Percy   Novel / U.S.   12

This fine and funny exploration of the existential ennui of America in the late 1950s tells the story of a small-time stockbroker in search of something more who finds it during a Mardi Gras weekend. (1961)

Mrs. Dalloway

Virginia Woolf   Novel / Britain   📖   11, 12

Woolf's masterpiece creates a "stream of consciousness" during one June day in London shortly after World War I when Clarissa Dalloway gives a party. (1925)

Murder Must Advertise

Dorothy Sayers   Novel / Britain   10, 11, 12

This classic Lord Peter Wimsey detective novel is full of insight into the weavings of the human subconscious. (1933)

Mutiny on the Bounty

Charles Nordhoff and James N. Hall   Novel / Britain   9, 10

Twelve members of the crew of a British war vessel, the *H.M.S. Bounty*, led by Masters mate Fletcher Christian, rise against the cruel commander, Captain William Bligh. Bligh is cast adrift with 18 loyal men in the South

Pacific. This is the first book in the *Bounty Trilogy,* based on accounts of actual events in the 18th century. (1932) See *Men Against the Sea* and *Pitcairn's Island.*

My Antonia

Willa Cather   Novel / U.S 📖   9, 10, 11, 12

A spirited immigrant girl from Bohemia learns about friendship, love and forbearance as she makes her way in the beautiful wilds of 18th-century Nebraska among immigrants from other parts of the world. (1918)

Mythologies

W. B. Yeats   Short Stories / Ireland   10

These short writings by one of the greatest writers of the 20th century includes "The Celtic Twilight," a collection of Irish folk stories, as well as "The Secret Rose," "Rosa Alchemica" and other semi-fictional stories based on esoteric thought and traditional tales. (1959)

Nabokov's Dozen: A Collection of Thirteen Stories

Vladimir Nabokov   Short Stories / Russia   📖   11

The reader has an opportunity to experience Nabokov through the era of Stalin, the rise of the Nazis, World War II, and McCarthyism in the U.S. as the writer continues to search for meaning through art. It contains the often anthologized "Signs and Symbols." (1958)

Native Son

Richard Wright   Novel / U.S.   11

This vivid and suspenseful portrayal of slum conditions in the South is an intense psychological and sociological study of the African American experience. (1940)

Native Speaker

Chang-Rae Lee   Novel / U.S.   9, 10, 11, 12

Henry Park has spent his entire life trying to become a true American, a native speaker. But even as the essence of his adopted country continues to elude him, his Korean heritage seems to drift further and further away. (1996)

Natural, The

Bernard Malamud   Novel / U.S.   ⌒   9, 10, 11, 12

Roy Hobbs is a talented athlete whose promising career is suddenly cut short; Roy makes a comeback as an aging player in what has been described as the best baseball story ever written. (1952)

Nectar in a Sieve

Kamala Markhandaya   Novel / India   9, 10

This is the moving story of a peasant woman in a primitive village in India, whose whole life is a battle to care for those she loves. Her friendship with a white doctor is a poignant portrait of the costs of both traditionalism and modernization. (1955)

Nicholas Nickleby

Charles Dickens   Novel / Britain   10, 11, 12

The adventures of young Nicholas after his father dies and he, his mother and sister are left penniless are as entertaining as anything Dickens ever wrote. The novel is full of wonderful characters, struggles between good and evil, and vivid descriptions of Victorian England. (1839)

Night and Day

Virginia Woolf   Novel / Britain   12

Woolf's second novel, set in London, explores the relationship between two women, one an artist, the other a feminist. (1919)

Night Flight

Antoine de Saint-Exupè   Novel / France   10, 11

Based on the author's experiences as a mail pilot in South America, this is the story of two men: Fabien, a pilot flying the Patagonia mail, and Riviere, his boss. (1932)

Nine Stories

J. D. Salinger   Short Stories / U.S.   📖   10, 11, 12

Salinger considers these nine stories the only ones he has written that are worth preserving. Included is the much-praised "A Perfect Day for Bananafish." (1953)

Nine Tailors

Dorothy Sayers   Novel / Britain   9, 10

A disfigured corpse, the local rector, and countryside bell ringing draw Lord Peter Wimsey into one of his most exciting cases. (1934)

Nineteen Eighty-Four (1984)

George Orwell   Novel / Britain   11, 12

Orwell offers a chilling vision of a world where private life and love become impossible as Big Brother watches all, and language itself is reduced to utilitarian bleakness. (1949)

No Longer at Ease

Chinua Achebe   Novel / Nigeria   10

A high-ranking and respected Ibo villager's Western education separates him from his tribal culture and makes him part of a corrupt ruling elite he despises. This novel can be considered the second in a sequence in which Achebe re-creates Africa's journey from traditional to modern times. (1960)

Northanger Abbey

Jane Austen   Novel / Britain   11, 12

Probably the earliest of Austen's delightfully witty novels, this is the story of young Catherine Morland who, somewhat unbalanced by reading too many popular tales of romance and terror, imagines that the father of her new friends is involved in a mystery. (1818)

Northwest Passage

Kenneth Roberts   Novel / U.S.   9, 10, 11, 12

This classic historical novel set in the wilderness of 18th-century North America covers the adult life of Robert Rogers, founder of Rogers' Rangers. It spans the French and Indian Wars through the Revolution. (1937)

Norton Anthology of Short Novel

R. V. Cassill and Richard Bausch, eds.   Anthology   📖   10

Now in its sixth edition, containing 125 stories from 115 authors, the

Norton Anthology is an excellent choice for classic and contemporary short stories.

Nose, The

Nikolai Gogol   Novel / Russia   📖   12

Gogol's satirical fantasy is set in a strange city where nothing is as it seems. (1936)

Nostromo

Joseph Conrad   Novel / Britain   📖   11, 12

A revolution in an imaginary South American country threatens a silver mine; Nostromo, an Italian sailor, is drawn into a plot to seize the silver. Conrad's vivid descriptions of the escape by sea are as gripping now as when they were first written. (1904)

Not For Publication and Other Stories

Nadine Gordimer   Short Stories / South Africa   10

This is a remarkable collection of short stories inspired by the author's life in South Africa. Many of her themes revolve around the tensions of race. (1965)

Notes From the Underground

Fyodor Dostoevsky   Novel / Russia   📖   12

In this tragic-comic story, an alienated individual's obsessions destroy his chance for love. He is one of the greatest anti-heroes in all literature, (1864)

Nothing But the Truth: A Documentary Novel

Avi   Novel / U.S.   ✑   9

High school freshman Philip Malloy is suddenly swept up by national media coverage of a school protest because he likes to hum along to the national anthem. (1991)

Nymph and the Lamp, The

Thomas Head Raddall   Novel / Canada   9, 10

A young working girl's sudden marriage to a middle-aged lighthouse keeper on Sable Island, the "graveyard of the Atlantic," is rich in detail and a masterpiece of psychological tension. (1950)

O Pioneers!

Willa Cather   Novel / U.S.   📖   9, 10, 11, 12

A determined young woman becomes a wealthy landowner on the Nebraska prairie showing the social and economic changes brought on by the industrialization of farming in America. (1913)

Of Human Bondage

Somerset Maugham   Novel / Britain   11, 12

This semi-autobiographical novel describes the lonely childhood and coming-of-age of Philip Carey, a sensitive boy with a clubfoot raised by a religious aunt and uncle in a small English town. At 18, Philip leaves home to become an artist in Paris. When he returns to London to study medicine, he begins a doomed love affair that will change the course of his life. (1915)

Of Mice and Men

John Steinbeck   Novel / U.S.   9, 10

Two Californian migrant farm workers, George, the planner and dreamer, and Lennie, large and simpleminded, become tragically embroiled in a murder. (1937)

Old Curiosity Shop, The

Charles Dickens   Novel / Britain   10, 11, 12

Angelic Little Nell and her grandfather wander the countryside after the evil moneylender, Quilp, turns them out of their Curiosity Shop. Considered by some to be Dickens' most sentimental novel, it is still worth reading for the unforgettable characters he creates. (1841)

Old Gringo, The

Carlos Fuentes Novel / Mexico   12

Using the mysterious disappearance of writer Ambrose Bierce as a starting point, this is a powerful love story set within the rebel army of Pancho Villa during the Mexican civil war of 1913. (1985)

Oliver Twist

Charles Dickens Novel / Britain 📖 ᧸   9

Dickens' classic tale about a workhouse boy who runs away, falls into a gang of thieves, and is finally rescued by a wealthy gentleman is still a longtime favorite. (1838)

On the Beach

Nevil Shute Novel / Britain   9, 10

Radioactive fallout from a nuclear war has wiped out the entire northern hemisphere and survivors in Australia gather for their last days of life. (1957)

On the Road

Jack Kerouac Novel / U.S. 📖   9, 10, 11, 12

The classic semi-autobiographical story of the "Beat" generation describes the wanderings, friendships, and affairs of a young writer and his friend. (1957)

Once and Future King, The

T. H. White Novel / Britain ᧸   9, 10, 11

This delightful retelling of the Arthurian legends is the story of young Arthur, nicknamed Wart, and his teacher, Merlin the Magician, who lives life backwards, growing younger every day. (1958)

Once in Europa

John Berger Novel / Britain   11, 12

The second volume in Berger's trilogy chronicles the impact of the forces of modern life on a peasant community. (1983) See *Pig Earth* and *Lilac and Flag*.

One Day in the Life of Ivan Denisovich

Aleksandr Solzhenitsyn　Novel / Russia　📖　　　12

Solzhenitsyn's own life provided the background for this simple tale of a single day of suffering and humiliation in a Soviet Labor camp. (1962)

One Flew Over the Cuckoo's Nest

Ken Kesey　Novel / U.S.　　　9, 11

This classic parable about freedom and totalitarian control follows the experiences of Randle Patrick McMurphy, an irrepressible good-timer who has been transferred from a minimum-security prison to a mental hospital, where he initiates a series of rebellions against the head nurse, Miss Ratched. (1962)

One Hundred Years of Solitude

Gabriel Garcia Marquez　Novel / Columbia　　　12

Marquez' masterpiece of magical realism chronicles the fantastic history and idiosyncratic inhabitants of the village of Macondo. (1967)

Ordinary People

Judith Guest　Novel / U.S.　　　9

This compelling look at a family dealing with the tragic loss of one son while another is coping with suicidal depression became an instant best seller. (1976)

Orlando

Virginia Woolf　Novel / Britain　　　12

Woolf may have been at her most experimental in this novel that traces the central character through four centuries of both male and female incarnations. (1928)

Our Mutual Friend

Charles Dickens　Novel / Britain　　　11, 12

John Harmon's father engages him to Bella, a woman he has never met. Harmon contrives to meet her in disguise and to test her love for him. (1865)

Out of Africa
Isak Dinesen   Short Stories / Denmark   11

Dinesen, the pen name of Baroness Karen Blixon, owned and operated a coffee plantation in East Africa. Her stories reveal the attitudes of pre-World War II British colonialism as well as the beauty of the land and animal life. (1937)

Out of the Silent Planet
C. S. Lewis   Novel / Britain   9, 10, 11, 12

The first of Lewis' *Space Trilogy* tells how the remarkable linguist Dr. Ransom is abducted by aliens and taken via spaceship to the red planet of Malacandra (Mars). He learns that Thulcania (Earth) is called the silent planet. (1938) See *Perelandra* and *That Hideous Strength*.

Oxbow Incident, The
Walter van Tilburg Clark   Novel / U.S.   9, 10

The sheriff and a posse in a small frontier town reluctantly set off to find cattle rustlers and, instead, find out truths about themselves. (1943)

Panther in the Sky
James Alexander Thom   Novel / U.S.   10, 11, 12

Thom offers a well-written story of the Shawnee chief, Tecumseh and his vision of the union of all Indian tribes. (1989)

Parrot in the Oven
Victor Martinez   Novel / U.S.   11, 12

Manny Hernande is a 14-year-old Mexican American boy living in an urban California housing project; in this coming-of-age novel he faces the confusing world of family and community. (1996)

Passage to India, A
E. M. Forster   Novel / Britain   11, 12

A young Muslim doctor in India during the time of the Raj loses his admiration for the English after his pride has been hurt; he is falsely accused of molesting an Englishwoman in the famous caves of Marabar.

What follows is a story that plumbs the depths of colonialism and the racism that sustains it. (1924)

Path of the Pale Horse

Paul Fleischman   Novel / U.S.   ⌒   9, 10

Lep, a doctor's apprentice, assists his master in treating victims of yellow fever in Philadelphia during the epidemic of 1793. (1983)

Peace Like a River

Leif Enger   Novel / U.S.   10, 11, 12

Set in a small town in Minnesota in 1962, a family's tragedy is told in the straightforward, unsentimental narration of 11-year-old Rube Land. Rube's older brother escapes jail after being arrested for shooting two intruders; Rube, his father, a widowed school custodian, and his sister, search for him. This beautifully written novel was one of the most popular releases in 2001.

Pearl, The

John Steinbeck   Novel / U.S.   ⌒   •   9

A pearl diver and his family 's lives are changed forever after finding a pearl of exceptional size and beauty. The allegory reveals the conflict of greed and deception contrasted with the power of family love in this Mexican folktale. (1945)

People Could Fly, The: American Black Folktales

Virginia Hamilton   Short Stories / U.S.   📖   12

This collection of African American folktales contains beautifully told traditional trickster tales, ghost tales, and tales of the quest for freedom. (1985)

Pere Goriot

Honore de Balzac   Novel / France   10, 11, 12

This story about an ambitious aristocrat and his financial ruin is one of the interconnected novels in Balzac's *Human Comedy* that give authentic pictures of French society in the first half of the 19th century. (1834)

Perelandra

C. S. Lewis   Novel / Britain   10, 11, 12

In the second novel in Lewis' trilogy, Dr. Ransom is sent on a mission to Venus where he experiences temptation as intense as that in the Garden of Eden. (1944) See *Out of the Silent Planet* and *That Hideous Strength*.

Persian Boy, The

Mary Renault   Novel / Historical / Ancient Greece   9, 10

The second in the trilogy about Alexander the Great tells of the last seven years of his life and the conquering of Persia. (1988) See *Fire from Heaven* and *Funeral Games*.

Persuasion

Jane Austen   Novel / Britain   10, 11, 12

Austen's last novel is the story of Anne Elliot who has been persuaded to break off an engagement to the man she loves because of his lack of prospects. Will true love prevail? (1818)

Pickwick Papers

Charles Dickens   Novel / Britain   10

Dickens creates the entertaining adventures of Mr. Pickwick and his associates who belong to an English gentleman's club in the early 1800s. (1837)

Pig Earth

John Berger   Novel / Britain   11, 12

The first volume in the trilogy, *Into Their Labours*, a brilliant blend of fiction and non-fiction, chronicles the lives of the inhabitants of the small peasant village in the French Alps where Berger has lived for over 30 years. (1979) See *Once in Europe* and *Lilac and Flag*.

Pilgrim's Progress, The

John Bunyan   Novel / England   11, 12

While in prison, Bunyan claimed to have a dream that inspired the allegory of Christian who flees his family and the City of Destruction and makes his pilgrimage through the Slough of Despond, the Valley of Humiliation, Vanity Fair, Doubting Castle, and on to the Celestial City. (1684)

Pitcairn's Island

Charles Nordhoff and James N. Hall   Novel / Britain   9, 10

In the final book of the *Bounty Trilogy,* Christian takes charge of the ship after Captain Bligh and men loyal to him are cast adrift. With the remaining crew members, Christian discovers and inhabits an uncharted Pacific island. (1934) See *Mutiny on the Bounty* and *Men Against the Sea.*

Plague, The

Albert Camus   Novel / France   11, 12

In this classic modern parable, a town in France is overwhelmed and isolated by bubonic plague; focusing on a core of characters, Nobel Prize-winner Camus describes the duality of life through, on one side, fear, confusion, isolation, and intense loneliness and, on the other, self-sufficiency and compassion. (1947)

Player Piano

Kurt Vonnegut   Novel / U.S.   📖   12

Vonnegut's first novel, considered by many to be his best, is a horrifying picture of a fully automated totalitarian future. (1952)

Point Counter Point

Aldous Huxley   Novel / Britain   9

Huxley's portrayal of the hypocrisy and selfish betrayals of the literary and social elite in early 20th-century England continues to strike a disturbing chord in the early 21st. (1929)

Poisonwood Bible, The

Barbara Kingsolver   Novel / U.S.   11, 12

Nathan Price, a Baptist minister from Georgia, takes his wife and four daughters to a remote village on a twelve-month mission although he has been advised against it. The story is told in the five distinct voices of the women. Set against a backdrop of the struggle for independence in the Congo in the 1960s, this is a brilliant portrayal. (1998)

Poland

James Michener   Novel / U.S.   11, 12

This best-selling sweeping epic covers eight centuries during which three Polish families live out their destinies. (1983)

Portrait of a Lady, The

Henry James   Novel / U.S.   11, 12

Isabel Archer is an attractive American girl transplanted into a European environment; in her naivete, she turns down two honest suitors to marry a scoundrel. (1881)

Portrait of the Artist as a Young Dog

Dylan Thomas   Short Stories / Britain   11, 12

Thomas describes the scenes from his young adulthood in these loosely autobiographical short stories. (1955)

Portrait of the Artist as a Young Man

James Joyce   Novel / Britain / Ireland 📖   11, 12

Joyce's autobiographical story of Stephen Dedalus traces his journey from early childhood through his schooling and crisis in faith, leading him to recognize that to survive as an artist, he must leave Dublin and possibly Ireland. (1915)

Possession

A. S. Byatt   Novel / Britain   10

Two young literary scholars unexpectedly become figures of romance as they discover a surprising link between the two poets on whom they are authorities; Byatt's genius lies in the way she brings both stories to life and intermingles them. (1990)

Potlach Family, the

Evelyn Sibley Lampman   Novel / Native American   11, 12

A young Chinook girl has a difficult time trying to fit in with her school-mates because she has dark skin and her father is an alcoholic. Things change for the better when her brother returns home from Vietnam. (1976)

Power and the Glory, The

Graham Greene   Novel / Britain   12

Greene tells the story of the last desperate days in the life of a dissolute Roman Catholic priest in Mexico, of his involvement with a dying criminal, and of his ultimate betrayal. (1940)

Power of One, The

Bryce Courtenay   Novel / Australia   11

A boy growing up in South Africa prior to World War II finds boxing to be his way into the world. Once in, he battles to eliminate apartheid. (1998)

Practical Magic

Alice Hoffman   Novel / U.S.   10, 11, 12

One of Hoffman's best-loved novels tells the story of the Owens sisters who are raised by two aunts gifted with knowledge of magic; after years apart, they return home to the aunts for help with a highly unusual difficulty. (1996)

Prester John

John Buchan   Novel / Britain   9

An exciting adventure story that pits the dream of Scottish fortune against the vision of a liberated black Africa. (1910)

Pride and Prejudice

Jane Austen   Novel / Britain   📖   10, 11, 12

This perennially popular classic set in early 19th century England is the story of Elizabeth Bennet and Fitzwilliam Darcy told with Jane Austen's inimitable acerbic wit. (1813)

Pride's Fancy

Thomas Raddall   Novel / Canada   9, 10

This adventure tale of Nova Scotia and Haiti in the 1790s was based on the log of a Spanish brigantine, brought north from the Caribbean by Nova Scotia Privateers. (1946)

Promise, The

Chaim Potok   Novel / U.S.   9

This book follows the two boys introduced in *The Chosen,* as they become young men; although they follow different paths, their fates are intricately linked. (1969) See *The Chosen.*

Property Of

Alice Hoffman   Novel / U.S.   9, 10, 11, 12

A young woman in a New York suburb becomes involved in the gang world she previously looked down upon when she falls in love with a gang leader. The first novel of this contemporary author. (1977)

Pudd'nhead Wilson

Mark Twain   Novel / U.S.   9, 10

Twain's biting satire on race involves the difference in fortunes of baby boys switched at birth; one grows up as a slave, the other as a master's son. (1894)

Rabbit Angstrom

John Updike   Novel / U.S.   12

The four Harry Angstrom novels chronicle the lives of middle-class Harry, his wife, and his friends from their youth in the 1950s, through the social upheavals of the '60s and '70s and to the compromises of middle age. This quartet won Updike a solid reputation as one of America's best writers. *Rabbit Run* was the first book (1960), followed by *Rabbit Redux* (1971), *Rabbit is Rich* (1981) and *Rabbit at Rest* (1990). The final book won Updike a Pulitzer Prize.

Ragtime

E. L. Doctorow   Novel / U.S.   10

Set in the Progressive Era in the early years of the 20th century, this remarkable novel combines real historical figures with a fictitious New York family to bring out the diverse mix of individuals; real people who appear in the book include Harry Houdini, Andrew Carnegie, J. D. Rockefeller, Booker T. Washington, and Evelyn Nesbit. (1975)

Rainbow, The

D. H. Lawrence   Novel / Britain   12

This saga of three generations of a rural English Midlands family between the years 1840 and 1905 is a classic exploration of the quest for identity and individualism. (1915)

"Raise High the Roofbeams, Carpenter" and "Seymour: An Introduction"

J. D. Salinger   Novel / U.S.   11, 12

Buddy Glass narrates these two stories introducing readers to the Glass family of *Franny and Zooey*. They were originally published in *The New Yorker.* (1963)

Raj

Gita Mehta   Novel / India   11, 12

India's early struggle for independence from Britain is seen through the eyes of a young woman born into Indian nobility. (1989)

Raven's Eye

Philip Thatcher   Novel / Canada   10, 11, 12

Nathan Solomon Jacob, born in an aboriginal village on the west coast of British Columbia, grows up full of riddles. To find the answers, he travels to Wales and Ireland in this poetic blend of West Coast Native and Celtic legends. (2000)

Red and the Black, The

Stendhal   Novel / France   12

The rise and fall of a young man at the time of the French Restoration in 1813 has become a classic. (1830)

Red Badge of Courage, The

Stephen Crane   Novel / U.S.   📖   9, 10, 11, 12

This novel of intense psychological realism follows an inexperienced young soldier into the horrors of battle during the American Civil War. (1895)

Red Clay: Poems and Stories

Linda Hogan   Short Stories / Native American   📖   12

These stories and poems by Chickasaw poet, novelist, essayist, playwright, and activist reflect her concerns with native issues and the environment. (1991)

Red Pony, The

John Steinbeck   Novel / U.S.   ⌢   9

The setting is a ranch in northern California where Jody, a young boy, raises a high-spirited pony while learning hard lessons about the nature of humans and horses. (1937)

Red River Story

Alfred Silver   Novel / Native Canadian   9, 10, 11, 12

This novel about life on the northern Great Plains shows three groups competing for the land: the half-Indian buffalo hunters, the settlers who want to farm, and the great fur companies seeking profit. (1988)

Red Sorghum

Mo Yan   Novel / China   10

A novel of three generations told through a series of flashbacks depicts the Chinese battle against Japanese invaders in the 1930s. (1993)

Refiner's Fire: The Life and Adventures of Marshall Pearl, a Foundling

Mark Helprin   Novel / U.S.   11, 12

This superbly written and highly recommended novel is a modern Odyssey of a young man's restless quest through a series of extraordinary adventures. (1977)

Reivers: A Reminiscence

William Faulkner   Novel / U.S.   📖   12

Faulkner's last novel is narrated by 11-year-old Lucius and tells of his adventure with two of his grandfather's servants after they "borrow" the family motorcar to go from Mississippi to Memphis in 1905. (1962)

Return of the King, The

J. R. R. Tolkien   Novel / Britain   12

Frodo and Sam realize that the only way to defeat the Dark Lord is to destroy the accursed Ring of Power in the fires of Mount Doom. This is the final volume of the *Lord of the Rings Trilogy*. (1955)

Return of Martin Guerre, The

Natalie Davis   Novel / U.S.   11, 12

Peasants in 16th-century rural France struggle to discover the truth surrounding the return, after many years, of Marin Guerre. Is he the real Martin or an imposter? Davis combines the tale with scholarly attention to the details of social and legal history to make this much richer than a simple narrative. (1983)

Return of the Native, The

Thomas Hardy   Novel / Britain   10, 11, 12

The tragic lives of mismatched lovers convey the conflict between passion and dreams that go unfulfilled, yet end with hope for true meaning in life. (1878)

Riddley Walker

Russell Hoban   Novel / U.S.   10

This astonishing novel is set in England among the ruins of society some centuries after a nuclear Armageddon. Twelve-year-old Riddley becomes "connexion" man for his tribe. Written in a remarkably devolved English, the book is rich in allusions to our own time and centuries past. (1980)

River Between, The

(James) Ngugi wa Thiong'o   Novel / Kenya   9, 10

Set in the 1920s and 1930s, this is the story of an unhappy love affair in a rural community divided between Christianity and traditional African beliefs. (1965)

River King, The

Alice Hoffman   Novel / U.S.   10, 11, 12

The town of Hadden is home to the prestigious Hadden School; contact between the "locals" and the school community, normally minimal, suddenly intensifies when an inexplicable death brings them together. (2001)

River Sutra, A

Gita Mehta   Novel / India   11, 12

A widower and former bureaucrat has taken a position at the Government rest house, situated on the banks of the famed Narmada River, to become a vanaprasthi, "someone who has retired to the forest to reflect." But he finds himself besieged by people whose lives have been very different from his own. (1993)

Riversong

Craig Lesley   Novel / Native American   11, 12

Set in Oregon, this is the story of a footloose young Nez Perce and his father as they search for meaning through their tribal heritage. (1989)

Robber Bridegroom, The

Eudora Welty   Novel / U.S.   10

Once upon a time, many, many years ago in old Mississippi, there lived a beautiful young girl whose name was Rosamond; this is Welty's delightful fairy tale of the daughter of a wealthy planter in love with a bandit. (1942)

Robinson Crusoe

Daniel Defoe   Novel / Britain   📖   9

A shipwrecked sailor struggles to survive after being marooned on a deserted island. (1719)

Roll of Thunder, Hear My Cry

Mildred D. Taylor   Novel / U.S.   9

This insightful tale of a black family's struggle to survive prejudice in Mississippi in the 1930s is an inspiring story that reflects the virtues of pride, dignity, and strength. (1977)

Romance of Leonardo da Vinci, The

Dmitri Merejkowski   Novel   11, 12

Merejkowski creates a provocative, behind-the-scenes account of the Renaissance and its most universal man; loosely based on da Vinci's life. (1928)

Room with a View, A

E. M. Forster   Novel / Britain   11

This delightful English novel tells of the awakening of a young woman to love on a trip to Italy, her return to conventional life, and, finally, her breaking away to find her own happiness. (1908)

Runner in the Sun

D'Arcy McNickle   Novel / Native American   9, 10

Salt, a young pre-Columbian Indian boy in the American Southwest struggles to save his people and their village against the ravages of drought and the internal turmoil of the tribe. (1987)

Sabbatical: A Romance

John Barth   Novel / U.S.   11

A young literature professor and her much older ex-CIA husband, after seven years of marriage, go on a sailing adventure to sort out their lives. (1983)

Saint Maybe

Anne Tyler   Novel / U.S.   **11, 12**

Ian Bedloe, at 17, considers himself responsible for the death of his brother who has a young wife and three children. When his sister-in-law also dies, Ian drops out of college to parent the young orphans and seek forgiveness in the Church of the Second Chance. Tyler's characters and her unusual and endearing families are instantly engaging. (1991).

Sanctuary

William Faulkner   Novel / U.S.   **12**

A young debutante takes a wrong turn and meets a sadistic gangster. (1931)

Sara Bastard's Notebook

Marion Engel   Novel / Canada   **11, 12**

A 30-year-old teacher of English literature living in Toronto finds that her life is a mess and sets out to discover how it got that way. (1967)

Saturnalia

Paul Fleischman   Novel / U.S.   **9, 10**

Set in Puritan Boston of 1861, this is the story of a Native American apprenticed to the town printer. (1992)

Scarlet Letter, The

Nathaniel Hawthorne   Novel / U.S.   📖   **10, 11, 12**

The novel's theme of conscience dealing with hidden guilt portrays the public and private costs of illicit love in Puritan Salem, Massachusetts. While Hester redeems her sin, her lover suffers from self-condemnation. (1850)

Scarlet Pimpernel, The

Baroness d' Orczy   Novel / Britain   **9, 10**

A band of Englishmen pledges to rescue the innocent victims of the Reign of Terror in France between 1793 and 1794. This is a semi-historical novel about the Comte de St. Germaine, known to the British as the Scarlet Pimpernel. (1905)

Schindler's List

Thomas Keneally   Novel / Australia   9, 12

Oskar Schindler, a Catholic war profiteer risked his own life and eventually went bankrupt to save the lives of more than 1,000 Jews who worked in his factory. Booker Prize-winner. (1982)

Sea of Grass, The

Conrad Richter   Novel / U.S.   9, 10

A New Mexico cattle baron faces heartbreak when he is torn between his love for his land, his discontented wife, and his wayward son. (1933)

Sea-Wolf, The

Jack London   Novel / U.S.   9, 10

A well-educated, shipwrecked journalist gets an education at sea on a seal hunter's ship. (1904)

Search for America, A

Frederick Philip Grove   Novel / Canada   11, 12

This epic novel, one of Grove's most powerful works, speaks of the longings of immigrants for the realization of an ideal. (1927)

Second Nature

Alice Hoffman   Novel / U.S.   10, 11, 12

Robin Moore surprises herself when she befriends a man raised in the wilderness by wolves and learns profound lessons about love and humanity. (1994)

Secret Life of Walter Mitty, The

James Thurber   Novel / U.S.   9, 10, 11, 12

Mitty is a repressed, ordinary man who daydreams about doing great things. (1932)

Secret Sharer, The

Joseph Conrad   Novel / Britain   📖   9, 10, 11, 12

A ship captain who befriends a mysterious stowaway becomes involved in a shared life of ambition, uncertainty, murder, and loyalty. (1911)

Seed and the Sower, The

Laurens van der Post   Novel / South Africa   📖   12

This compelling story of captors and captives in a Japanese POW camp is based on the author's own World War II experiences. (1963)

Segu

Maryse Conde   Novel / Guadeloupe   12

Several generations of the Bambara tribe, the present Mali of West Africa, encounter white slave traders and Muslim converters in the 18th and 19th centuries. (1987)

Selected Short Stories: De Maupassant

Guy de Maupassant   Short Stories / France   📖   10

De Maupassant's (1850–1893) short stories were among the earliest of the genre, yet they remain popular today. His subjects range from everyday life in Paris to tales of suspense and horror.

Sense and Sensibility

Jane Austen   Novel / Britain   10, 11, 12

Elinore and Marianne Dashwood embody, respectively, sense and sensibility, or emotional excess; Austen, with her usual dry wit, contrasts their responses to disappointed love and eventual marriages. (1811)

Separate Peace, A

John Knowles   Novel / U.S.   📖   9

Gene, the protagonist recounts through flashback life at an all-boys' private school during World War II and the event that shattered the peace of that "world apart." (1959)

Seven Arrows

Hyemeyohsts Storm   Novel / Native American   10, 11, 12

This is the sorrowful struggle of Night Bear and his people on the land they fought for and lost. (1972)

Seventeen

Booth Tarkington   Novel / U.S.   9

A delightful story describes what it was like to be a 17-year-old male and in love for the first time in middle America at the beginning of the 20th century. (1916)

Seventh Heaven

Alice Hoffman   Novel / U.S.   10, 11, 12

When a liberated woman comes to a small suburban town in the 1950s everyone begins to learn new things about themselves and each other. (1990)

Shadows on the Rock

Willa Cather   Novel / U.S.   📖   9

French Catholics in 17th-century Quebec adapt to the harsh northern realities of what is now Canada in this powerful story. (1931)

Shane

Jack Schaeffer   Novel / U.S.   ⌒   9, 10

A drifter comes to a Wyoming town and tries to head off a war between cattle ranchers and farmers. (1949)

Shikasta

Doris Lessing   Novel / Britain   12

At times epic, at times grippingly real, the story begins before birth as souls undertake their mission on earth; how they succeed or fail and the effect on world history is compelling. (1979)

Shipping News, The

E. Annie Proulx   Novel / U.S.   11, 12

A slow-thinking man learns his way to love in Newfoundland; a Pulitzer Prize-winner in 1994.

Shoeless Joe

W. P. Kinsella   Novel / Canada   9, 10

A magical blend of fantasy and reality, this is the story of a farmer who plows down his crops because he hears a voice that tells him to; Shoeless Joe Jackson, his Black Sox teammates, and other athletes mystically arrive to play baseball. (1982)

Short Stories: Poe

Edgar Allan Poe   Short Stories / U.S.   10, 11, 12

Poe (1809–49), along with French author Guy de Maupassant and Russian author Anton Chekhov, is credited as being the originator of the short story.

Siddhartha

Hermann Hesse   Novel / Germany   10, 11, 12

Based on the story of Buddha, a young man's quest for enlightenment brings him understanding of the desires of the flesh as the cause of human suffering. He also comes to understand the futility of following even a great teacher. He rejects both worldly pleasure and his great teacher to find truth and peace out of his own experience and understanding. (1922)

Silas Marner

George Eliot   Novel / Britain   9, 10, 11, 12

A miserly English linen-weaver's gold is stolen from him, but through a twist of fate, his happiness is restored as he raises a foundling. (1861)

Simple Stories of Langston Hughes

Akiba Sullivan Harper, ed.   Short Stories / U.S.   📖   10, 11, 12

Poet, novelist, and playwright Langston Hughes is the most prominent figure in the literary, artistic, and intellectual movement known as the Harlem Renaissance. Volume 7 (*The Early Simple Stories*) and Volume 8 (*The Later Simple Stories*) are part of *The Collected Works of Langston Hughes*. (1902–67)

Single Pebble, A

John Hersey   Novel / U.S.   10, 11, 12

A young American engineer, hoping to tame the "raw, naked, cruel power" of the Yangtze, travels upriver in a junk to search out the perfect spot for a hydroelectric project. (1956)

Sister Carrie

Theodore Dreiser   Novel / U.S.   11

A young working girl in 19th-century Chicago and New York gains worldly success, as the fortunes of her lover and protector decline. (1900)

Slaughterhouse Five

Kurt Vonnegut   Novel / U.S.   11, 12

This mixture of science fiction, satire, fantasy, and realism revolves around the fire bombing of Dresden during World War II. With the help of aliens, a witness to the events reviews his experience. (1969)

Small Room, The

May Sarton   Novel / U.S.   11

This novel by one of America's best-loved poets is about women in academic life; set on the campus of a New England college, it examines the precarious relationship between teachers and students. (1976)

Smoke on the Water

John Ruemmler   Novel / Native American   9, 10

A 13-year-old English colonist and a 15-year-old Powhatan brave become friends and face the racism, bitterness, and parent-child relationships in parallel coming-of-age stories before the massacre of 300 colonists by the Indians. It presents a sympathetic view of both sides involved in the struggle. (1992)

Snow Goose, The

Paul Gallico   Novel / Britain   9

An unforgettable story set in southern England tells of the unlikely friendship between a recluse artist and a young girl culminating in an act of heroism at the Battle of Dunkirk during World War II. (1942)

Snow in August

Peter Hamill   Novel / U.S.   9

A fatherless Irish Catholic boy in 1940's Brooklyn exchanges life lessons with a rabbi, who is a survivor of the Holocaust. (1997)

Snows of Kilimanjaro and Other Stories, The

Ernest Hemingway   Short Stories / U.S.   9, 10, 11, 12

Readers will find this an ideal introduction to ten of Hemingway's best short stories. (1938)

Soldier of the Great War, A

Mark Helprin   Novel / U.S.   11, 12

This novel weaves a journey of immense courage with a profound love story; it contrasts the beauty of Italy and its art with the horrors of World War I. (1991)

Something to Be Desired

Thomas Mc Guane   Novel / U.S.   9, 10

A sharp and funny novel set in Montana about a man who is thrown into questioning his own life. (1984)

Something Wicked This Way Comes

Ray Bradbury   Novel / U.S.   📖   10, 11, 12

The carnival rolls into Greentown, Illinois, rushing in Halloween a week early. Two boys discover the secret of its mazes and mirrors as well as the heavy cost of wishes. (1962)

Song of Bernadette, The

Franz Werfel   Novel / Germany   9

In the small town of Lourdes, where millions still come to seek a miracle, the virtuous Bernadette received visions of the Virgin Mary; this is her story. (1941)

Song of Solomon

Toni Morrison   Novel / U.S.   📖   11, 12

A family chronicle culminates in the attempts of an upper-class Northern black businessman to try to protect his family, causing his son to take a path opposite to the one his father had hoped for. (1977)

Sophie's World

Jostein Gardner   Novel / Norway   11

Within the framework of a romantic adventure, a philosopher explains the great philosophers to his young protégé. (1994)

Sorrows of Young Werther, The

Johann Goethe   Novel / Germany   11, 12

Goethe's semi-autobiographical novel caused a sensation throughout Europe when it was published. Sensitive, artistic, shy Werther is hopelessly in love with a young woman engaged to someone else. (1774)

Sot-Weed Factor, The

John Barth   Novel / U.S.   12

Readers will take an indescribable but thoroughly delightful romp through early colonial Maryland with Ebenezer Cooke, the sot-weed factor (tobacco salesman). (1960)

Sound and the Fury, The

William Faulkner   Novel / U.S.   11, 12

In this classic American South "stream-of-consciousness novel" three brothers each describe the life of their unconventional sister from a different perspective; a fourth section gives a somewhat detached view from the point of view of a black servant. (1929)

Sound of the Flutes, The

Richard Erdoes   Short Stories / Native American   📖   10, 11, 12

This is a poetically written collection of Native American legends. (1976)

Southern Mail

Antoine de Saint-Exupéry   Novel / France   9

A novel based on Saint-Exupéry's flights as a mail pilot reveals the importance of responsibility and the fellowship it nurtures among men. (1933)

Spartacus

Howard Fast   Novel / U.S.   10

This fictionalization of a slave revolt in ancient Rome in 71 B.C.E. tells the story of Spartacus, born a slave and trained as a gladiator. (1953)

Sport of Nature, A

Nadine Gordimer   Novel / South Africa   11

A "sport of nature" is an animal or plant starkly different from the rest of its species. Gordimer's central character is a young woman named Hillela who is abandoned by her mother, and becomes a major player in the struggle against apartheid. (1987)

St. Mawr

D. H. Lawrence   Novel / Britain   9, 10

A young woman considers a horse superior to the men in her life. (1925)

Steppenwolf

Hermann Hesse   Novel / Germany   📖   10, 11, 12

The classic "outsider" novel follows Harry Haller's search; caught in a mid-life crisis, he feels that he has two beings inside him and faces his shadow self who introduces him to drinking, dancing, music, sex, and drugs. (1927)

Stone Angel, The

Margaret Laurence   Novel / Canada   9, 10

Hagar Shipley, in her 90th year, runs away hoping to avoid an old-people's home and finds she must face her past in one of Canada's best loved novels. (1964)

Stone Carvers, The

Jane Urquhart   Novel / Canada   11, 12

Real-life Canadian sculptor Walter Allward carved a huge stone monu-
ment to Canada's war dead in Vimy, France, after World War I. This is
the backdrop against which Urquhart places her fictional characters, a
brother and a sister from a small Ontario town, whose lives are deeply
affected by the war. (2002)

Stories

O. Henry   Short Stories / U.S.   10, 11, 12

In 1896, William Sydney, under the pseudonym of O. Henry, began writing in prison. After his release, he published 11 volumes of short stories
between 1904 and 1910, widely read for their ironic coincidences and
surprise endings. Among his most popular is "The Gift of the Magi."

Stories Of Eva Luna, The

Isabel Allende   Short Stories / Chile   📖   12

Eva Luna tells these twenty-three stories to her European lover, refugee
and journalist Rolf Carle; each one has a touch of magic realism mixed
with vivid portrayals of South American life. (1990)

Story Like the Wind, A

Laurens van der Post   Novel / South Africa   9, 11

Francois, a young European boy, becomes a child of the African bush in
an agricultural oasis created by his father. This beautifully told story
continues in the sequel, *A Far Off Place*. (1972)

Story of an African Farm, The

Olive Schreiner   Novel / South Africa   12

Hailed as an early feminist masterpiece, this is the story of the independent Lyndall, an orphan. She breaks away from her Bible-loving relatives and becomes pregnant by a lover whom she refuses to marry. (1883)

Stotan!

Chris Crutcher   Novel / U.S.   9

The story of four high school seniors and their marathon week-long aquatic training exercises is told with profound understanding and humor. (1987)

Stranger, The

Albert Camus   Novel / France   **10, 11, 12**

In this classic of existentialist literature, an ordinary man who unwittingly gets drawn into a senseless murder on a sun-drenched Algerian beach faces the absurd realities of life in the face of death. *L' Etranger* was written in French in 1942 and translated into English as *The Outsider.* (1946)

Subtle Knife, The

Philip Pullman   Novel / Britain   **11, 12**

The second part of the trilogy that began with *The Golden Compass* is set partly in our own world and introduces Will, who lives in modern Oxford. He discovers a way to enter the parallel world portrayed in the first book where he meets Lyra and joins her in a quest to discover more about "Dust" and the struggle between good and evil. (1997) See *The Golden Compass* and *The Amber Spyglass.*

Such Is My Beloved

Morley Callaghan   Novel / Canada   **11, 12**

An idealistic young priest attempts to redeem the lives of two down-and-out prostitutes and encounters a cruel and uncaring world. (1934)

Summer of My German Soldier

Bette Greene   Novel / U.S.   **9**

A 12-year-old Jewish girl forms a relationship with a soldier in a German prison camp near a small town in Arkansas during World War II and risks her family, friends, and freedom. (1973)

Sun Also Rises, The

Ernest Hemingway   Novel / U.S. 📖   **9, 10, 11, 12**

This classic novel of the post-World War II "lost generation" follows the aimless wanderings of Lady Brett Ashley and her friends in war-torn Europe. (1926)

Surfacing

Margaret Atwood   Novel / Canada   11, 12

A young commercial artist travels to a remote lake in Northern Ontario to search for her widowed father who has mysteriously disappeared; she finds instead that she is confronted by long-dormant emotions and repressed memories that transform her life. (1972)

Swiftly Tilting Planet, A

Madeleine L' Engle   Novel / U.S.   9, 10

In the third book of L' Engle's classic fantasy series, young adventurers face the question of how the course of history might be altered by traveling backward in time. (1978) See *A Wind in the Door, A Wrinkle in Time,* and *Many Waters.*

Sword in the Stone, The

T. H. White   Novel / Britain   9, 10, 11

The first book in White's quartet retelling the legend of King Arthur was originally published separately in 1937. See *The Once and Future King.*

Tale of Two Cities, A 📖

Charles Dickens   Novel / Britain   9

Dickens uses the French Revolution to draw unforgettable characters whose choices make them heroes and victims of revenge against the aristocracy. (1859)

Tales of Burning Love

Louise Erdrich   Short Stories / Native American   12

The short stories in this collection by the popular Chippewa writer are interwoven in character and content with her novels. (1996)

Tales of Hulan River

Xiao Hong   Novel / China 📖   12

This collection of short fiction by one of China's best writers describes life in China in the 1920s and '30s. (1942)

Tanglewood Tales

Nathaniel Hawthorne   Short Stories / U.S.   📖   12

Hawthorne's retelling of the great legends of Greek mythology has fed the minds of young people for over a 100 years; they are still well worth reading. (1853)

Tar Baby

Tony Morrison   Novel / U.S.   11

A beautiful young black woman, protégé of a white millionaire and his wife and molded by white culture, falls in love with a black man who represents everything she both fears and desires. The resulting relationship rocks a tranquil world, challenging much of what previously had been accepted. (1981)

Taras Bulba

Nikolai Gogol   Novel / Russia   12

This novella portrays strong heroism against a panoramic canvas of the Setch, the military brotherhood of the Cossacks. (1835)

Tender is the Night

F. Scott Fitzgerald   Novel / U.S.   📖   10, 11, 12

A psychiatrist and his schizophrenic wife live on the Riviera with other American expatriates in this classic of the "lost generation." (1934)

Terra Nostra

Carlos Fuentes   Novel / Mexico   10

The life and times of Philip II of Spain form the core of Fuentes's novel, but chronological time and conventional history are ignored as Philip marries England's Elizabeth Tudor and witnesses the discovery of the New World. (1975)

Tess of the D' Urbervilles

Thomas Hardy   Novel / Britain   10, 11, 12

Hardy's independent female protagonist shows the triumph of the spirit over the repression of society and the cruelty of two men who wrong her. (1891)

That Hideous Strength

C. S. Lewis   Novel / Britain   9, 11, 12

The last novel in Lewis' trilogy describes the deification of science at the expense of reducing the dignity of human life and the importance of the individual. (1945) See *Perelandra* and *Out of the Silent Planet*.

Their Eyes Were Watching God

Zora Neale Hurston   Novel / U.S.   📖   9, 10, 11, 12

This classic novel traces the journey of a powerful black woman through the rural South in the 1920s. (1937)

Things Fall Apart

Chinua Achebe   Novel / Nigeria   9, 10, 11, 12

A modern Nigerian makes his way between timeless tradition and modern change. Although written first, this novel may be considered the third of a sequence in which Achebe re-creates Africa's journey from traditional to modern times. (1958)

Third Life of Grange Copeland, The

Alice Walker   Novel / U.S.   10

A black tenant farmer leaves his wife and son in Georgia to head North and returns years later to find his son imprisoned for the murder of his wife; in looking after his youngest granddaughter, he sees a renewed sense of life. (1970)

Three Candles of Little Veronica: The Story of a Child's Soul in This World and the Other

Manfred Kyber   Novel / Germany   9

This fairytale in which Veronica encounters fairies, demons, sylphs, and ghosts, all during her seemingly normal life, has become a classic of spiritual growth. (1920)

Three Musketeers, The

Alexandre Dumas   Novel / France   ᐤᐤ   9

Set in 17th-century France, this begins the story of d'Artagnon's adventures when he joins the king's musketeers under Louis XIII; in subsequent books, he adventures together with Athos, Porthos, and Aramis for over 20 years. (1844)

Through the Looking Glass and What Alice Found There

Lewis Carroll   Novel / Britain   9, 10, 11, 12

Alice's delightful adventures continue as the chess pieces come to life, especially the Red and White Queens and the White Knight, and she meets Tweedledum, Tweedledee, and Humpty Dumpty. (1871)

Thurber Carnival, The

James Thurber   Short Stories / U.S.   9, 10

Thurber has been called a genius of American humor; this anthology brings together a number of his short stories as well as selections from his modern fables and cartoons. (1945)

Till We Have Faces

C. S. Lewis   Novel / Britain   9, 11, 12

Lewis retells the myth of Psyche and Eros from the point of view of one of Psyche's sisters. (1956) See *Out of the Silent Planet, Perelandra,* and *That Hideous Strength.*

Time Machine, The

H. G. Wells   Novel / Britain   9

Set in the year 802,701, this is Wells' vision of a society divided into two classes: the subterranean workers called the Morlocks, and the decadent Eloi, their masters. (1895) See *The Island of Dr. Moreau.*

Tin Drum, The

Gunter Grass   Novel / Germany   12

This semi-biographical novel about growing up in Nazi Germany has absurdist themes that have made it a classic. (1959)

To Have and Have Not

Ernest Hemingway   Novel / U.S.   11, 12

Henry Morgan is forced into crime in the 1930s by running contraband
between Key West and Cuba. Hemingway is at his realistic best in describing Morgan's fall. (1937)

To Kill A Mockingbird

Nell Harper Lee   Novel / U.S.   📖   9, 10

A young white girl growing up in the deep South in the 1930s shows the
prejudice her family faced when her father, a well-respected lawyer, defends an innocent black man accused of rape. (1960)

To the Lighthouse

Virginia Woolf   Novel / Britain   📖   10, 11, 12

Woolf's masterpiece weaves together present, past, and future in three
sections. The first is one day in the life of the Ramsays on holiday in the
Hebrides; the second, an account of the death of Mrs. Ramsay and her
son Andrew who is a soldier in World War I; and the third, the creative
strivings of a friend of the Ramsay's, the painter Lily Briscoe. (1927)

Tombs of Atuan, The

Ursula Le Guin   Novel / U.S.   9, 10

The second volume in *The Earthsea Trilogy* tells the story of Tenar who
has been brought up as a priestess and lives in the dark tombs of Atuan
until Ged arrives and brings her into the world of the light. (1971) See *A
Wizard of Earthsea* and *The Farthest Shore*.

Too Late the Phalarope

Alan Paton   Novel / South Africa   9

In the apartheid era in South Africa, Pieter, a white policeman, has an
affair with a native girl and is betrayed and reported. (1953)

Town, The

Conrad Richter   Novel / U.S.   9, 10

The third volume in Richter's trilogy, *The Awakening Land,* is considered
his finest novel and won the Pulitzer Prize in 1951. It gives an extraor-

dinary picture of Ohio on the eve of the Civil War. See *The Trees* and *The Fields. (1950)*

Tracks
Louise Erdrich   Novel / Native American   11

Told in Erdich's rich and inimitable style, this is the story of the Chippewa Indians in the early 20th century at a time when epidemics, harsh winters, and the greed of white men are rapidly destroying the land and its Native American people. The story is told through the antagonism of Fleur and her daughter Pauline. (1988)

Travels of Jamie McPheeters, The
Robert Lewis Taylor   Novel / U.S.   9

This Pulitzer Prize-winner, touching and humorous, follows Jaimie and his father, Sardius, on the long trek to California's El Dorado in 1849. (1959)

Treasure Island
Robert Louis Stevenson   Novel / U.S.   9

The swashbuckling adventure of treasure seekers on a pirate ship captained by Long John Silver is seen through the eyes of the young cabin boy, Jim Hawkins. (1883)

Treasure of Sierra Madre, The
B. Traven   Novel / U.S.   9

Three gold prospectors, all down-and-outers, head to Mexico as buddies with dreams of riches. Instead, they become entangled in treachery and murder. (1935)

Tree Grows in Brooklyn, A
Betty Smith   Novel / U.S.   10, 11, 12

This well-loved, touching, and insightful classic is the story of Francie Nolan as she grows into a young woman in Brooklyn in the early part of the 20th century. Loss, struggle and pain are balanced by Francie's unsentimental clarity and basic optimism. (1943)

Tree of Man, The

Patrick White   Novel / Australia   11, 12

A young man and his family attempts to farm in the Australian wilderness at the beginning of the 20th century. This epic account has become a world-renowned classic. (1955)

Trees, The

Conrad Richter   Novel / U.S.   9, 10

This is the first volume of the trilogy, *The Awakening Land*, about early pioneer life in Ohio. Here, the Luckett family migrates from Pennsylvania to southeastern Ohio and begins their life there. (1940) See *The Fields* and *The Town*.

Trial, The

Franz Kafka   Novel / Czechoslovakia (German)   11

A bank clerk, known as K, is arrested on the morning of his 30th birthday; he is aware only that he is guilty, but not of the nature of the crime for which he is being tried. (1930)

True and Untrue and Other Norse Tales

Sigrid Undset, ed.   Short Stories / Norway   9

The 1928 Nobel Prize winner wrote this excellent collection of Scandinavian myths. (1945)

True History of the Kelly Gang

Peter Carey   Novel / Australia   10, 11, 12

Ned Kelly is an Australian folk hero because of his defiance toward the authority of the English. Carey's book, winner of the 2000 Booker Prize, is a fictional account based on what is known of his life told in an authentic voice with humor, passion, and wisdom. (2000)

Trumpeter of Krakow, The

Eric Kelly   Novel / U.S.   9

In 1461, Joseph and his parents are hoping to make it to Krakow, Poland, after the Tartars burn their home to the ground. (1928)

Turn of the Screw, The

Henry James   Novel / U.S.   10, 11, 12

James called this novel a ghost story; it tells the tale of a young governess and her intimations of the evil presence of the ghosts of two former servants whom she feels are a danger of the worst kind to the two children in her care. (1898)

Turtle Moon

Alice Hoffman   Novel / U.S.   10, 11, 12

Hoffman's deft blend of magic and realism teaches readers to look beneath the surface of ordinary lives. In this book, Lucy Rosen and her 12-year-old son move from New York to rural Florida and find their expectations turned upside down. (1992)

Twenty-one Great Stories

Abraham Lass and Norma L. Tasman, eds.   Anthology   📖   9

These are chosen from classic authors especially for young adults. (1991)

Twice-told Tales

Nathaniel Hawthorne   Short Stories / U.S.   12

This famous collection of some of Hawthorne's best short stories illustrates his recurrent themes of pride and guilt. (1852)

Twilight in Delhi

Ahmed Ali   Novel / India   12

Set in Delhi, this is the story of an upper middle-class Muslim family witnessing the destruction of the old ways as the British Occupation begins destroying their heritage and culture. (1940)

Two Solitudes

Hugh MacLennan   Novel / Canada   9, 11, 12

The classic novel of the two cultures of Quebec, English and French, is set between the years 1917 and 1939, in the rural countryside and in the city of Montreal. The book's ending with the intermarriage of two young people, one French and one English, offers a possible resolution to longstanding conflict. (1945)

Two Towers, The

J. R. R. Tolkien   Novel / Britain   12

The second volume of Tolkien's masterpiece, *Lord of the Rings*, sees the Fellowship scattered, while Frodo and Sam, with the deceitful Gollum as their guide, travel alone to Mordor to destroy the Ring of Power. (1954)

Typee or a Peep at Polynesian Life

Herman Melville   Novel / U.S.   10

Two young men jump ship hoping to find a paradise and discover instead the cannibalistic Typees. (1846)

Unbearable Lightness of Being, The

Milan Kundera   Novel / Czechoslovakia   11, 12

Set within the framework of the political repression in Czechoslovakia under Communism, this novel explores the psyche of a young Czech physician. He engages in erotic adventures over which he thinks he has some control while ignoring what is happening to his country, where he feels he can have no power or freedom. (1984)

Uncle Tom's Cabin

Harriet Beecher Stowe   Novel / U.S.   9, 10, 11, 12

Stowe's abolitionist novel tells the moving story of Tom, a noble slave, whose life is subject to the whims of kindness and cruelty as he passes from one master to another. (1852)

Under the Eye of the Clock

Christopher Nolan   Novel / Ireland   11, 12

This is a poetic autobiographical novel by a young writer who escapes the isolation of cerebral palsy by typing with a pencil attached to his head. (1987)

Vanity Fair

William M. Thackeray   Novel / Britain   11, 12

This satirical picture of worldly society, published in installments in

Victorian England, is set at the time of the Napoleonic Wars; it follows the rise and fall in fortunes of two young women, the orphan Becky Sharp and the daughter of a rich merchant, Amelia Sedly. (1848)

Vendor of Sweets, The

R. K. Narayan   Novel / India   12

Mali, the son of a sweet vendor, travels to America for a course in creative writing. He unexpectedly returns with a Korean American girlfriend, setting off family struggles with modernity and the class of cultures. (1967)

Victory

Joseph Conrad   Novel / Britain   📖   10, 11, 12

An idealistic Swedish baron in the East Indies rescues a young cockney woman from a dissolute life and finds himself in the grip of an evil plot of revenge. (1915)

Violent Bear It Away, The

Flannery O'Connor   Novel / U.S.   11, 12

O'Connor's second and final novel follows young Francis Tarwater who is filled with doubt about following his great-uncle, a mad prophet, until he receives a vision. (1960)

Virginians, The

William Makepeace Thackeray   Novel / Britain   11, 12

This continuation of Thackeray's famous novel, *The History of Henry Esmond, Esq.,* details the events after Henry marries Rachel and emigrates from England to Virginia. (1859)

Voss

Patrick White   Novel / Australia   11, 12

A German visionary leads an epic expedition across the Australian continent in 1845 and is bound in a mystic union with a woman he has left behind in Sydney. (1957)

Voyage Out, The

Virginia Woolf   Novel / Britain   12

The first of Woolf's novels is a realistically intense story of a young English woman who travels to South America, becomes engaged, catches a fever, and dies. (1915)

Waimea Summer

John Dominis Holt   Novel / U.S.   9

In this first novel written in English by a writer of Hawaiian ancestry, a young man discovers his ethnic heritage. At the same time he has spiritual and ghostly encounters during a summer spent on the Big Island. (1976)

Waiting for the Barbarians

J. M. Coetze   Novel / South Africa   11, 12

A Magistrate in a nameless Empire grows increasingly suspicious of the treatment of the Barbarians whom he has known only as peaceful people; when he protests he faces torture and humiliation that raises this parable to the archetypal. (1980)

Waiting Year, The

Fumiko Enchi   Novel / Japan   11, 12

Set in 19th-century Japan, a wife buys the first of a series of concubines for her husband and finds herself caught in a traditional female role with no escape. (1994)

Walk in the Night and Other Stories, A

Alex La Guma   Short Stories / South Africa   10

La Guma's short stories give vivid details of ordinary people struggling with biracial life in South Africa. (1962)

Wall, The

John Hersey   Novel / U.S.   11

This is a moving account of the destruction of the Jewish community in Warsaw by the Nazis. (1950)

War and Peace

Leo Tolstoy   Novel / Russia   11, 12

This epic novel follows the lives of three aristocratic families in Russia during the Napoleonic invasion. (1869)

War at the End of the World, The

Mario Vargas Llosa   Novel / Peru   11, 12

In this story of a revolt against the Brazilian government in the late 19th century, a religious leader known as the "Counselor," attracts a band of followers from among the outcasts of society; together they build a town with a magnificent cathedral attracting the suspicions of the conservative authorities. (1981)

Washington Square

Henry James   Novel / U.S.   10, 11, 12

Catherine Sloper is the plain daughter of a rich doctor who is courted by a fortune seeker and then dropped when her father threatens to disinherit her; years later, he returns, and is dismissed by a clearer-sighted, older Catherine. (1881)

Waterlily

Ella Cara Deloria   Novel / U.S.   10

Written in 1944 but published 40 years later, this is the story of the childhood, adolescence, and early adulthood of a young woman growing up in the middle of the 19th century in a Dakota community just before white settlers appear and change the life of her people forever. (1984)

Watership Down

Richard Adams   Novel / Britain   9, 10, 11, 12

This animal fantasy became an immediate best seller when it was first published. A group of rabbits, threatened by the encroaching dangerous world of humans, sets off to find a new place to build a safe world of their own. The epic stories told in the dark caves underground are especially compelling. (1972)

Waves, The

Virginia Woolf   Novel / Britain   10

Considered by many to be Woolf's masterpiece, this novel traces the lives of six friends from childhood to late middle age written in a poetic stream-of-consciousness style. (1931)

Way of All Flesh, The

Samuel Butler   Novel / Britain   10, 11, 12

A semi-biographical novel about an awkward, unhappy young man, the son of a tyrant, who reveres his great-grandfather's simple virtues but suffers multiple misfortunes before he is able to approximate such a life. (1903)

Way to Rainy Mountain, The

N. Scott Momaday   Novel / Native American   10, 11, 12

Momaday tells this collection of oral stories in three voices. The first voice is the voice of his father, the ancestral voice of the Kiowa oral tradition. The second is the voice of historical commentary, and the third is that of his personal reminiscence. (1969)

Weep Not Child

Ngugi WaThiong'o   Novel / Kenya   9, 10, 12

This powerful novel shows the effects of the Mau Mau war in Kenya on the simple people forced to choose between loyalty and progress. (1964)

What Maisie Knew

Henry James   Novel / U.S.   12

The child of divorced parents, Maisie becomes increasingly aware of a world where mothers and fathers keep changing their sexual partners and even their names. In spite of it all, she retains her openness and humor. (1897)

When the Tree Flowered: The Fictional Autobiography of Eagle Voice, A Sioux Indian

John Neihardt   Novel / U.S.   9

This collection of stories is based upon interviews with the Sioux Indians on the Pine Ridge Reservation in 1944. Eagle Elk is the central figure of the work. (1950)

Where I'm Calling From: New and Selected Stories

Raymond Carver   Short Stories / U.S   📖   12

Carver, often described as a minimalist, writes about the lives of ordinary people, including the marginally employed, alcoholic, or those dealing with loss. (1989)

Where the Ghost Horse Runs

Alfred Silver   Novel / Native Canadian   9, 10, 11, 12

Cuthbert Grant, known as "Chief of all the Half-breeds," dreams of creating an Eden for his half-Indian people on the Northern Great Plains in the third and final book of the *Red River Trilogy*. (1991)

Where the Rivers Flow North

Howard Frank Mosher   Short Stories / U.S.   10

These six stories are set in the fictional Kingdom County, an amalgam of northern Vermont, Quebec, northern Maine, and the Catskills. The title story about an old logger in 1927 who fights a power company that wants to build a dam was made into an excellent movie. (1978)

Who Has Seen the Wind?

W. O. Mitchell   Novel / Canada   📖   9, 10, 11, 12

In one of Canada's most beloved novels, young Brian O'Connal grows from age four to twelve in a small Saskatchewan town in the 1930s. His search for "the ultimate meaning in the cycle of life" is profound. (1947)

Wide Sargasso Sea

Jean Rhys   Novel / Dominican Republic   12

A short novel derived from Jane Eyre shows Mrs. Rochester enslaved as a young woman by the arrogant Rochester as revenge for her family's past. (1966)

Wife of Martin Guerre, The

Janet Lewis   Novel / U.S.   📖   **10**

Set in the 16th-century French Pyrenees, this is the story of justice and love. Martin leaves home after a dispute with his father. Many years later, a man claiming to be Martin comes to the village and is accepted by all, including Martin's wife, Bertrande. When doubts are raised, Bertrande has the returned "Martin" arrested for impersonation. You may also want to read *The Return of Martin Guerre* by Natalie Zemon Davis. (1941)

Wind in the Door, A

Madeleine L' Engle   Novel / U.S.   **9, 10**

L' Engle's classic fantasy series continues with the story of two young people's journey into their brother's body when he becomes critically ill. (1973) See *A Wrinkle in Time, A Swiftly Tilting Planet,* and *Many Waters.*

Winesburg, Ohio

Sherwood Anderson   Short Stories / U.S.   **9, 10, 11, 12**

This collection of stories portrays life in a small mid-western town early in the 20th century. (1919)

Winged Pharoah

Joan Grant   Novel / U.S.   **9**

An evocative portrayal of life in ancient Egypt under the First Dynasty is told through the experiences of a royal woman. (1937)

Wings of the Dove, The

Henry James   Novel / U.S.   **12**

Milly Theale, an heiress with a short time to live and a passion for experiencing life to its fullest, falls in love with Merton Densher, who is persuaded by the woman he loves, Kate Croy, to pretend to love her back in the hope that she will leave them money. Densher's moral torment leads to an inescapable conclusion. (1902)

Winner Take Nothing

Ernest Hemingway   Short Stories / U.S.   11, 12

Hemingway is a master of the short story; this is one of his finest collections. (1933)

Winners, The

Julio Cortazar   Novel / Argentina   9

A cross-section of the citizens of Buenos Aires wins a luxury cruise in a state lottery. Once aboard the boat, they are told that a mysterious and highly infectious disease has broken out; their individual reactions to the confinement explore the widest range of emotional response. (1965)

Winter in the Blood

James Welch   Novel / Native American   11, 12

Welch's humorous novel reveals the guilt of survivors and the way contemporary Native Americans deal with their history of genocide. It is based on an understanding of Blackfoot stories about Old Man and Old Woman. (1974)

Winter of our Discontent, The

John Steinbeck   Novel / U.S.   11, 12

Set in an East Coast town after World War II, this is the story of Ethan Hawley and his gradual entrapment in an unethical life for the sake of material gain. (1961)

Winter People

John Ehle   Novel / U.S.   9, 10

In North Carolina in the 1930s, Collie Wright, an unmarried mother, chooses between a quiet man who loves her and the wild father of her child. (1982)

Winterkill

Craig Lesley   Novel / Native American   11, 12

Lesley's realistic portrait of contemporary reservation life describes the painful relationship of a Native American father and son who struggle against the heritage and history of former generations. (1984)

Winter's Tale

Mark Helprin   Novel / U.S.   9, 10, 11, 12

An unlikely love affair begins between a thief and the terminally ill daughter of the house he is robbing; magical realism hits New York City, complete with angels, gangsters, and flying horses. (1983)

Winter's Tales

Isak Dinesen   Short Stories / Denmark   11

This is one of several collections of excellent short stories by the author of *Out of Africa*. Haunting and magical, one can imagine listening to a storyteller beside a warm fire. (1942)

Wise Blood

Flannery O'Connor   Novel / U.S.   11, 12

O'Connor's first novel is a subtle mix of satire and religious passion. Protagonist Hazel Motes returns from the Korean War determined to dedicate his life to evil, but finds that to be not quite as simple as it seems. (1952)

Wizard of Earthsea, A

Ursula Le Guin   Novel / U.S.   9, 10

The protagonist Ged is tested and learns to use power to restore balance rather than for personal gain. This is the first book of an excellent fantasy series. (1968) See *The Tombs of Atuan* and *The Farthest Shore*.

Woman Hollering Creek and Other Stories

Sandra Cisneros   Short Stories / U.S.   9, 10, 11, 12

The title short story tells of the romantic dreams of a young Mexican woman who travels to Texas with her new husband, a relative stranger. She finds herself trapped in alcoholism and abuse but, through facing her own lies, manages to escape. (1992)

Woman in the Dunes, The

Abe Kobo   Novel / Japan   📖   11

This haunting novel is the story of a young entomologist who is taken prisoner in a seaside town and lowered into a sandpit with an outcast woman. Together they must shovel the sand that threatens to bury them. (1962)

Woman of Andros, The

Thornton Wilder   Novel / U.S.   9, 10

Based on a comedy by the Roman playwright Terence, this is a story set in classical Greece about a young man who avoids an arranged marriage in order to marry the woman he loves, the mother of his child. (1930)

Women in Love

D. H. Lawrence   Novel / Britain   12

Lawrence's powerful novel explores the positive and negative aspects, of love, and includes what Lawrence hoped could be the model for a new intimacy between men. (1921)

Work

Louisa May Alcott   Novel / U.S.   12

The author of *Little Women* writes about the lives of young women trying to find a place in the harsh realities of 19th-century America. (1873)

World of Wonders

Robertson Davies   Novel / Canada

In the third book of *The Deptford Trilogy*, Dunstan Ramsey discovers that the baby prematurely born after the fateful snowball hit the baby's mother has become the famous magician Magnus and records Magnus's memories. (1975) See *Fifth Business* and *The Manticore*.

Worm Ouroborus, The

Eric Rucker Eddison   Novel / Britain   11, 12

One of the earliest fantasies, this novel has become a classic. An English gentleman is whisked off to the planet Mercury by a winged chariot to witness the events of a great war between the inhabitants of Demonland and Witchland. (1922)

Wreath for Udomo, A

Peter Abrahams   Novel / South Africa   12

This black South African novel describes British-educated young revolutionary leaders at odds with both colonialism and the tribalism of their elders. (1956)

Wrinkle In Time, A

Madeleine L' Engle   Novel / U.S.   9, 10

The first of a classic science fiction series tells of a brother and sister as they experience altered time and space to save the world. (1962) See *A Wind in the Door, A Swiftly Tilting Planet,* and *Many Waters.*

Wuthering Heights

Emily Bronte   Novel / Britain   9, 10, 11, 12

Emily Bronte's powerful novel describes the profound connection between an orphan waif, Heathcliff, and Catherine, the daughter of a gentleman. Their spirits continue to be bound after Catherine marries another man, and even from beyond the grave after she dies. (1847)

Year of Living Dangerously, The

Christopher Koch   Novel / Australia   12

Two Australians, a journalist and his cameraman, work in the capital city of Jakarta during the reign of Sukarno. The famous September coup and subsequent massacre, which conclude the tale, are a prelude to a much greater Asian cataclysm, alluded to throughout the text: Vietnam. (1998)

Yearling, The

Marjorie Kinnan Rawlings   Novel / U.S.   9

A young boy raises a tame fawn in the backwoods of Florida in a story that reflects the beauty of nature and the human heart. (1938)

Yellow Raft in Blue Water

Michael Dorris   Novel / Native American   11, 12

A young woman of mixed blood, Black and Native American, returns to her grandmother's Plains reservation to face several mysteries, unraveled for the reader through the stories of her mother and grandmother. (1988)

You Can't Keep a Good Woman Down

Alice Walker   Short Stories / U.S.   📖   12

African American activist and Pulitzer Prize-winner Walker offers 14 provocative and humorous stories that show women "oppressed but not defeated." (1981)

Zanoni

Edward Bulwer Lytton   Novel / Britain   11, 12

Zanoni, a Rosicrucian initiate, has to decide between immortality and human love. (1842)

Zen and the Art of Motorcycle Maintenance: An Inquiry into Values

Robert M. Pirsig   Novel / U.S.   12

As much a journey of discovery within as it is a tale of travel, this novel has become a classic. Phaedrus takes a cross-country motorcycle trip with his son. In taking care of their motorcycles, they experience, the combining of technology and art, as a Zen experience. (1974)

Zorba the Greek

Nikos Kazantzakis   Novel / Greece   11, 12

A scholarly teacher from England learns the dance of life from a Greek laborer, dreamer, and lover of life. (1946)

BIOGRAPHY AND HISTORY

Reader's Road Map

History began as a record of contemporary events kept by small groups as a thread of connection with their collective past. In the beginning, those who "read" this history were also those who made it, and one can presume that there was general agreement within the community that what was recorded was absolute fact, "the way it was."

Time passed and these records came to be viewed by those outside the communities that recorded them; it became increasingly obvious that there was more than one way to tell the story of the same event. We now know clearly that there can be no such thing as an unbiased report; that all recorded history is seen through the lens of the individual or group writing it down. Much more enticing than a collection of facts and dates are books by individual historians whose questions lead to passionate research that uncovers evidence supporting new theories of how events were shaped.

Very often, events occur as a direct result of the actions of one individual. That is why we have included biography in this section. Great human beings are often recognized in their greatness only after their death. Their stories, written retrospectively by others, inspire our own lives as we seek to discover our own unique contribution to human history. As someone pointed out, history is *his* story; yes, and *her* story, too.

Since history is *my* story as well, autobiography is part of this section. Every life is worth recording, and it is fortunate for readers that both important and ordinary individuals have been willing to invite us into their lives, to tell us their stories, often in intimate detail. In reading autobiography, we begin to recognize that each moment of every life is rich in observations that are unique.

As we read autobiographies, biographies, and histories, we come to see that individual lives follow the small pathways that create the well-trod roads of history. The books in this section invite us to walk for a bit along the highways and byways of humanity's journey and to reflect on where our own path is leading.

Abe Lincoln Grows Up
Carl Sandburg   Biography   9, 10

Thoroughly researched, beautifully told, and written especially for young readers, Sandburg's biography of the young Abe remains a classic. (1928)

Abraham Lincoln
Benjamin P. Thomas   Biography   9, 10

A well-respected Lincoln biographer writes this colorful account of the man who kept the vision of a United States alive during the tumult of the Civil War. (1979)

Abraham Lincoln: Prairie Years
Carl Sandburg   Biography   11, 12

Sandburg tells the engaging story of Lincoln's early life and how he becomes President. (1926)

Abraham Lincoln: The War Years
Carl Sandburg   Biography / U.S.   11, 12

Praised for its readability, this volume of Sandburg's biography traces Lincoln's career from the time of his departure for the White House to May 4, 1865, the day of his assassination. (1939)

All But My Life
Gerda Weissman Klein   Autobiography   9, 10

This true account of a six-year ordeal as a victim of Nazi cruelty begins when young Gerda is taken from Poland, losing everything she holds dear. Her liberation by American troops, including the man who became her husband, seems miraculous. Throughout, the author manages to convey great strength of spirit and faith in humanity. (1995)

Always Running: La Vida Loca: Gang Days in L. A.
Luis Rodriguez   Autobiography   11, 12

This brutally honest account of a boy involved in Latino gangs in Los Angeles from the age of 11 has become a best seller. (1993)

American Conservation Movement, The: John Muir and His Legacy

Stephen Fox   Biography   12

Fox tells the story of the Scottish-born "Father of the Modern Conservation Movement" who, more than anyone, is responsible for the U.S. National Park Service. (1981)

And There Was Light

Jacques Lusseyran   Autobiography   12

After Lusseyran became blind at the age of eight, he discovered new ways of knowing. These enable him to maintain an inner light through the darkness of resistance fighting in World War II France and the horrors of Buchenwald. (1963)

Angela's Ashes

Frank McCourt   Autobiography   10, 11, 12

This Pulitzer Prize-winner is a heart-wrenching yet surprisingly warm and amusing account of growing up in the slums of Ireland. (1997) McCourt's story continues in the sequel 'Tis.

Anne Frank: Diary of a Young Girl

Anne Frank   Autobiography   📖   9, 12

The journal of Anne Frank, published after her death, gives an intimate portrayal of her two years in hiding during the Nazi occupation of the Netherlands. It reveals the hardships and joys of Anne's daily life growing up as a sensitive and spirited young woman. (1953) A new translation in 1996 includes previously excluded entries about her emerging sexuality and her relationship with her mother.

ArtBook Series

DK Publishing   Biography   9, 10, 11, 12

This beautiful series is designed for the general reader as well as art-history students. With glorious illustrations, each volume tells the story of an individual artist's life and works within the historical and cultural context of their time. Series includes: Bosch, Caravaggio, Cezanne, Durer,

Friedrich, della Francesca, Gauguin, Giotto, van Gogh, Goya, Kandinsky, Matisse, Rembrandt, Titian, da Vinci, and Velazquez. (1999)

Autobiography, An
Chuck Yeager   Autobiography   9, 10

General Chuck Yeager, World War II flying ace and the first man to fly faster than the speed of sound, tells his story. (1985)

Autobiography of a Face
Lucy Grealy   Autobiography   9, 10

A young girl from Spring Valley, New York, coping with cancer of the jaw and enduring thirty operations over twenty years, comes to understand beauty. (1994)

Autobiography of Benjamin Franklin, The
Benjamin Franklin   Autobiography   10, 11, 12

This classic offers a pithy and colorful account of the life and times of America's first great scientist and man of culture. (1791)

Autobiography of Bertrand Russell, The
Bertrand Russell   Autobiography   12

"Three passions, simple but overwhelmingly strong, have governed my life: the longing for love, the search for knowledge and unbearable pity for the suffering of mankind." Mathematician, philosopher, and peace-activist Russell completed the final book in his three-volume autobiography just a year before his death. (1967–1969)

Autobiography of Malcolm X, The
Alex Haley   Biography   📖   11,12

Malcolm X, assassinated in 1965, was born in poverty, became a petty criminal, converted to Islam while in jail, and became a courageous black leader in the 1960's. He told the story of his life and the growth of the Black Muslim movement to journalist Alex Haley over a period of two years. (1965)

Babe: The Legend Comes to Life

Robert W. Creamer   Biography   &&   9

Sport's Illustrated calls this "the best biography ever written about an American sports figure." It moves behind the legend to reveal Ruth's early days in a Baltimore orphanage, to the glory days with the Yankees, and on to his later years. (1974)

Balm in Gilead: Journey of a Healer

Sara Lawrence-Lightfoot   Biography   11, 12

The struggles of the author's mother, a black woman, who becomes a pediatric psychiatrist in the early 20th century is a heartwarming example of dedication and courage. (1989)

Barrio Boy

Ernesto Galarza   Autobiography   12

An important cultural and historical chronicle, this memoir tells of a young boy and his family who are forced to move from a small Mexican village to escape the Revolution and the Diaz dictatorship. Life in Sacramento, California in the early 20th century is very different from the one they left behind. (1971)

Big Change, The: America Transforms Itself 1900–1950

Frederick Lewis Allen   History / U.S.   12

Allen gives a lively and entertaining account of the remarkable changes that took place during the first half of the 20th century in politics, finance, business, literature, the arts, and sports. (1952)

Biko

Donald Woods   Biography   11, 12

Written by Stephen Biko's friend and confidante, this is an essential book about apartheid in South Africa. The movie *Cry Freedom* was based on this book. (1987)

Black Boy: A Record of Childhood and Youth

Richard Wright   Autobiography   10, 11, 12

This classic vividly describes a black child's experiences growing up in the Southern U.S. in the first part of the 20th century. (1945)

Black Elk Speaks

John G. Neihardt, ed.   Biography   📖   9, 10, 11, 12

This is a first-hand account of Lakota life before and after the fight for the Black Hills. Black Elks' eloquent and historic accounts are easily understood, but native visions and dreams may require discussion and understanding of native cultural beliefs to reveal the inner spiritual nature of their struggles. (1932)

Black Like Me

John Griffin   Autobiography   9, 10, 11, 12

The sad and shocking story of a white writer who travels across the south in 1959 after chemically darkening his skin in order to experience the country's attitude toward black people. (1961)

Broken Cord, The

Michael Dorris   Biography   11, 12

This heartbreaking story, full of compassion and anger, tells of Adam, a Native American child who is disabled due to Fetal Alcohol Syndrome. It is told through his own words and the words of Dorris, who adopted him. (1989)

Bury My Heart at Wounded Knee

Dee Brown   History / Native American   9, 11

A powerful account describes the systematic destruction of the Native American peoples through the treachery of broken treaties, massacres, and accounts given by the great chiefs as they faced their demise. (1971)

Case of the Mid-Wife Toad, The
Arthur Koestler   Biography   11, 12

The tragic story of the Austrian biologist Paul Kammerer is a remarkable description of persecution and jealousy in the scientific community over rival theories of evolution. (1971)

Caspar Hauser: The Enigma of a Century
Jakob Wasserman   Biography   12

Casper Hauser was locked away from all human contact through his entire early life, yet he exhibited remarkable capacities when he was released. (1928)

Cezanne
Meyer Shapiro   Biography   11, 12

The early part provides a comprehensive overview of his work. The rest showcases one painting per page with appropriate commentary. This treasury from the Master of Art Series is accessible for the general reader as well as art students. (1988)

Cheaper by the Dozen
Frank and Ernestine Gilbreth   Autobiography   9

The authors humorously recall growing up at the turn of the 20th century in a family of 12 children, with an efficiency expert for a father. (1948)

Cheyenne Autumn
Mari Sandoz   History / Native American   11, 12

A small proud band of Northern Cheyenne face the military might of the U.S. government in a poignant battle in 19th-century America. Their suffering and humiliation make the reader's heart ache for the loss of their land and heritage as they are hunted to near extermination. (1953)

Childhood
Leo Tolstoy   Autobiography   10, 11, 12

Published in 1852, this is the first of a trilogy that captures life in Tolstoy's early years. The other titles are *Boyhood* (1854) and *Youth* (1857).

Christopher Columbus, Mariner

Samuel Eliot Morison Biography 9, 10, 11

Morison wrote his prize-winning, 680-page definitive biography of Columbus, *Admiral of the Ocean Sea,* after he himself had sailed Columbus' original courses. He considers Columbus one of history's most remarkable mariners and navigators. This is an excellent condensed version of the original biography that is much more accessible to the general reader than the lengthier version. (1955)

Citizen Tom Paine

Howard Fast Biography 10, 11, 12

Fast follows revolutionary Tom Paine from his sordid beginnings in London, through his coming to the New World, and on to his writings that inspired the American Revolution. (1943)

Color of Water: A Black Man's Tribute to his White Mother

James McBride Biography 9

As an adult, McBride, one of a family of 12 children, discovered that his mother, who had always denied that she was white, was the daughter of an Orthodox rabbi from rural Virginia. She had run away to Harlem, married a black man, and founded an all-black Baptist church in Brooklyn. (1996)

Colored People: A Memoir

Louis Gates Autobiography 11,12

Gates, now a university professor, traces his experiences as an African American in a small West Virginia town in the 1950s and 60s. (1994)

Concerning the Spiritual in Art

Wassily Kandinsky Biography 11, 12

Kandinsky sought a return to the spiritual in art in an age where science and materialism result in a culture without soul. He was a passionate, radical artist considered to be the father of abstract art. (1910)

Crazy Horse: The Strange Man of The Oglalas
Mari Sandoz   Biography   11, 12

This superb biography describes one of the last great war chiefs of the Oglala Sioux. Sandoz lived at a time when she could interview those who lived and knew this great Lakota warrior. (1942)

Creators, The: A History of Heroes of the Imagination
Daniel Boorstin   History / Art   11, 12

Boorstin explores the development of artistic innovation over 3,000 years by focusing on the lives of individual artists. This title is the second of a trilogy that follows *The Discoverers* and precedes *The Seekers*. (1992)

Daily Life in Medieval Times: Life in a Medieval City
Joseph and Frances Gies   History / Middle Ages   📖   11

Subtitled *A Vivid, Detailed Account of Birth, Marriage and Death; Food, Clothing and Housing; Love and Labor in the Middle Ages,* this volume shows 13th-century European life is shown through historic pictures, period illustrations, and detailed descriptions of real places. (1979–1989)

Dear Theo: The Autobiography of Vincent van Gogh
Vincent van Gogh   Irving and Jean Stone, eds.   Biography   12

Van Gogh's letters to his confidant and brother Theo vividly describe his everyday life as well as his most profound feelings. An intimate portrait of a tormented soul. (1937)

Death Be Not Proud
John Gunther   Biography   9, 10

A journalist chronicles his 17-year-old son's fiercely intrepid battle with cancer. A deeply moving memoir. (1949)

Deep Cover
Michael Levine   Autobiography   11, 12

Levine recounts the true story of harrowing challenges in the life of an undercover agent for the Drug Enforcement Agency. (1990)

Democracy in America
Alexis de Tocqueville History / U.S. 19th Century **12**

A young French aristocrat tells of his visit to America in 1831 during which he "sought the image of democracy itself, with its inclinations, its character, its prejudices, and its passions, in order to learn what we have to fear or hope from its progress." (Published in two volumes: 1835 and 1840)

Diary of Samuel Pepys, The
Richard La Gallienne, ed. History / Britain 17th century **11, 12**

Pepys began his remarkable diary in 1660 in London when he was 27. His eyewitness accounts of the Plague (1665) and the Great Fire (1666) are remarkable reports. But no less interesting are Pepys' daily doings: visits to the theatre, his delight in singing, dancing, and drinking, and his comments on current fashions. The one-volume Modern Library edition (1991) gives an excellent abridgement of the six-volume original.

Discoverers, The: A History of Man's Search to Know His World and Himself
Daniel Boorstin History / Science **11, 12**

Boorstin relates human invention, such as the development of the calendar, clock, microscope, telescope, medicine, vaccines, the understanding of genetics, and many other scientific and cultural subjects to historical change and progress. (1983) See *The Creators* and *The Seekers*.

Disraeli: A Picture of the Victorian Age
Andre Maurois Biography **12**

Maurois gives a vivid picture not only of the life of Benjamin Disraeli, Prime Minister under Queen Victoria at the height of the British Empire, but of the Victorian Age as well. (1927)

Diving Bell and the Butterfly, The
Jean-Dominique Bauby   Autobiography   10, 11, 12

When the author, editor of French magazine *Elle*, suffers a permanently paralyzing stroke at age 43, he is able to communicate only by blinking his left eye. He thus composed this eloquent, triumphant memoir celebrating the liberating power of consciousness and human spirit. It was published two days before his death and became an international best seller. (1995)

Down and Out in Paris and London
George Orwell   Autobiography   12

Orwell chronicles his eighteen months of living in extreme poverty in these two cities as the Depression gripped Europe. (1933)

Down These Mean Streets
Piri Thomas   Autobiography   9, 10

A story of Puerto Rican immigrants living in the tenements of New York in the 1940s is particularly honored for its blend of street language and poetic descriptions. (1967)

Elinore of Aquitaine and the Four Kings
Amy Kelly   Biography   11

Eleanor (1122–1204), the mother of Richard the Lionhearted and his inept brother King John, began her political career at the age of 15 as the ruler of France's largest kingdom, and went on to become one of the most influential people of her time. (1959)

Elizabeth the Great
Elizabeth Jenkins   Biography   11, 12

Sixteenth-century life in the court of Good Queen Bess is brought to life in this fascinating account of not only the excitement of great events, but also the intimate details of daily activities. The Elizabethan Age was a glorious time for England, the Queen herself a complex and powerful ruler as Jenkins' biography richly illustrates.(1959)

Emerson: The Mind on Fire
Robert Richardson   Biography   **12**

Richardson's task was to find out "what kind of individual was this prophet of individualism"? His book is a remarkable account of Emerson's emotional as well as intellectual life. (1995)

Endurance
Alfred Lansing   Biography   **10, 11, 12**

Lansing tells the story of the British explorer Shackleton and his men who, in 1914, spent five months ice-locked in Antarctica, one of the most savage regions of the world. (1999)

Esoteric Emerson, The
Richard G. Geldard   Biography   📖   **12**

Through the example of his life, Emerson showed that "holy and mysterious forces" are present for us all if we will listen for the right word. Geldard shows how such a practice of listening can lead to the emergence of the true Self. (1993)

Farewell to Manzanar
Jean Wakatsuki Houston   Autobiography   **9, 10, 11, 12**

Uprooted from their home in California, a young woman and her family spend the years of World War II living in an internment camp with 10,000 other Japanese Americans. (1973)

Fear No Evil: The Classic Memoir of One Man's Triumph Over a Police State
Anatoly Sharansky et al   Autobiography   **12**

In this rare true story, a Soviet political dissident survives nine years of imprisonment through wits, courage and faith. (1998)

First Hundred Years of Nino Cochise: The Untold Story of an Apache Indian Chief

Ciye Nino Cochise   Biography / Native American   9, 10

The story of the great Apache Chief Cochise is told by his grandson who was raised in the mountains of Mexico, where he fought with Theodore Roosevelt and struggled to understand the ways of the white man. (1971)

Flame Trees of Thika

Elspeth Huxley   Autobiography   9

Huxley pens an autobiographical account of her extraordinary adventures as a child in Kenya in the early 1900s. It is a picture of a vanished Africa. (1959)

Galileo's Daughter: A Historical Memoir of Science, Faith, and Love

Dava Sobel   Biography 📖   12

This unusual biography of Galileo is based on the 124 surviving letters of his illegitimate daughter Virginia, who became Sister Maria Celeste. Her father described her as "a woman of exquisite mind, singular goodness, and tenderly attached to me." (1999)

Gandhi, the Man: The Story of His Transformation

Eknath Easwaran   Biography 👓   9, 10

As a young man, Eknath Easwaran visited Gandhi because "I wanted to know the secret of his power." This book tells what he learned. (1984)

Gandhi's Autobiography: The Story of My Experiments with Truth.

M. K. Gandhi   Autobiography   11

Gandhi is one of the most inspiring figures of the 20th century. In his classic autobiography, he tells the story of his life with astonishing honesty. Especially interesting is how he developed his concept of active nonviolent resistance, which won the Indian struggle for independence. (1954)

Genghis Khan: The Emperor of All Men
Harold Lamb   Biography   10

This is an exciting account of the warrior and visionary leader who captured half of Europe in the 13th century. (1927)

George Washington Carver
Rackham Holt   Biography   9

America's first great African American botanist rose above the segregation of the deep South to achieve world-wide fame. (1943)

Georgia O'Keefe: Portrait of an Artist
Laurie Lisle   Biography   11, 12

Legendary Georgia O'Keefe is remembered as one of the original painters of the 20th century. Lisle examines the girlhood, the romance with famed photographer Alfred Stieglitz, and the unique vision of this strong and independent woman. (1986)

Girl, Interrupted
Susanna Kaysen   Autobiography   10

In this insightful memoir, a teenage girl describes her treatment for mental illness at McLean Hospital in the 1960s. (1993)

Grandfather Stories
Samuel Hopkins Adams   Biography   9

Originally published in *The New Yorker* in the 1950s, Adams' grandfather's stories go back to the 1830s, when his family helped to create the Erie Canal. (1955)

Great Conductors, The
Harold C. Schonberg   Biography   12

Schonberg was a music critic for the *New York Times* for 30 years and wrote several books on the history of music. His love of music comes through his informative and engaging text. See *The Great Pianists* and *The Lives of the Great Composers*. (1967)

Great Pianists, The: From Mozart to the Present

Harold C. Schonberg   Biography   9, 10, 11, 12

The author has written 12 books and some reviewers consider this his best work. Covering a period of 200 years, Schonberg once again brings a lively and informative account of the lives, performances, and personalities of the great pianists. See *The Great Conductors* and *The Lives of the Great Composers*. (1987)

Great Rehearsal: The Story of the Making and Ratifying of the Constitution of the United States

Carl Clinton van Doren   History / U.S. Revolution   9

This highly regarded history of the first (1881) Constitutional Convention was written during the period of history when the United Nations was being formed, a time when people were considering how to think internationally, not nationally. (1948)

Greeks, The

H. D. F. Kitto   History / Classic Greece   📖   10, 11, 12

Kitto's detailed exploration of the life, culture, and history of classical Greece is considered by many to be the best overall introduction to the epoch that has shaped so much of the modern world. (1957)

Grey Is the Color of Hope

Irina Ratushinskaya   A. Kojevnikov, trans.   Biography   11, 12

A young Russian poet and human rights activist, imprisoned in a harsh Siberian camp with other females during the 1980s, writes this memoir of courage, survival, and humor. (1988)

Growing Pains

Emily Carr   Autobiography   9, 10

One of Canada's most innovative and treasured artists tells of her girlhood in late 19th-century Victoria, British Columbia. (1945) See also *Klee Wyck*.

Growing Up

Russell Baker   Autobiography   9

With ironic wit, Baker describes growing up during the Great Depression in Baltimore. (1982)

Gulag Archipelago, The

Aleksandr Solzhenitsyn   Autobiography   12

Published in Britain in three volumes between 1974 and 1978, this "history and geography" of the Soviet Union's prison and forced labor camp system was the cause of Solzhenitsyn's deportation from Russia to West Germany.

Having Our Say: The Delaney Sisters' First 100 Years

Amy Hill Hearth   Biography   ᘓᔿ   10, 11, 12

The gutsy, humorous and revealing memoir of Bessie and Sadie Delanie, 103 and 105-year-old sisters, reflects the struggles of women and of African Americans in this century. First written as a drama. (1993)

Headmaster, The: Frank L. Boyden of Deerfield

John McPhee   Biography   11, 12

McPhee writes an inspiring biography of Boyden, an educator with a vision who was headmaster of Deerfield Academy for over 60 years. (1966)

Henry Thoreau: A Life of the Mind

Robert Richardson   Biography   12

This detailed biography explores the intellectual life of the leading 19th-century Transcendentalist philosopher, whose independent thinking and reflections on nature continue to fascinate us over 150 years later. (1986)

Hiroshima

John Hersey   History / World War II   📖   10, 11, 12

The atomic bomb that was dropped on Hiroshima hastened the end of World War II. Hersey recorded what the bomb meant to the lives of ordinary civilians in that city. (1946)

History of the English-Speaking Peoples, A

Winston Churchill   History / Britain   12

Churchill was the Prime Minister of Britain during World War II; his classic history is a thorough and highly readable four volumes. (1956–1958)

Homage to Catalonia

George Orwell   Autobiography   11, 12

Orwell, like many other young idealists in the 1930s, went to Spain to fight in the Civil War where he saw the confusion first hand and was wounded in the throat. (1938)

Hour of Gold, Hour of Lead

Anne Morrow Lindbergh   Biography   11, 12

In her journal, Lindbergh describes her life as co-pilot for Charles Lindbergh, and as wife and mother. She writes of the tragic kidnapping of her son and of her search for meaning in life. (1973)

Howard Pyle's Book of Pirates

Howard Pyle   Biography   9

Subtitled *Fiction, Fact and Fancy Concerning the Buccaneers and Marooners of the Spanish Main*, Pyle's work remains an exciting, page-turner, richly illustrated by his own paintings and drawings. (1921)

Hummingbird and the Hawk

R. C. Padden   History / Central America   9, 10

This graphic history recounts the sacrifice of thousands of slaves and natives from hostile provinces by the great Aztec chiefs. It is considered controversial for its interpretation of Aztec society. (1967)

Hunger of Memory: The Education of Richard Rodriguez

Richard Rodriguez   Autobiography   11, 12

Rodriguez began his schooling in California, knowing just 50 words of English, and went on to earn a Ph.D. in English Renaissance Literature. His success was bought at the cost of a painful alienation from his past, his parents, and his culture. (1982)

I Have Spoken: American History Through the Voices of the Indians

Virginia Irving Armstrong   History / Native American   **11, 12**

This excellent collection of primary sources, speeches, and treaty interpretations shows the changing posture of Native Americans as they moved from peaceful to more aggressive negotiations with the white government. This happened during the time their land was being taken and the true chiefs were left out of negotiations. The 1971 and 1972 editions include powerful photographs that have been omitted from more recent editions. (1971)

I Know Why The Caged Bird Sings

Maya Angelou   Autobiography   **9, 10, 11, 12**

Poetically written and brutally honest, Angelou describes her life from her arrival in Stamp, Arkansas, at age three, to giving birth to her only child in San Francisco when she was 16. Angelou provides an unforgettable memoir of growing up black in the 1930s and 1940s. (1969)

I Rode with Stonewall

Henry Kyd Douglas   Biography   **9, 10**

Douglas gives a lively first-hand account of life with one of history's greatest generals, "Stonewall" Jackson of the Civil War. (1940)

I Send a Voice

Evelyn Eaton   Autobiography   **11, 12**

The Caucasian author, at the age of 63, seeks healing with Native American ritual, attends sweat lodges, fasts, and becomes a medicine woman who helps heal others. This story takes the reader on her journey of Native American spirituality. Indians later shunned her because of political issues between the races. (1978)

I, Rigoberta Menchu

Rigoberta Menchu   Autobiography   **12**

Menchu, a Guatemalan Indian woman, received the Nobel Peace Prize in 1992 and is dedicated to improving the lives of indigenous people. (1983)

In the Days of Vittorio

Eve Ball   History / Native American   9, 10

During the turbulent period between 1876–1886, the Apache were a hunted people. James Kaywaykla gives a first-hand account of the last years of Warm Springs Apache Chiefs Vittorio and Nana, in the time of Geronimo. (1970)

In the Spirit of Crazy Horse

Peter Mathiessen   History / Native American   11, 12

Mathiesson recounts the history of the Lakota tribe versus the U.S. government from Red Cloud's War to the FBI shoot-out near Wounded Knee in 1975. His work shows the powerful injustices that still remain against the Native Americans. (1983)

Indeh, An Apache Odyssey

Eve Ball, Nora Henn, & Lynda A. Sanchez History / Native American
9, 10

The authors present an engrossing oral history of Apache survivors across the U.S. (1980)

Interrupted Life: The Diaries of Etty Hillesum, 1941–1943

Etty Hillesum   Autobiography   12

A young Dutch Jewish lawyer wrote these diaries before and during the Holocaust, when she was imprisoned in Auschwitz. They tell of an inner strength that allowed her to find moments of joy in the face of horror. She subsequently died in Auschwitz. (1983)

Invisible Africa: Contributions to a Coming Culture

Ralph Shepherd, ed.   History / Africa   10, 11, 12

These essays explore intuitive insights into historical events in Africa, and South Africa in particular, inspired by the humanism of Stephen Biko and Mahama Gandhi, and the spiritual insights of Rudolf Steiner. (1996).

Ishi, The Last of His Tribe

Theodora Kroeber   Biography   ᘓᕁ   9

The Yahi, a sub-group of the Yand Indian tribe of northern California, lived in virtual isolation from white society and pursued their traditional way of life well into the 20th century. The last surviving member of the tribe came to live in the University of California anthropology museum in San Francisco in 1911. (1964)

Jackson's Track

Daryl Tonkin and Carolyn Landon   Biography   10, 11, 12

Bushman Daryl Tonkin and his beloved aboriginal wife, Euphemia, lived and worked along Jackson's Track in Gippsland, South Eastern Victoria, Australia from the 1930s onwards, (2000)

Jim Bridger, Mountain Man

Stanley Vestal   Biography   9, 10

An accurate history of the early 1800s in the American West, Vestal chronicles the life of a great American explorer, trapper, and scout. (1946)

Johann Sebastian Bach —As His World Knew Him

Otto L. Bettman   Biography

Think of this as a portrait of Bach composed of snapshots taken at myriad angles during his life and organized into a magnificent collage. The bonus of this biography is that as you learn who Bach the man and artist was, you also get to stroll through 17th-century Europe. (1995)

John Adams

David McCullough   Biography   12

McCullough's biography of the second President of the United States from his earliest days in Massachusetts as a country lawyer to the American Revolution includes a full picture of his marriage to the remarkable Abigail. (2001)

Joys and Sorrows: Reflections

Pablo Casals and Albert Kahn   Autobiography   9, 10, 11, 12

The great cellist reflects on his life, music, politics, and humanity over the first 70 years of this century. A profound and inspiring story of a musical humanitarian. (1974)

Kaffir Boy: The True Story of a Black Youth's Coming of Age in Apartheid South Africa

Mark Mathabane   Autobiography   10, 11, 12

Mathabane moved from poverty in a South African black township to a tennis scholarship in the U.S. (1986)

Käthe Kollwitz: Life in Art

Mina C. Klein   Biography   12

Kollwitz was a famous German artist who lived from 1867–1945. Her work serves as an indictment of the social conditions in Germany during the late 19th and early 20th centuries. (1972)

Klee Wyck

Emily Carr   Autobiography   9, 10

The now-famous artist travels through the villages of British Columbia, Canada, where the Nuu-chah-nulth natives called her Klee Wyck, "laughing one." (1924) See *Growing Pains.*

Lakota Woman

Mary Crow Dog   Autobiography   11, 12

Crow Dog dramatically tells of difficulties and hardships of a Native American woman growing up on the Rosebud Sioux Indian Reservation in South Dakota. She traces her life from its start in 1953, through growing up fatherless in a one-room cabin, to her discovery of purpose and involvement in the American Indian Movement. (1990)

Lame Deer, Seeker of Visions
John Lame Deer and Richard Erdoes   Biography

11, 12

Erdoes tells the story of John Lame Deer who was born on the Rosebud Reservation in South Dakota but lived a riotous life in the white man's world. Lame Deer's story contrasts his life as a Lakota medicine man with his life as a rodeo clown, painter, and prisoner. (1992)

Land of Our Own, A
Golda Meir   Autobiography

9, 10

Meir tells how she went from being a Milwaukee, Wisconsin schoolteacher to becoming Prime Minister of Israel. The conflict in Palestine is carefully and thoughtfully discussed. (1973)

Last Algonquin, The
Theodore Kazimiroff   History / Native American

9, 10

The author retells the story told to him by his father who befriended Joe Two Trees, an old Algonquin believed to be the last of his tribe. The story reflects both the oral tradition and cultural heritage of the Algonquin. (1982)

Last American Man, The
Elizabeth Gilbert   Biography

9, 10

Eustace Conway discovered his love of nature growing up in South Carolina during the 1960s. He decided to live in the woods, and by the time he finished high school had moved into a teepee where he lived for 17 years, developing wilderness skills unknown to most modern Americans. He considers the wasteful habits of modern America catastrophic and advocates a return to nature as a solution. (2002)

Leg to Stand On, A
Oliver Sacks   Autobiography

11, 12

Sacks describes with inimitable insight his own crisis and recovery when his leg is injured on a desolate mountain in Norway. (1984)

Legacy: A Search for the Origins Of Civilization

Michael Wood   History / Ancient Civilizations 📖   10

This text was published to accompany the British television series of the same name. It explores the six great civilizations of Iraq, India, China, Egypt, Central America, and the Barbarian West in an attempt to discover the essential nature of civilization. (1992)

Letter From the Birmingham Jail

Martin Luther King. Jr.   History / U.S. Civil Rights 📖   11

King joined thousands of demonstrating blacks in downtown Birmingham, Alabama in 1963 and was arrested. When he was criticized by a group of white clergymen for his unwise and untimely actions, he smuggled a letter to them on any scraps of paper he could find, including toilet tissue and the margins of newspapers, justifying his moral concern for oppressed humanity. (1963)

Letters of Wolfgang Amadeus Mozart

Hans Mersmann, ed., M. M. Bozman, trans.   Biography 📖 11, 12

Mozart left an incredible legacy of letters, which cover his entire life. Written to a wide circle including his father, friends, patrons, and his wife, they are often moving and sometime ribald correspondence of the musical genius. (1929)

Life on the Mississippi

Mark Twain   Autobiography 📖   10

Twain's recollections of his steamboat pilot days make for delightful reading. (1883)

Light from the Yellow Star: A Lesson of Love from the Holocaust

Robert O. Fisch   Autobiography   9, 10, 11, 12

Through his own paintings, memories and quotations from gravestones in the Budapest memorial concentration camp cemetery where his father is buried, Fisch gives us a memoir of hope; "What could those silent, slaughtered millions ask us now? I believe they would want us to have understanding, compassion, and love." (1994)

Lives of the Great Composers, The

Harold C. Schonberg   Biography   9

A Pulitzer Prize-winning *New York Times* critic brings lively, anecdotal and eminently readable brief biographies of composers from Monteverdi to Arnold Schoenberg with a wonderful bibliography. (1997) See *The Great Conductors* and *The Great Pianists*.

Long Journey Home: Stories from Black History

Julius Lester   Biography   9

These are six excitingly told real-life stories about the contributions of little known but important figures in African American history. (1972)

Longest Day, The

Cornelius Ryan   History / World War II   10, 11, 12

On D-Day, June 6, 1944, the Allied invasion of German-occupied northern France began when British, U.S., and Canadian forces landed on the beaches of Normandy. (1959)

Longitude: The True Story of a Lone Genius Who Solved the Greatest Scientific Problem of His Time

Dava Sobel   History / Science   11, 12

Eighteenth-century scientist and clockmaker William Harrison solved one of the most perplexing problems of history: how to determine east-west location at sea. (1995)

Madame Curie

Eve Curie   Biography   9, 10

Curie's daughter tells of the life and work of her mother, a Nobel Prize-winner in both chemistry and physics. (1938)

Madame Sun Yat-Sen

Jung Chang and Jon Halliday   Biography   9

In this fascinating account, young Soong Ching-ling returns to China from school in America and becomes passionately involved in the Chinese Revolution. (1986)

Mahatma Gandhi: His Life and Message to the World
Louis Fischer   Biography   9, 11, 12

Fischer writes an accessible account of the man who sparked a quiet revolution in the hearts of the people of India and led to its liberation. (1954)

Man's Search for Meaning
Victor Emil Frankl   Autobiography   12

The eminent psychiatrist Victor Frankl was imprisoned in concentration camps. His groundbreaking theory proposes that the most basic human motivation is the will to find meaning. (1963)

Maps and Dreams: Indians and the British Columbia Frontier
Hugh Brody   History / Canada / First Nations   11, 12

This important study describes Canada's West Coast First Nations people, their relationship to the land, their history, and their future. (1998)

Marbacka
Selma Lagerlof   Autobiography   9

Selma Lagerlof (1858–1940) was the first woman author to receive the Nobel Prize for Literature. She tells how she became partially lame at age three and how her early desire to be a writer was prompted by her grandmother's stories. A rich and rewarding memoir. (1922)

Markings
Dag Hammerskjold   Autobiography   12

Hammerskjold's life was given to public service, first as a member of the Swedish government, where he is credited with having coined the term "planned economy," and then as the Secretary General of the United Nations from 1953 until his death. This remarkable little book, published after his death, is his private diary containing, as he put it, his "negotiations with himself and with God." (1964)

Martin Luther King, Jr.: Spirit-Led Prophet

Richard L. Deats and Coretta Scott King   Biography   9, 10, 11, 12

Civil rights leader King practiced spiritual non-violence in his fight for freedom. He was arrested over 25 times and was assassinated at the age of 39. His legacy lives on through his strong example and the stirring clarity of his writing and oratory..(1997)

Medieval People

Eileen Power   History / Middle Ages   📖   11

Power explores the lives of six ordinary people who lived between the 9th and 16th centuries, including a peasant on a country estate in Charlemagne's time, a Venetian traveler of the 13th century, and a middle-class Parisian housewife of the 14th century. (1924) Also of interest is her book *Medieval Women*.

Memoirs of Chief Red Fox

Chief Red Fox   Autobiography   9, 10

On the eve of his 101st birthday Native American Chief Red Fox recounts the events of his life and the changes created by the westward movement of settlers. He was a Hollywood actor in 1913 and a member of Wild Bill's West Show. (1971)

Memories, Dreams and Reflections

Carl Jung   Autobiography   11, 12

The great psychiatrist tells his life story through his dreams, visions, premonitions, and insights into the mythic dimension of human experience. (1961)

Memories of a Catholic Girlhood

Mary McCarthy   Autobiography   11, 12

One of America's most well respected writers focuses on her childhood from age six after her parents die in a flu epidemic. (1957)

Mortal Lessons: Notes on the Art of Surgery
Richard Selzer   Autobiography   9, 10, 11, 12

Through four stories of loss, Selzer, as surgeon, moves from despair to acceptance and redemption. (1976)

Mountains of California, The
John Muir   Autobiography   📖   10

The Scottish-born "Father of the Modern Conservation Movement" movingly describes the Sierra Nevada mountains through which he traveled in the late 1800s. (1894)

Moveable Feast, A
Ernest Hemingway   Autobiography   11, 12

Published after his death, this is an account of Hemingway's life in Paris where he met Gertrude Stein, Ford Maddox Ford, Ezra Pound, and others. (1964)

My Family and Other Animals
Gerald Durrell   Autobiography   10

Durrell amusingly recalls growing up on the island of Corfu in the middle of an eccentric family. (1956)

My Left Foot
Christy Brown   Autobiography   9, 10, 11,12

Irish painter and author Brown was born with severe cerebral palsy, leaving him almost completely paralyzed; he began to communicate by writing and drawing with a pencil gripped in his left foot. (1954)

Names, The
N. Scott Momaday   Autobiography   10, 11, 12

Momaday's memoir looks back on growing up in New Mexico and on the Native American's connection to the land, and includes his genealogy and photos of his family. (1976)

Narrative of the Life of Frederick Douglas: An American Slave

Frederick Douglas   Autobiography   9, 11

Douglas recounts his trials as a slave and his escape from slavery to the North where in his freedom he becomes an eloquent spokesperson for abolition. (1845)

New England Indians, The

C. Keith Wilbur   History / Native American   9, 10

This rich source book of information about the every-day lives of New England Indians contains detailed illustrations and maps. The work uncovers the prejudice against and mystery about these early native peoples. (1996)

Nicholas and Alexandra

Robert K. Massie   Biography   12

This story of the extraordinary imperial dynasty of Tsar Nicholas II of Russia, his doomed empire, and the Russian Revolution became a best seller; Massie gives a sympathetic account of Nicholas, his wife Alexandra, their love for their children and their struggles with their son's hemophilia. (1967)

Night

Elie Wiesel   Autobiography   9

Weisel gives a horrific and detailed account of himself and his father in a Nazi concentration camp. (1958)

Night to Remember, A

Walter Lord   Social History   9

An account of the sinking of the Titanic, based on interviews with the survivors, remains unsurpassed in presenting the reality of that unimaginable disaster. (1955)

No Place For A Nervous Lady
Lucy Frost   Autobiography   11, 12

Thirteen women describe life en route to and in Australia between the 1840s and 1880s through diaries, autobiographical sketches, photographs, drawings and letters home. (1984)

Not Without My Daughter
Betty Mahmoody   Autobiography   11

An American housewife is trapped with her daughter in Iran during a visit to her husband's family in 1984. Her husband, influenced by his Muslim relatives, forces her to wear a veil, tells her they are never returning to the United States, and threatens to kill her if she tries to escape. (1991)

Notebooks of Leonardo da Vinci , The
Leonardo da Vinci   Biography   9, 10

These notebooks were assembled after the artist's death. They reflect his ideas, his thoughts on all subjects imaginable as well as his sketches, drawings, and mathematical notes. One page is in the original Italian and the opposite is the English translation. (ca. 1508)

Of Water and the Spirit: Ritual, Magic, and Initiation in the Life of an African Shaman
Malidorma Patrice Some   Biography   📖   11, 12

Burkina Faso was still a French colony when Some, born in 1956, was taken from his village at four years by the local Jesuit missionary to prepare him for the priesthood. When he grew old enough, he rebelled and returned to his original home where he underwent the traditional month-long Dagara initiation rite. He then acted as mediator with the whites to help his tribe survive. (1994)

On the Black Hill
Bruce Chatwin   Biography   10

Identical twins lived for 80 years on a few square miles of Welsh countryside. (1982)

Once to Every Man: An Autobiography
William Sloane Coffin   Autobiography   12

Coffin has been a long-time civil rights advocate and international peace movement activist. He served as chaplain at Yale University for 18 years and rose to prominence during the 1960s and '70s as a leader in the Civil Rights and anti-Vietnam War movements. (1977)

One Writer's Beginnings
Eudora Welty   Autobiography   11, 12

A beautifully written account by one of America's best-loved writers of her early life in Jackson, Mississippi is actually a series of three lectures delivered at Harvard University in 1983 when the author was 74. It includes "Listening", "Learning to See", and "Finding a Voice." (1984)

Only Yesterday: An Informal History of the 1920's
Frederick Allen   History / 20th Century   12

Popular historian Allen describes with remarkable detachment everything from politics to prohibition, the economy, sweeping social changes, the coming of radio, syndicated columnists, the movies, the red scare, the rise of business, science, and religion. (1931)

Ordeal by Hunger: The Story of the Donner Party
George Stewart   History / U.S. Westward Expansion   10

A group of 87 pioneers set out for California from Illinois in the spring of 1846 and were trapped in the Sierra Nevada during the worst-ever recorded winter. Half the party who survived did so by yielding to the necessity of cannibalism. (1936)

Oregon Trail, The
Frances Parkman   Autobiography   11

A primary resource for American history is the eyewitness account of Parkman's 1846 trek across the High Plains of Nebraska, Wyoming, Colorado, and Kansas. (final revision 1892)

Out of Africa

Isak Dinesen   Autobiography   9, 10, 11, 12

Danish writer, Karen Blixen, ran a coffee plantation in Kenya with her husband and continued to do so on her own after her divorce; this book tells her story and is a detailed and vivid account of East Africa in the early 20th century. (1937)

Out of My Life and Thought

Albert Schweitzer   Autobiography   11, 12

Humanitarian Schweitzer tells the story of his life and the development of his philosophy from his earliest memories, through his medical training, and his first 16 years as a doctor in Africa. His life has inspired millions. (1933)

Outermost House: A Year of Life on the Great Beach of Cape Cod

Henry Beston   Biography   10

This nature classic is elegantly written by Beston, who, planning to spend only two weeks at the house becomes so entranced by the birds, the wind, the sand, and the sea, that he spends an entire year. (1928)

Passion of the Western Mind: Understanding the Ideas That Have Shaped Our World View

Richard Tarnas   History / Philosophy   📖   11, 12

Described as "a complete liberal education in a single volume," Tarnas' book gives a highly readable account of the great minds of Western Civilization and their pivotal ideas, from Plato to Hegel, from Augustine to Nietzsche, from Copernicus to Freud; his epilogue remains unsurpassed as a description of the radical changes facing humanity at the close of the 20th century. (1991)

Paula

Isabel Allende   Autobiography   12

Chilean author Allende wrote this moving story of her own life while facing the tragedy of her 28-year-old daughter's sudden coma and death. (1995)

Pictorial Autobiography, A

Barbara Helpworth Autobiography 📖 **11, 12**

Hepworth (1903-1975) is considered to be one of the foremost sculptors of the 20th century. Her powerful work explores form in life and in mathematics. As well as working in stone, she experiments in new substances such as sheet metal, wire and bronze. (19895)

Pilgrim at Tinker Creek

Ann Dillard Biography **12**

A woman in her mid-20s keeps a journal of her daily walks along Tinker Creek in the Blue Ridge Mountains of Virginia. It has become a classic among environmentalists and nature lovers. (1974)

Portable Medieval Reader, The

James B. Ross and Mary M. McLaughlin, eds.
History / Middle Ages 📖 **11**

Contemporary accounts of the Crusades, the first trade missions to Cathay, the persecution of Jews and heretics, the delights of courtly pageants, and the confusion of popular uprisings. Chaucer, Petrarch, Boccaccio, Saint Francis of Assisi, Thomas Aquinas and Abelard, and lesser-known writers, bring the medieval world alive for the modern reader. (1949)

Portable Renaissance Reader, The

James B. Ross and Mary M. McLaughlin, eds.
History / Renaissance 📖 **11**

Subtitled *The Golden Age of Italy and Northern Europe, 1400–1600*, this is a window into the European Renaissance in the words of more than a hundred of its monarchs, prelates, merchants, scholars, artists, poets, and ordinary citizens. (1953)

Portable Roman Reader, The

Basil Davenport, ed. History / Ancient Rome 📖 **11**

A collection of 18th and 19th-century translations of Roman literature includes *Juvenal's Satires* by Dryden, *Ovid's Metamorphoses* by Addison, and Walter Pater's rendition of *The Golden Ass*. (1951)

Prisoner without a Name, Cell without a Number

Jacobo Timerman   History / Argentina   12

A journalist documents Argentina's institutionalized violence against political dissidents who disappeared in the 1970s and '80s, at least 100 of whom were journalists. (1981)

Prodigal Genius: The Life of Nikola Tesla

John O'Neill   Biography   11, 12

This popular biography tells the story of the great electrical engineer and inventor, Nicholas Tesla. (1944)

Profiles of Courage

John F. Kennedy   Biography   9, 10

Kennedy's Pulitzer Prize-winning book tells the stories of courageous, self-sacrificing American leaders who shaped the United States. (1956)

Pueblo Nations

Joe S. Sando   History / Native American   11, 12

Sando, a Native American elder, writes about the history and ethnography of Pueblo civilization, including the Spanish conquest and American government policies and how they affected the Pueblo culture. The 1992 version includes new photographs and history of recent events. (1991)

Quest: The Life of Elisabeth Kubler-Ross

Derek Gill   Biography   11, 12

This book tells the story of the inspiring physician whose work with the terminally ill has indicated that there is an observable and meaningful pattern in the process of dying. (1980)

Railway Man: A True Story of War, Remembrance and Forgiveness

Eric Lomax   Autobiography   9, 10

A young man with a passion for trains was stationed in Malaysia as a member of the Royal Signal Corps when the Japanese took Singapore at the start of World War II. He was sent to Thailand as a prisoner of war to work on the infamous Burma-Siam railroad. (1995)

Rain of Gold

Victor Villasenor   Biography   11, 12

This account of the journeys of two Mexican families through the generations from the 1870s to the 1940s culminates in the birth of the author himself in California. (1991)

Rembrandt's Eyes

Simon Schama   Biography   9, 10

Shama creates a stunning biography of the enigmatic Dutch artist, Rembrandt van Rijn, within the context of the whirl of the 17th-century Low Countries. This is also a biography of Peter Paul Rubens, his rival artist and countryman. Lavishly illustrated. (1999)

Return from Tomorrow

George Ritchie   Autobiography   9, 11

At the age of 20, George Ritchie died in an army hospital; he came back to life nine minutes later. This is the story of what he experienced during those nine minutes. (1985)

Rights of Man, The

Thomas Paine   History / 18th Century / Revolution   📖   9, 10

Paine's classic work defended the French Revolution and resulted in his indictment for treason by the British. (1791)

Rise and Fall of the Third Reich

William L. Shirer   History / World War II   12

As a journalist assigned to Berlin, Shirer tells his account of the early days of the Nazis and World War II. It was one of the first major historical works on the subject and is still very highly regarded. (1959)

Road From Coorain, The

Jill Ker Conway   Autobiography   9, 10, 11, 12

Conway's exceptionally well-written autobiography portrays a woman's uneasy odyssey from the Australian outback to the presidency of Smith College. (1989)

Rolling Thunder

Doug Boyd   History/ Native American   11, 12

Boyd's book captures the simple wisdom of John Pope, Rolling Thunder, who is a medicine man of the Cherokee tribe. Through a series of episodes and dialogue, Boyd raises awareness as he recounts the plight of reservation Indians in the 1970s. (1974)

Roman Way, The

Edith Hamilton   History / Ancient Rome   10

Hamilton's readable prose gives an account of Roman history from its founding until its collapse with an emphasis on the great writers Cicero, Catullus, Horace, Virgil, Livy, Seneca, Tacitus, and Juvenal. (1932)

Romance of Leonardo da Vinci, The

Dmitri Merejkowski   Biography   11, 12

The Renaissance and its most universal man are described in this provocative, behind-the-scenes account. (1928)

Roots

Alex Haley   Biography   9, 10, 11, 12

An American's memory of his family's oral history leads him on a journey, back through generations, to his roots in West Africa. (1976)

Russian Century: A History of the Last Hundred Years

Brian Moynahan   History / Russia   📖   12

Through extensive use of contemporary accounts, Moynahan traces Russia's stormy 20th century, from the last days of Tsarist rule, to the Bolshevik Revolution, through both world wars, the Cold War, and to the overthrow of Communism. (1995)

Russians, The

Hendrick Smith   History / Russia   12

This excellent and thorough description of Russia and the Russians was published before the fall of the Berlin Wall; Smith's book *The New Russians* (1996) describes the post-communist era. (1976)

Saga of Chief Joseph

Helen Addison Howard   History / Native American   11, 12

Howard's revised version of the story of Chief Joseph and the five bands of the Nez Perce tribe who fought with him is told from three views: the Nez Perce, the military, and the settlers. (1978)

Schoolteacher in Old Alaska, A

Hannah Bryce   Autobiography   9

An adventurous young woman's memoir, based on letters to her niece, tells about teaching Aleuts, Indians, Inuits, and Russians in the desolate wilderness of Alaska from 1904–1918. (1995)

Seed of Sarah: Memoirs of a Survivor

Judith Isaacson   Autobiography   12

While teaching at Bates College in Maine, Isaacson was asked by a student, "How can you smile after Auschwitz?" It was that question that prompted her to write this stunning, detailed memoir. (1991)

Seekers: The Story of Man's Continuing Quest to Understand His World

Daniel Boorstin   History / Philosophy   11, 12

From the prophets of the Holy Land and the philosophers of ancient Greece, through the Renaissance, to the modern era of the social sciences, Boorstin contends, "In this long quest [for understanding], Western culture has turned from seeking the end or purpose to seeking causes, from the Why to the How." (1998) See *The Creators* and *The Discoverer*.

Shadows on the Grass

Isak Dinesen   Autobiography   9

This book continues the life story of Dinesen (Karen Blixen) on a coffee plantation in Kenya. (1960) See *Out of Africa*.

Showdown at Little Big Horn

Dee Brown   History / Native American   11, 12

Brown uses primary sources of journals, diaries, letters, and testimony to recount the history from May 17, 1876 through June 25, when General Custer's cavalry troops met defeat at the Little Bighorn River in Montana. (1964)

Snakes and Ladders: Glimpses of Modern India

Gita Mehta   History / Social Issues   11, 12

With humor, wisdom, compassion, and perspective, Mehta's essays are intended to explain India as it enters the 21st century, both to Westerners and to fellow Indians. (1997)

Soccer War, The

Ryszard Kapuscinski   History / Revolution   11, 12

Covering 27 revolutions and coups in Africa, Latin America, and the Middle East as a reporter, Kapuscinski combines journal entries with journalistic accounts to reveal the human dramas behind the official press releases. (1991)

Sorrow in Our Heart, A

Allan W. Eckert   Biography   9, 10, 11, 12

This is a well-researched and accurate account of Tecumseh, the Shawnee chief who successfully united a Northern alliance of Native Americans to defeat the American military power, driving them from the Northwest Territory in the middle of the 18th century. He was recognized as a military genius, orator, diplomat, and visionary. (1992)

Spirit of St. Louis, The

Charles Lindbergh   Autobiography   9, 10

Charles Lindbergh's marvelous account of his famous first flight to Paris is interspersed with colorful memories of his earlier years as a barnstorming pilot. (1953)

Spirit of Survival
Gail Sheehy　Biography　　11, 12

The author of *Passages* writes about her adoption of an extraordinary Cambodian girl who lived through the genocidal regime of Pol Pot. (1987)

Stillness at Appomattox, A
Bruce Catton　History / U.S. Civil War　　11

This prize-winning history of the Civil War documents the conflicts between Grant and Lee and details the end of hope for the Confederacy. (1953)

Story of Civilization, The
Will and Ariel Durant　World History　　📖　　10

The Durants' 11-volume comprehensive survey of humankind published over the course of 40 years has become an enduring classic. (1935–1972)

Story of My Life, The
Helen Keller　Autobiography　　9, 10

The courageous story of Helen Keller, who overcame the darkness of being blind and deaf, has made her one of the world's most inspirational figures. (1903)

Such a Vision of the Street: Mother Teresa—The Spirit and the Work
Eileen Egan　Biography　　11

A co-worker tells the story of one of the most remarkable women of the 20th century, Mother Teresa, who worked among the poor and dying in Calcutta and won the Nobel Peace Prize in 1979. (1985)

"Surely You're Joking, Mr. Feynman!": Adventures of a Curious Character

Richard P. Feynman   Autobiography   11, 12

This is a hilarious yet moving account of an outspoken, non-conforming, Nobel Prize-winning physicist's love for science, his outrageous exploits, and his curiosity about everything he came into contact with. (1985)

Talks with Great Composers

Arthur M. Abell   Music   11, 12

Abell, a young American, travels to Europe between 1890–1917 and records his conversations with the most prominent composers of the time including Brahams, Puccinni, Richard Strauss, Humperdinck, and Grieg about their intellectual and spiritual ideas and what they considered to be the source of their creativity. The book largely disappeared from the public attention until its recent re-publication in 1992. (1950s)

Testimony: The Memoirs of Dmitri Shostakovich

Shostakovich and Volkov   Antoninaw Bovis, trans.

Biography   10, 11, 12

With directions that this be published after his death, Shostakovich reveals a picture of 55 years under the musical bureaucracy of Stalinist Russia. Dictated to a young journalist who smuggled it to the West. (1979)

This Hallowed Ground: The Story of the Union Side of the Civil War

Bruce Catton   History / U.S. Civil War   11, 12

Prize-winning author Catton gives an account of the battles of the Civil War from the Union perspective. (1956)

'Tis

Frank McCourt   Autobiography   12

Frank McCourt's sequel to *Angela's Ashes* continues his story as he returns to America and becomes a teacher; his ability to delight in life whatever befalls continues to inspire his readers. (1999) See *Angela's Ashes.*

To Be Young, Gifted and Black: Lorraine Hansberry in Her Own Words

Robert Nemiroff   Biography   10, 12

Robert Nemiroff put together a stage play of Hansberry's memoirs and letters to give a full picture of the life of the writer of *A Raisin in the Sun*; the book is adapted from the play. (1969)

Tracker, The

Tom Brown   Autobiography   9

This inspirational autobiographical account tells the story of a boy from New Jersey in the 1960s, whose life is changed when he meets the 80-year-old Apache grandfather of a friend and learns how to track animals and live self-sufficiently. (1978)

Trail of Tears: Rise and Fall of the Cherokee Nation

John Ehle   History / Native American   11, 12

The Cherokee Indians tried to adapt to European ways and coexist with the white settlers of the East by educating their children and farming on plantations. Ironically, these Indians were then moved out by land-hungry Georgians and forced by Andrew Jackson to make the arduous and long journey west to relocate in a much different environment. (1988)

True Adventures of John Steinbeck, Writer, The

Jackson Benson   Biography   11, 12

This is the authoritative biography of America's revered writer, John Steinbeck, author of *The Grapes of Wrath* and *Cannery Row*, among other books. (1984)

Two Years Before the Mast

Richard Henry Dana   Autobiography   9

First published anonymously, this is a true account of an adventurous journey from Boston around Cape Horn to California. (1840)

Uncle Tungsten

Oliver Sacks   Autobiography   10, 11, 12

The Uncle Tungsten of the book's title is Sacks' Uncle Dave, who manufactured light bulbs with filaments of fine tungsten wire, introducing Sacks into the mysteries of science. Sacks writes of his childhood in wartime England and his early scientific fascination with light, matter and energy. (2001)

Unfinished Woman

Lillian Hellman   Biography   11, 12

This is the first of the memoirs of American dramatist Lillian Hellman (1907–1984) and includes her experiences in Europe during the years of World War II. (1969)

Up From Slavery

Booker T. Washington   Biography   &   10

An ex-slave struggles to achieve his own education and then devotes his life to opening doors of learning to fellow blacks in the South. (1901)

We

Charles Lindbergh   Autobiography   9

Three weeks after the first historic transatlantic nonstop flight from New York to Paris in 1927, Lindbergh wrote this exciting, easy-to-read autobiography.

Week on the Concord and Merrimac Rivers, A

Henry David Thoreau   Autobiography   12

Thoreau, a self-described "mystic, transcendentalist, and natural philosopher," describes a journey with his brother in 1839 on two northern Massachusetts rivers. A metaphor into Thoreau's mind.

West with the Night

Beryl Markham   Autobiography   9, 10

This is the memoir of Kenyan flyer Markham (1902–1986) who made aviation history in 1936 when she became the first person to fly solo across the Atlantic Ocean from East to West. (1942)

When Heaven and Earth Changed Places

Le Ly Hayslip   Autobiography   11

Hayslip grew up in rural Vietnam and became caught in the Vietnam War when she tried to please both sides in the battle. This book describes her growing-up years and her war experiences including torture by both the American-backed South Vietnamese and the Viet Cong. (1989)

Wild Swans: Three Daughters of China

Jung Chang   Biography   12

Chang writes a memoir of three generations of Chinese women from Imperial China through and beyond the Cultural Revolution. (1991)

Wind, Sand and Stars

Antoine de Saint-Exupéry   Autobiography   9, 10

The famous author of *The Little Prince* gives an autobiographical account of early mail flights across the Andes and Pyrenees. (1930)

Wolf Willow

Wallace Stegner   Autobiography   10, 11, 12

Stegner's account of growing up in a pioneer community in Saskatchewan, Canada, has become a classic. (1963)

Wolfgang Amadeus Mozart

Johannes C. Jansen   Biography.   10, 11, 12

Jansen follows Mozart's work from his astonishing performances at the age of five through his turbulent life as he changed the dominant forms of the time to become the most widely admired composer in western music. His symphonies and operas, such as *The Magic Flute* and *Cosi Fan Tutte,* remain much-loved works. The book is enhanced by many excellent illustrations. (1999)

Woman Warrior

Maxine Hong Kingston   Autobiography   9, 10, 11, 12

Kingston's memoir about life in California as a Chinese American woman is powerfully crafted to reflect both traditional values of ancestry and contemporary issues of feeling like a powerless ghost in American culture. (1976)

NONFICTION

Reader's Road Map

Fiction invites us into imaginative worlds unlike our own; nonfiction insists on a closer exploration of this world. Through the eyes of travelers and naturalists, we see the Earth and its wonders anew. Scientists, inventors, and artists take us with them as they describe the growing excitement or apprehension of patterns of discovery. Philosophers invite us into the most profound questioning as they attempt to untangle the definition of reality, the reason for existence, the possibility of God, or the nature of good and evil.

Reading nonfiction is different from reading stories, poetry, or drama. It is often a good idea to preview a nonfiction book, looking through the sections or chapters, getting an overview of the basic ideas. Often we can find what we want to know by looking through the table of contents or the index, or by simply focusing on the illustrations, photographs, maps and charts. Sometimes, the reader is interested only in a particular section of the book, and that's fine.

The pace of reading nonfiction is different, too. The reader usually needs to slow down in order to carefully follow the writer's building up of ideas. You may find yourself silently asking the writer questions: "Why do you say that? How do you know? What would lead to that conclusion?" This is an indication of the intense engagement reading nonfiction requires.

Rather than being "long ago" or "far away" as we might be with a poem or novel, we are very much "here" in the books in this section. The rewards are multi-faceted and manifold.

Ages of Gaia, The
James Lovelock   Biology   11, 12

In 1979, atmospheric scientist Lovelock published *The Gaia Hypothesis*, in which he gave evidence for his theory that the Earth itself is a self-evolving and self-regulating living system, a living being. This second volume encompasses Lovelock's extensive further search for evidence to support his idea. (1988)

Aku-Aku: The Secret of Easter Island
Thor Heyerdahl   Exploration   10, 11, 12

Norwegian Heyerdahl and a team of archaeologists spent many months on Easter Island in an attempt to understand the "giant heads." Heyerdahl's theory is that there is a link between these and the artifacts of ancient Peru. (1958)

Algeny
Jeremy Rifkin   Genetic Engineering   11, 12

This survey of technology, culminating in warnings about the dangers of genetic engineering, is written by the leading figure trying to slow down such research. (1983)

American Scholar, The
Ralph Waldo Emerson   Philosophy   11

The "Father of Transcendentalism" delivered this oration to the Phi Beta Kappa Society at Harvard. (1837) See *Essays* by Emerson.

Amusing Ourselves to Death
Neil Postman   Technology   12

Postman's premise is that our present and future resemble the predictions in *Brave New World* more than those of *1984*. Technology, in particular television, has shaped every aspect of our world including politics, news, religion, and education. This is an excellent media awareness resource. (1986)

Animal Camouflage
Adolph Portman   Biology   11, 12

This classic phenomenological study describes animal adaptations. (1959)

Animal Forms and Patterns
Adolph Portman   Biology   12

A richly illustrated scientific account describes how animals worldwide share forms and patterns. (1967)

Arctic Assignment: The Story of the St. Roch
Sergeant F. S. Farrar   Exploration   10

Farrar tells the exciting story of the historic first trip through the Northwest Passage from west to east by the Canadian police vessel that was also the first to circumnavigate North America. (1959)

Arctic Dreams: Imagination and Desire in a Northern Landscape
Barry Lopez   Natural History   11, 12

A 1986 National Book Award Winner, this natural history of the Canadian Arctic and its inhabitants—narwhals, polar bears, beluga whales, musk oxen, and caribou—has become a classic in ecology.

Artist's Book of Inspiration, An
Astrid Fitzgerald   Anthology / Art / Philosophy   11, 12

Fitzgerald has assembled a collection of the best thoughts on art, artists, and the creative process drawn from varying traditions, times, and places. (1996)

Assembling California
John McPhee   Geology   📖   9

This fourth book in McPhee's geological history of the United States, he describes current knowledge about the formation of California. McPhee's style is noted for its humor and accessibility. The other three books are *Basin and Range, In Suspect Terrain,* and *Rising from the Plains.* (1993)

Awakenings
Oliver Sacks   Medicine   11, 12

Sacks writes powerfully about the relationship between medical science and the human spirit. This book chronicles his work at a long-term care facility in the late 1960s, as the first exciting results using L-dopa to treat comatose states became known. (1973)

Basin and Range
John McPhee   Geology   9, 10

McPhee gives a clear, detailed, yet often poetic description of plate tectonics as revealed in the contorted and tilted rocks seen in the road cuts we drive by each day. This is the first book in McPhee's monumental series, *Annals of the Former World*. (1981) See *In Suspect Terrain, Rising from the Plains,* and *Assembling California.*

Biosphere Politics: A Cultural Odyssey from the Middle Ages to the New Age
Jeremy Rifkin   Ecology   11, 12

The president and founder of the Foundation on Economic Trends explores the way humans have related to nature over the past five centuries and the resulting environmental disaster. Rifkin's solution is to promote the idea of the entire earth as a living organism. (1991)

Birth of Tragedy, The
Friedrich Nietzsche   Philosophy   12

Considered revolutionary when it was published, Nietzsche believed that the art (especially literature) of the Greek civilization could not exist without a mixture of the influence of the Greek gods, Dionysis and Apollo. (1872)

Black Dawn Bright Day
Sun Bear with Wabun Wind   Spirituality   11, 12

This collection of Indian prophecies details the environmental future of major landmasses as learned through Sun Bear and other Native American's visions and dreams. (1992)

Blue Nile, The
Alan Moorehead   Exploration   10, 11, 12

Moorehead continues the story of the early exploration of the Nile as begun in *The White Nile*. He describes adventuring into the Nile's major tributary by four explorers in the first half of the 19th century. (1980)

Body of Frankstein's Monster, The
Cecil Helman   Medicine   10, 11, 12

Helman, a doctor, poet, and painter, explores the idea that our overall perception of health and well-being is informed by concepts, words, and images rather than just facts. (1991)

Bones of Contention
Roger Lewin   Paleoanthropology   11, 12

Lewin writes a fascinating account of the personalities and struggles of scientists as they interpret human and proto-human fossils. (1987)

Book of the Hopi
Frank Waters   Spirituality   📖   11, 12

Thirty Hopi elders tell the world-view of their people. Waters' collection includes Hopi art, history, folklore, ceremonies, and traditional beliefs. (1963)

Brief History of Time: From the Big Bang to Black Holes
Stephen Hawking   Physics   📖   12

Cambridge University physicist Stephen Hawking contends that the basic ideas about the origin and fate of the universe can be stated without mathematics in a form that people without scientific education can understand. This overview of the current understanding of the origin and evolution of the universe, black holes, and the theory of relativity achieves his purpose. Hawking describes how he arrived at his own discovery that black holes emit particles as well as explaining the contributions of others. (1988)

Brunelleschi's Dome: How a Renaissance Genius Reinvented Architecture

Ross King   Architecture   12

Between 1418–1446, Filippo Brunelleschi, a goldsmith and clockmaker in Florence, Italy, worked at solving the puzzle of how to vault the dome of the cathedral Santa Maria del Fiore, still the largest dome (143 feet in diameter) in the world. In the process, he revolutionized the field of architecture. (2001)

Catching the Light: The Entwined History of Light and Mind

Arthur Zajonc   Cultural History   12

Zajonc explores the history of light through a remarkable blend of mythology, religion, science, literature, and painting revealing the evolution of consciousness of human beings in their quest to answer one of life's enduring mysteries. (1993)

Changing Bodies, Changing Lives: A Book for Teens on Sex and Relationships

Ruth Bell   Health   📖   9, 10, 11, 12

Teens appreciate this excellent resource of honest, accurate, and nonjudgmental information on everything they need to know about both emotional and physical changes that occur at puberty. (1987)

Changing Woman and Her Sisters

Sheila Moon   Social Issues / Spirituality   11, 12

Native American stories about feminine deities are linked to stories from other continents and the dreams and experiences of modern women, showing the universal search for meaning. (1985)

Chaos: Making A New Science

James Gleik   Science   📖   12

The new science of chaos theory blankets such diverse fields as meteorology, economics, physiology, molecular physics, and astronomy. The theory proposes that order underlies what appear to be chaotic systems. (1989)

Civil Disobedience
Henry David Thoreau   Philosophy   📖   11, 12

Thoreau argues the right to refuse to pay taxes when conscience dictates against government policy. (1849)

Closing Circle, The: Nature, Man and Technology
Barry Commoner   Ecology   9, 10, 11, 12

In this highly influential ecological work, Commoner argues that the environmental crisis cannot be traced to biological causes such as population growth but to economic, social, and political forces. (1980)

Collected Essays, Journalism and Letters of George Orwell
Sonia Orwell and Ian Angus, eds.   Essays   12

George Orwell was one of the great minds of the 20th century; his essays include "Shooting an Elephant" and "Politics and the English Language." (1968)

Comet
Carl Sagan and Ann Druyan   Astronomy   11, 12

Pulitzer Prize-winning astronomer Sagan and writer Druyan explore the myths, origins, and nature of comets. Enhanced with lavish illustrations, it reads like an exciting adventure. (1986)

Complexity: Life at the Edge of Chaos
Roger Lewin   Science   11, 12

This readable overview of a new approach to scientific understanding explains how systems self-organize, innovate, and adapt. (1993)

Conquest of Everest, The
John Hunt   Exploration   9

A first-hand account published in Britain as *The Ascent of Everest* tells the exciting adventure of the first ascent of the world's tallest mountain with a chapter by Sir Edmund Hillary. Hunt always refused to call the climb a "conquest." (1953)

Cosmos
Carl Sagan   Astronomy   11, 12

Astronomer Sagan's award-winning television show *Cosmos* was the most watched series in public-television history at the time of its showing. The accompanying book was on *The New York Times* bestseller list for 70 weeks and is the best-selling science book published in English to date. (1980)

Custer Died for Your Sins: An Indian Manifesto
Vine Deloria, Jr.   Social Issues   11, 12

With humor and irony, Deloria uncovers the American politics and perpetuated stereotypes that seem to have fostered the corruption of Native American people and culture. (1969)

Dancing Wu Li Masters: An Overview Of The New Physics
Gary Zukav   Physics / Spirituality   11, 12

This remarkably accessible reference has become a classic in the new blending of science and spirituality; Zukav suggests that consciousness states and matter are dependent on one another, and share a common force field. (1984)

Dangerous Summer, The
Ernest Hemingway   Adventure   10, 11, 12

Hemingway was hired by *Life* magazine in 1959 to spend the summer with two Spanish bullfighters. The account of their lives and actions in the ring is as powerful as any of Hemingway's fiction. (1985)

Darwin Retried
Norman Macbeth   Evolution   11, 12

Macbeth presents an objective analysis of the evidence for and against evolution from the perspective of a jurist. He argues that Darwinian theory is a tautology and that the scientific community is not honestly publicizing its own doubt about the theory of natural selection. (1977)

Death in the Afternoon

Ernest Hemingway   Adventure   11, 12

Hemingway believed that bullfighting was more than "mere sport." Here he describes the emotional and spiritual intensity of bullfighting. This was his last work. (1932)

Declaration of a Heretic

Jeremy Rifkin   Genetic Engineering   11, 12

The President of the Foundation of Emerging Technologies, Rifkin pleads for humility in scientific investigation, particularly genetic engineering. (1985)

Delicate Arrangement: The Untold Story of the Darwinian Conspiracy and Cover-Up

Arnold Brackman   Evolution   11, 12

Is it possible that Charles Darwin stole the theory of natural selection from Alfred Russel Wallace? This book explains how that could have happened. (1980)

Digging Dinosaurs: The Search That Unraveled the Mystery of Baby Dinosaurs

John Horner, et al   Paleontology   10

Horner has been called the most influential paleontologist alive today. In this highly readable account, he describes the day-to-day frustrations and trials of analyzing fossil remains and the pure joy of a breakthrough. (1988)

Double Helix: A Personal Account of the Discovery of the Structure of DNA

James Watson   Genetics   📖   12

Watson gives us a remarkably compelling description of scientific process and human betrayal in the discovery of the structure of the DNA molecule. (1968)

Dream of the Earth, The
Thomas Berry   Ecology / Spirituality   📖   10

Berry was among the first to recognize that the environmental crisis facing our planet is fundamentally a spiritual crisis. (1988)

Edge of the Sea
Rachel Carson   Biology   11, 12

Carson provides an excellent practical guide to identifying the flora and fauna of the sea, and the marshes and tide pools that border it, particularly the tide zone of the northeastern U.S. (1955)

Essays
Ralph Waldo Emerson   Philosophy   12

Emerson published his first collection of essays, including "Self-Reliance", in 1841 and his second, in 1844; in both he reflects on the themes of leadership, obedience to inner law, truth, and the individual integrity of one's own mind. "American Scholar" and "Nature" are widely read.

Essays of E. B. White
E. B. White   Philosophy   📖   12

White, perhaps best known for his children's books *Stuart Little, Charlotte's Web,* and *The Trumpet of the Swan,* is also one of the 20th-century's finest essayists, respected for his clarity and loved for his wit and insight. This is a collection from over 50 years of his writing life. (1999)

Evolution's End: Claiming the Potential of Our Intelligence
Joseph Chilton Pearce   Education .   📖   12

Through 20 years of research into human intelligence and development, Pearce claims that since the end of World War II contemporary hospital birthing techniques, extended daycare, premature schooling, and television have seriously impeded children's vital neurological development and killed creative play. Such damage threatens the future of the human race itself. (1995)

Flamingo's Smile, The: Reflections in Natural History
Stephen Gould   Natural History   11, 12

Gould's essays explore an astonishingly broad range of subjects, from the mistakes of Audubon (the flamingo doesn't have a smile) to dinosaurs, killer meteors, jellyfish as well as to current theories of evolution. What science believes says as much about cultural prejudices as about the object of investigation. Gould writes beautifully and always weaves history into his science. (1985).

Free to Choose
Milton and Rose Friedman   Economics   12

Nobel Prize-winning economist Friedman gives a history of the market economy from the 18th century to the present. This refreshing book accompanied the video series of the same name. Timely even today. (1980)

Friday Night Lights: A Town, A Dream & A Team
H. G., Bissenger   Social issues / Sports   ᕦ   11, 12

Bissinger's insightful delving into the culture of high school football in Odessa, Texas focuses on six young men during the dramatic 1987–88 season. He explores issues of community, culture, racial and sexual stereotypes, and politics raising significant questions about the price paid for a brief moment of glory. The tenth-anniversary edition (2000) includes an *Afterword* with updates on the continuing lives of the core of the team. (1990)

Gift from the Sea, A
Anne Morrow Lindbergh   Reflections   11, 12

Lindburgh's elegant descriptions of the small miracles of everyday life by the sea ring true as analogies for the striving for peace and independence still sought so fervently today. (1955)

Go Ask Alice

Anonymous   Drugs   10, 11, 12

With over a million copies in print, this book has had a profound impact on countless readers. It is a powerful true diary of a 15-year-old girl's struggle with drugs and addiction. (1971)

God is Red: A Native View of Religion

Vine Deloria, Jr.   Spirituality   11, 12

In his work on the tenets of native religion, Deloria argues that Christianity has failed society and explains how the underlying principles of native religion, which connect human life to the land, support the environmental awareness that we need today. In the updated edition, he asks new questions about the future of our species and our fate. (1994)

Gods, Graves, and Scholars: The Story of Archaeology

C. W. Ceram   Archaeology   10, 11

Ceram's book reads like a novel yet contains true accounts of many of the most important discoveries of ancient civilizations, including Troy and the Rosetta Stone. (1954)

Goethe the Scientist

Rudolf Steiner   Olin D. Wannamaker , trans.   Biology 📖 12

Steiner's understanding that Goethe was able to perceive the spiritual in nature is reflected in his introductions to several volumes and selections of Goethe's scientific writings (1883–1897). Collected by Wannamaker. (1950)

Great Dialogues

Plato   Philosophy   11, 12

It has been said that all philosophy can be seen as a footnote to Plato. In his famous dialogues, Socrates, the principal speaker, asks a chain of questions to discover truth. (ca. 370 B.C.E.)

Green Hills of Africa
Ernest Hemingway   Adventure   9, 10, 11, 12

In 1933, Ernest Hemingway and his wife, Pauline, set out on a two-month safari in the big game country of East Africa, camping at the foot of Mount Kilimanjaro. This is the true account of that adventure. (1935)

Hakluyt's Voyages
Richard Hakluyt   Exploration   9

These classic accounts of the voyages of English seamen and explorers in the 16th century include those made by John Cabot, Francis Drake, and Sir Walter Raleigh among many others. (1598–1600)

Heart of the Hunter, The
Laurens van der Post   Anthropology   10

Van der Post takes a profound look into the Bushmen's customs and mythological life in the continuation of *The Lost World of the Kalahari*. (1961)

History of Western Philosophy, The
Bertrand Russell   Philosophy   12

In 76 chapters, Russell traces the story of philosophy from the rise of Greek civilization to the emergence of logical analysis in the 20th century by describing the major philosophers in their social and cultural context. (1945)

Immense Journey, The
Loren Eiseley   Life Science   12

Eiseley's essays, written from a background in anthropology, geology and biology, encompass evolution, nature, and the human mind and continue to inspire nature lovers. (1957)

In Patagonia
Bruce Chatwin   Exploration   10

Chatwin journeys through the desolate tip of South America. (1977)

In Suspect Terrain
John McPhee   Geology   📖   9, 10

McPhee travels the eastern U.S. with a geologist who questions how plate tectonics can explain the complexity of the geology of this region. This 'suspect terrain' has been marked by many forces including volcanic activity, movement of the glacial ice sheets and erosion. The second of McPhee's quartet. See *Basin and Range, Assembling California, Rising from the Plains.* (1983)

In the Absence of the Sacred: The Failure of Technology and the Survival of the Indian Nations
Jerry Mander   Social Issues   12

Mander proposes that technology worship, economic expansion, and commodity accumulation have brought social disorder and global environmental devastation. (1991)

Indian Voices
First Convocation of American Indian Scholars   Anthology   11, 12

This is a collection of papers and presentations given at a convocation held at Princeton University. Contributors include N. Scott Momaday, Vine DeLoria, Jr., Alfonso Ortiz, Fritz Scholder and others. Subjects include:"American Indian Philosophy and its Relation to the Modern World," "Native American Studies Programs: Review and Evaluation," "Native Arts in America," and "The Urban Scene and the American Indian." (1970)

Into Thin Air: A Personal Account of the Mount Everest Disaster
Jon Krakauer   Adventure/Mountaineering   12

In 1996, *Outside Magazine* sent Krakauer along on an expedition to the summit of Mount Everest to report on high-altitude mountaineering. This book is an account of the expedition in which a storm took nine lives. (1997)

Journey to the Ants: A Story of Scientific Exploration
Bert Holldobler & Edward O. Wilson   Entomology   11, 12

Considered by some to be "the greatest of all entomology books," this is a fascinating account of the biology and ecology of ants. (1994)

Karma Cola: Marketing the Mystic East
Gita Mehta   Essays   11, 12

Humorous and witty, Mehta's satire on the major wave of foreigners swarming into India in the 1960s in search of India's spiritual powers is informative and insightful. (1979)

King Solomon's Ring: New Light on Animal Ways
Konrad Lorenz   Animal Behavior   9, 10

The classic book on animal behavior is easy to read and full of entertaining anecdotes. (1965)

Kon Tiki
Thor Heyerdahl   Exploration   9, 10, 11, 12

Norwegian explorer and anthropologist Heyerdahl gives a vivid account of a recreation of a sea voyage of the ancient Polynesians. (1970) See also *The Ra Expeditions* and *The Tigris Expedition*.

Life for the Spirit, A: Rudolf Steiner in the Crosscurrents of Our Time
Henry Barnes, ed.   Philosophy   11, 12

Rudolf Steiner is the originator of many practical cultural initiatives including Waldorf education, biodynamic agriculture, and anthroposophical medicine. Barnes follows this remarkable man from his early days as a Vienna student to the turn of the century in Berlin and on through Steiner's courageous responses to the needs of the first tumultuous 25 years of the 20th century. Includes extensive excerpts from Steiner's writings. (1997)

Lives of a Cell: Notes of a Biology Watcher

Lewis Thomas   Biology   11, 12

Lewis' collection of essays urges us to look critically, while remaining full of wonder, at the living world around us. (1978)

Lives of the Artists, The

Giorgia Vasari   Julia and Peter Bondanella, eds.

History / Art   10, 11, 12

Vasari invented the term "Renaissance" and his accounts of the lives of his contemporaries has long been considered the most important source of understanding such great artists as Giotto, Brunelleschi, Michaelangelo, da Vinci, and Raphael. This new translation, clearly accessible to modern readers, contains 36 of the important artists and is fully annotated by the translators. (1546)

Lost World of the Kalahari, The

Laurens van der Post   Anthropology   10

The author, a South African anthropologist, writer, and farmer, chronicles his search for and rediscovery of the Bushmen, then believed to be extinct. (1958)

Making Face, Making Soul

Haciendo Caras   Social Issues   11, 12

This anthology is a collection of essays and poems by women of color working for social change. It presents an inspiring and consciousness-raising perspective. (1990)

Man Who Mistook His Wife for a Hat and Other Clinical Tales, The

Oliver Sacks   Medicine   11, 12

Sacks is at his best as he describes the strange and bewildering problems of his brain-injured patients and how they can be treated medically and psychologically. (1987)

Marriage of Sense and Thought: Imaginative Participation in Science
Edelglass, Maier, Gebert & Davy   Science / Philosophy   11, 12

The authors' view of physiology, history, methodology, and philosophy of science recognizes the essential role of sense perception in scientific knowledge. (1992)

Medical Detectives, The
Berton Roueche   Medicine   11, 12

In this compelling and understandable account of the discoveries of medical researchers, *New Yorker* magazine writer Roueche traces, step-by-step, the efforts of doctors to solve a series of baffling medical cases, and provides an excellent introduction to the work of epidemiologists. It was first published as *Eleven Blue Men* in 1948. (1988)

Medusa and the Snail: More Notes of a Biology Watcher
Lewis Thomas   Medicine   12

Lewis, in his eloquent prose, gives the reader essays on, among other things, the genius of human error, cloning, disease and natural death. (1984)

Megatrends: Ten New Directions Transforming Our Lives
John Naisbitt   Social Issues   12

Futurist Naisbitt describes the changes that technology is bringing about and what they will mean for political and social structures. (1982)

Microbe Hunters
Paul de Kruif   Microbiology   10

In this highly accessible account of the early heroes of microbiology, de Kruif delights equally in their idiosyncrasies and their discoveries. (1926)

Naked Earth: The New Geophysics
Shawna Vogel   Geology   📖   12

Plate tectonics has answered many geological questions but has opened up still others, including the nature of the Earth's core and rocky mantle, and the mysteries of the geomagnetic field. This excellent introduction clearly outlines what is known and what is not. (1996)

Natural History of the Senses
Diane Ackerman   Natural History   9, 10, 11, 12

These delightful essays on the five senses—smell, touch, vision, hearing, taste—mix biology, psychology, history, and anthropology into a poetic blend. (1991)

Nature's Economy: A History of Ecological Ideas
Donald Worster   Ecology / Philosophy   12

In this classic treatise on streams of environmental thought in western culture, Worster focuses on the changing perception of nature, the rise of conservation and environmentalism, and particularly on the ways that the natural world has provided the context for human life over time. (1985)

Never Cry Wolf
Farley Mowat   Animal Behavior   9, 10

The Canadian North is the natural setting of this humorous and poignant chronicle of wolves in their native habitat. (1963)

New Science of Life, A
Rupert Sheldrake   Genetics   11, 12

Sheldrake's hypothesis suggests that morphogenetic fields pass the shapes and instincts of all living things to succeeding generations; this offers a radical alternative to current scientific thought. (1982)

Ocean in Mind, An
Will Kysalka   Exploration   10

Modern navigators recreate ancient voyages in the Pacific to discover a link with the past. (1997)

Of Wolves and Men
Barry Lopez   Ecology   12

In this careful study of the way wolves and humans have interacted over centuries, Lopez argues for the necessity of wolves in the world. (1978)

On Liberty

John Stuart Mill   Philosophy   12

Mill's famous essay claims that society should never interfere with the individual "for his own good." (1859)

On the Origin of Species: By Means of Natural Selection

Charles Darwin   Evolution   📖   11

Darwin's famous theory of evolution argues for a natural, not divine, origin of species based on a competitive struggle for existence, which gives advantage to creatures better able to adapt to changing environments. (1859)

Only One Earth: Care and Maintenance of a Small Planet

Barbara Ward and Rene J. Dubos   Ecology   11, 12

Author, scholar, friend and advisor of the world's decision-makers, and one of the 20th century's most persuasive writers, Dubos calls for a rational sharing of resources between rich and poor nations and peoples. Submitted to the United Nations Conference on the Human Environment in 1972.

Origin of Consciousness in the Breakdown of the Bicameral Mind, The

Julian Jaynes   Science / Consciousness   11, 12

Jaynes puts forth the revolutionary idea that our still-developing human consciousness did not begin far back in animal evolution but is a learned process. He argues that it was brought into being by cataclysm and catastrophe only 3000 years ago out of an earlier hallucinatory mentality. (1976)

Oxford Book Of Essays, The

John Gross, ed.   Anthology   📖   12

This inclusive collection ranges from the early 1600s through the 1980s and includes 140 essays by 120 of the finest writers in the history of the English language. Subjects range from history and travel to art, meditation, and book reviews and are brought together with introductory notes by John Gross, former book critic for *The New York Times* and former editor of *The Times Literary Supplement* (London). (1991)

Panda's Thumb, The: More Reflections in Natural History

Stephen Jay Gould   Evolution   **11, 12**

This second volume of popular essays by Gould supports the theory of natural selection, but with a complexity and several conclusions that would surprise Darwin. (1980) See *The Flamingo's Smile*.

Poverty of Power: Energy and the Economic Crisis

Barry Commoner   Ecology   **12**

Commoner describes how industrial methods, especially those involving fossil fuels, cause environmental pollution and how the quest for maximum profit currently takes priority over environmental reasoning. (1976)

Presence of the Past: Morphic Resonance and Habits of Nature

Rupert Sheldrake   Biology   **11, 12**

Sheldrake's new theory of biology suggests that nature itself has memory. He presents a radical alternative to materialistic reductionism. (1988) See *A New Science of Life*.

Prince, The

Niccolo Machiavelli   Philosophy   **11**

The 15th-century philosopher developed these guidelines for the rational use and maintenance of power. Although they appear autocratic and ruthless to modern western sensibilities, at the time they were a radically liberating proposal in contrast to the reactive personality politics of Florence. (1515)

Prisons We Choose to Live Inside

Doris Lessing   Essays / Philosophy   **11, 12**

A series of five lectures given on the Canadian Broadcasting Corporation explores how we can think for ourselves, understand what we know, and follow our own path in a world deluged with opinions and information. (1985)

Problems of Philosophy, The
Bertrand Russell   Philosophy   12

Lord Russell (1872–1970), the British philosopher, logician, essayist, and social critic, was best known for his work in mathematical logic and analytic philosophy. This simple, easy-to-read volume, however, is an excellent introduction to the main problems of epistemology. (1912)

Progress for a Small Planet
Barbara Ward   Ecology   11, 12

Ward tackles the three principal threats to the global environment: pollution, over-consumption by the affluent, and the growing tension between rich and poor nations. Refusing to accept these conditions as inevitable, she describes new technologies for recycling waste and efficient energy use, and links them to ordinary people's working lives. (1979)

Ra Expeditions, The
Thor Heyerdahl   Exploration   12

Heyerdahl vividly describes how he sailed in a papyrus boat from Morocco to Barbados, in an attempt to prove that ancient Mediterranean civilizations could have sailed in reed boats to America. (1971) See also *Kon Tiki* and *The Tigris Expedition*.

Reflections on Progress, Peaceful Coexistence, and Intellectual Freedom
Andrei Sakharov   Philosophy   📖   12

Following his work in helping to develop the Soviet atomic bomb, Sakharov became deeply convinced that the arms race was pointless and a threat to mankind. "I wanted to alert my readers to the grave perils threatening the human race: thermonuclear extinction, ecological catastrophe, famine, an uncontrolled population explosion, alienation, and dogmatic distortion of our conception of reality." (1968)

Republic, The
Plato   Philosophy   11

Socrates describes the ideal state; it includes Plato's famous allegory of the cave. See *Great Dialogues*. (4th c. B.C.E.)

Reviving Ophelia: Saving the Selves of Adolescent Girls
Mary Pipher   Psychology   11, 12

This psychologist's account of the problems facing modern young women today is movingly illustrated from her case studies. (1994)

Ring of Bright Water
Gavin Maxwell   Natural History   9, 10

The story of Maxwell's life with the otters in a wild area of the western highlands of Scotland has remained a bestseller. (1960)

Rising from the Plains
John McPhee   Geology   📖   9, 10

The third in his series, McPhee moves westward along Interstate Route 80 weaving the fascinating geological history of the Rocky Mountains and the terrain of Wyoming with the family history of geologist David Love. (1986) See *Basin and Range, In Suspect Terrain*, and *Assembling California*.

Roger's Recovery from AIDS: How One Man Defeated the Dread Disease
Bob Owen   Medicine   11

Owen offers a detailed account of a radical health regimen used by a medical doctor to defeat his own disease. (1985)

Room of One's Own, A
Virginia Woolf   Social Issues   📖   12

This fundamental feminist essay on the status of women, and women artists in particular, concluded that a woman must have money and a room of her own if she is to write. (1929)

Sacred Buffalo: The Lakota Way for a New Beginning
James G. Durham   Spirituality   10, 11, 12

The inspiration for the Sacred Buffalo, a carving of an entire buffalo skeleton with the seven sacred rites of the Lakota Sioux, was a seven-year quest. Lakota artists and Vietnam veterans did the carving. (1996)

Sacred Hoop, The
Paula Gunn Allen   Spirituality   11, 12

Allen examines the role of women's leadership in Native American society past and present in a collection of 17 essays, that include the work of many contemporary Indian writers. (1992)

Sacred Pipe, The: The Seven Sacred Rites,
Black Elk as told to Joseph E. Brown   Spirituality   11, 12

In this collection of spiritual wisdom, Black Elk shares seven rites of the sacred traditions of Oglala Sioux with Joseph Brown. (1989)

Sand County Almanac, A
Aldo Leopold   Ecology   11, 12

Leopold's remarkable description of plant and animal interactions in the Wisconsin countryside has become a classic in the ecology movement. (1970)

Sea Around Us, The
Rachel Carson   Marine Biology   10

Carson's story of the ocean and the mysteries of the natural world is a beautifully woven blend of science and imagination. An updated version of this classic of marine biology includes essays about later scientific discoveries. (1951)

Second Sex, The
Simone de Beauvoir   Social Issues   12

De Beauvoir's critique of the social condition of women is sometimes seen as the birth of "gender studies." (1953)

Selections from Ralph Waldo Emerson

Stephen Whicher, ed.   Philosophy   📖   12

Whicher subtitles his selections *An Organic Anthology*. He includes such famous essays as "The American Scholar," as well as many selections from Emerson's journals. (1960)

Self Reliance

See *Essays* by Emerson   11

Sensitive Chaos: The Creation of Flowing Forms in Water and Air

Theodor Schwenk   Life Science   11

This groundbreaking study of the form of fluidity or flow from physical, biological, aesthetic and spiritual viewpoints was inspired by the work of Rudolf Steiner. (1962)

Seven Years in Tibet

Heinrich Harrer   Exploration   11, 12

An Austrian escapes his captors in World War II and flees into the mountains of Tibet, where, amidst remarkable adventures, he encounters an extraordinary culture. (1953)

Sibling Society

Robert W. Bly   Philosophy   📖   12

Bly views current American culture as one of adults regressing toward adolescence by refusing to embrace adult responsibilities. This is fueled by such factors as insatiable greed and capitalism, an over-exaggerated emphasis on individualism, a lack of respect for and appreciation of elders, and the destructive influence of the media. (1996)

Silence

John Cage   20th-Century Music / Philosophy   11, 12

The philosopher composer discusses new frontiers in 20th-century music, such a electronic sound, ambient noise, silence and the role of "chance" in composition and performance. Sometimes called a "bible of the avant-garde". (1973)

Silent Spring
Rachel Carson   Ecology   9, 10, 11, 12

Carson describes the results of the indiscriminate use of pesticides and
weed-killers. Many credit her as launching the environmental movement in the U.S. with this book. (1963)

Sleepwalkers: A History of Man's Changing Vision of the Universe
Arthur Koestler   Astronomy   11, 12

This fascinating account of how humans have viewed the heavens from
the time of the Babylonians until Newton includes biographies of
Copernicus, Kepler, and Galileo. (1959)

Small is Beautiful: A Study of Economics As If People Mattered
E. F. Schumacher   Economics   12

Born from Schumacher's belief in human-scale, decentralized, and appropriate technologies, this book has been among the most influential
in moving readers toward economics from the heart rather than from
the bottom line. (1973)

Snow Leopard, The
Peter Matthiessen   Exploration   10, 11, 12

This prize-winning book is based on the journal of a man who climbs
the Himalayas in search of the snow leopard and his own clarity of spirit.
(1990)

So Human an Animal: How We Are Shaped by Surroundings and Events
Rene Dubos   Ecology   11

A renowned microbiologist argues that the environment human beings
have created is dehumanizing them. (1969)

Soap Bubbles and the Forces That Mould Them

C. V. Boys   Science   11, 12

This book explains the chemistry, mathematics, biology, and physics of soap bubbles. (1959)

Solzhenitsyn's Harvard Commencement Address

Aleksandr Solzhenitsyn   Philosophy / Spirituality.   📖   12

Solzhenitsyn proposes that the West has become decadent through too much comfort and that materialism has destroyed spiritual searching. The Russian people have achieved a much greater spiritual development, he says, through the suffering they have endured. (1978)

Songlines

Bruce Chatwin   Anthropology   10

Chatwin describes his journey to the Outback and his meetings with Australian aboriginals who remember their history by singing the ancient mythical song of the landscape. (1967)

Spirit Song: The Introduction of No-Eyes

Mary Summer Rain   Spirituality   11, 12

This is the first volume in a series of new-age books written about the author's journey into the ancient world of Native American medicine women. No-Eyes, a blind Chippewa visionary, and Many Heart, a dreamwalker, guide Mary Summer Rain on her personal journey into the spirit world. (1993)

Storyteller

Leslie Marmon Silko   Social Issues   📖   11, 12

Silko's opinions of the wrongs done to her Native American peoples may be considered alarming or confrontational to some readers, but her feminist view is also remarkable and intriguingly magical. This combination of poetry, stories, personal experience, and photographs begins in the middle of the book and should be read outward from the poem "Long Time Ago" in a spiral fashion. (1981)

Tao of Physics, The: An Exploration of the Parallels Between Modern Physics and Eastern Mysticism
Fritjof Capra   Physics / Spirituality   11, 12

Capra compares the concepts revealed by new discoveries in physics in the 20th century to the concepts of eastern mysticism and finds that they share a similar description of the universe. (1986)

Third Wave, The
Alvin Toffler   Social Issues   12

Toffler calls the electronic data communications revolution the Third Wave, paralleling its life-changing implications to those of the Agricultural Revolution and the Industrial Revolution. (1991)

Thirty Years that Shook Physics: The Story of Quantum Theory
George Gamow   Physics   11

In 1900 Planck proposed that light comes in discrete packages, or quanta, thus beginning the human adventure described in this book. By 30 years later Gamow claims that the investigation of quantum physics was in "tremendous difficulties" and that until the 1960s no further significant advances were made. (1966)

Tigris Expedition, The
Thor Heyerdahl   Exploration   9, 10

Heyerdahl journeyed from the Persian Gulf to the Red Sea, following a route he thinks might have been used by the ancient Sumerians. (1979) See also *Kon-Tiki* and *The Ra Expeditions*.

Time of Gifts, A
Patrick L. Fermor   Exploration   12

An 18-year-old boy sets out from London and walks to Constantinople, a journey of 1200 miles, in December 1933, the year Hitler came to power in Germany. (1978)

Time of our Lives: The Science of Human Aging

T. B. L. Kirkwood   Medicine   📖   12

What science knows about why and how we age is clearly presented in this understandable synthesis of biology, statistics, and social theory. (1999)

Treasury of Great Humor

E. B. Untermeyer   Anthology   10

A renowned critic, biographer, and teacher chooses this wit, whimsy, and satire from the remote past to the mid-20th century. (1972)

True Believer, The: Thoughts on the Nature of Mass Movements

Eric Hoffer   Philosophy   11, 12

Hoffer, one of the 20th-century's most important social philosophers, believes that the roots of fanaticism and self-righteousness begin and flourish in self-hatred, self-doubt, and insecurity. (1951)

Tycho and Kepler: The Unlikely Partnership That Forever Changed our Understanding of the Heavens

Kitty Gerguson   Astronomy   11, 12

In the late 1500s, Tycho Brahe, a Danish nobleman, built a variety of instruments for observing the heavens, later inviting Kepler, a brilliant young student, to carry on his work after death. Kepler went on to revolutionize 17th-century thought about the movement of the planets. Ferguson gives a full picture of the life and remarkable contributions of each. (2002)

Unanswered Question, The: Six Talks at Harvard

Leonard Bernstein   Music / Language   11, 12

An inspiring teacher, Bernstein explored music in an interdisciplinary spirit (with poetry, linguistics, physics) with great clarity in the Norton lecture series at Harvard. His "The Joy of Music" discusses music from ragas to symphonies and everything in between. (1981)

Under the Sea Wind
Rachel Carson   Marine Biology   9, 10, 11, 12

Carson's first book presents a naturalist's study of marine species along the shore, in the open sea, and at the sea bottom. (1941)

Understanding Media
Marshall McLuhan   Technology / Social Issues   12

McLuhan's view of a society affected by media speaks to issues reflected in today's media-driven culture that provoke discussion and new awareness. (1964)

Utopia
Sir Thomas More   Philosophy   📖   11, 12

More's imaginary perfect island society embraces communist rule, equal education for men and woman, and freedom of religion. More coined the name "Utopia" that means, literally, "no place." (1516)

Vision, The
Tom Brown   Spirituality   9, 10, 11, 12

Tom Brown reveals the secrets of the Vision Quest, a Native American spiritual journey of self-knowledge, through his own experience. The book makes several prophecies at the end that are a call to awaken readers to greater respect for our land and its resources. (1991)

Voice in the Margin, The
Arnold Krupat   Social Issues   11, 12

Krupat's critical work questions the white Eurocentric focus of the accepted literary canon and makes the case for the more than marginal placement of Native American oral narratives as a relevant and essential part of students' literary understanding. (1989)

Voyage of the Beagle
Charles Darwin   Natural History   12

Darwin's original title for this book was *Journal of Researches into the Geology and Natural History of the Various Countries Visited by H.M.S. Beagle.* Darwin served as naturalist aboard the *Beagle* for several years as it sailed around South America. Research on the Galapagos Islands proved crucial in the development of the theory of evolution. (1839)

Waking Up in Time: Find Inner Peace in Times of Accelerating Change
Peter Russell   Spirituality   📖   12

Russell investigates biology, physics, computer science, psychology, and philosophy in the evolutionary crisis of the human species resulting from the ever-accelerating pace of change. He calls for a spiritual renaissance to avoid catastrophe. (1998)

Walden: Or Life in the Woods
Henry David Thoreau   Philosophy / Ecology   11, 12

Thoreau built a cabin on the edge of Walden Pond near Concord, Massachusetts and lived there from 1845–1847. This is his account of that two-year experiment in self-sufficiency. (1854)

Walk in the Woods, The: Rediscovering America on the Appalachian Trail
Bill Bryson   Travel / Humor   10, 11, 12

Bryson documents his trek along the 2100-mile trail, from Georgia to Maine, with amusing and touching stories of the trail itself and the characters he encounters. The entire book serves as a fervent plea for conservation of wilderness. (1998)

What is Relativity?
L. D. Landau and G. B. Rumer   Physics   11, 12

Two leading Russian theoretical physicists give a lighthearted, simply written presentation of the theory of relativity. (1960)

White Nile, The
Alan Moorehead   Exploration   10

In the first half of the 19th century, against a background of slavery and massacre, political upheaval and all-out war, four European explorers ventured into the interior of Africa to find the source of the Nile. This is an excellent account of their journey. (1960) The story is continued in *The Blue Nile*.

Wild Animals I Have Known
Ernest Thompson Seton   Natural Science   9

An early self-educated naturalist and artist, Seton traveled throughout the wilderness in Canada, Mexico, and the United States; the stories in this collection are based on his first hand experiences. (1898)

Wisdomkeepers
Steve Wall and Harvey Arden   Spirituality   11, 12

His oral text expresses the spiritual world of the Native American elders who impart their wisdom, humor, insight, and inspirational philosophies to the two authors. They share natural healing remedies, visions, thoughts and feelings, and their apocalyptic prophecies. (1990)

Working
Studs Terkel   Social History / U.S.   12

The book's subtitle is *People Talk about What They do All Day and How They Feel About What They Do*. Terkel traveled throughout America interviewing people about their jobs; the result is particularly delightful because of the authenticity of voice Terkel captures. (1974)

Youngest Science, The: Notes of a Medicine Watcher
Lewis Thomas   Medicine   12

Through his own experience, Lewis compares what medicine was and what it has become between the time when his father was practicing and the time when he himself became a senior researcher; he laments the loss of the days when doctors gave comfort as often as prescriptions. (1983)

SENIORS LOOK BACK

Reader's Road Map

The final year of high school has a bittersweet quality. Excitement and apprehension about the future is balanced with nostalgia for the comfort of the familiar. This looking back and looking ahead at the same time is evident in the list of favorite books chosen by seniors in the schools we've contacted over the past five years. Treasured childhood books find themselves side-by-side with great classics from world literature and a healthy sprinkling of the most recent adult fiction.

Leaving high school often coincides with leaving home, so it is understandable that memories of the security of being read to while cuddled close to parents or grandparents would bring to mind special childhood books. And it is certainly true that many childhood classics such as *The Giving Tree* or *James and the Giant Peach* take on almost archetypal meaning when read again as one approaches adulthood.

Leaving home also means packing up treasures that have special significance, some to remain behind, but many to be tucked into boxes or backpacks, luggage destined for new places. There is no doubt that books will be included: a special volume of poetry; a collection of short stories; a book of philosophy as yet hardly opened; even, perhaps, a cookbook.

As a senior you may also be acutely aware that you and your classmates are moving into a future radically different from the world that existed when your parents were young. Some of these books raise issues that might make parents, and even teachers, a little uncomfortable. They are included here because students have found them meaningful.

We have sometimes thought that this section might be the first place students might look to for inspiration. It is intended as such. Each of these books has been endorsed and personally recommended by a student as a worthwhile companion on the journey.

Aeneid, The

Virgil   Epic / Ancient Rome

See *Drama, Mythology, Poetry, and Sacred Writing*

Age of Innocence

Edith Wharton   Novel / U.S.

See *Fiction*

Airframe

Michael Crichton   Novel / U.S.

A plane enroute from Hong Kong to Denver crashes. The investigation into the cause is both highly informative and gripping. (1996)

Alchemist, The

Paulo Coelho   Novel / Brazil

This much-loved fable tells the story of Santiago, a boy who has a dream and the courage to follow it. He undertakes an Ulysses-like journey of exploration and self-discovery. (1988)

American Psycho

Bret Easton Ellis   Novel / U.S.

In this shocking and satiric attack on the materialism of 1980s New York, a seemingly normal man turns out to be a serial killer. (1991)

And Then There Were None

Agatha Christie   Novel / Britain

Guests at a weekend party on an island begin to die off one after another in ways predicted by a familiar nursery rhyme; it is clear that the murderer is among them. (1939)

Annapurna

Maurice Herzog   Exploration

Annapurna was the first 8000-meter peak ever climbed. This is the breathtaking account of Herzog's ascent of the North Face in 1950. (1952)

Another Roadside Attraction

Tom Robbins   Novel / U.S.

The first of Robbins' wildly funny and often bizarre novels is about the mummified corpse of Jesus, stolen from the Vatican, and the authorities' efforts to get it back from a roadside attraction. (1971)

Anthem

Ayn Rand   Novel / U.S.

In a distant collectivist future, every form and emblem of individualism has been erased. A young scientist discovers the meaning of individual freedom in a world where the pursuit of knowledge is a crime. (1946)

Archetypes and the Collective Unconscious, The

Carl Jung   Psychology

Jung (1875–1961) considered to be the founder of Analytical Psychology, believed that in addition to the purely personal unconscious hypothesized by Freud, a deeper unconscious exists which manifests itself in universal archaic images expressed in dreams, religious beliefs, myths, and fairytales.

Arctic Adventure: My Life in the Frozen North

Peter Freuchen   Adventure / Greenland

In 1910, Danish writer Freuchen established an exploring station in Thule, Greenland with Knud Rasmussen, 800 miles from the North Pole. He lived there with his Inuit wife for 15 years, taking part in seal and polar bear hunts. (1935)

Art of War, The

Sun-Tzu   Philosophy

Tzu was a military strategist who, legend has it, penned the Art of War doctrine for a Chinese warlord as a way to outwit, outlast, and outplay his opponents. It was translated from the Chinese into English by Lionel Giles in 1910 and gained a wide following in the last quarter of the 20th century among those wanting to succeed in business, politics, and athletics. (ca. 500 B.C.E.)

Autobiography of Malcolm X, The

Alex Haley   Biography

See *Autobiography, Biography, and History*

Bastard out of Carolina

Dorothy Allison   Novel / U.S.

Bone is the child of an unwed mother; as she grows up she is made painfully aware of her birth status, but that torment is nothing compared to the brutality inflicted on her by her mother's lover. (1996)

Beggar, The

FM2030   Novel / Iran

FM2030 changed his conventional name to reflect his confidence in the future, particularly in the magical time that is to come around the year 2030. Written by this self-described "international citizen", this is one of three novels through which he hoped to promote world peace and understanding. (1963)

Bell Jar, The

Sylvia Plath   Novel / U.S.

Plath's highly acclaimed and largely autobiographical novel follows college student Esther Greenwood as she begins to experience life in New York in 1953; following attempted suicide and a mental breakdown, she finds the strength to return to college. (1963)

Beowulf

Seamus Heaney, trans.   Epic / Old English

See *Drama, Mythology, Poetry, and Sacred Writing*

Best Short Stories of O. Henry, The

O. Henry   Short Stories / U.S.

This collection of 38 stories is chosen from over 600 that William Sidney Porter wrote under the pen name of O. Henry. They are clearly among the favorites of this master storyteller and include "The Gift of the Magi" and "An Unfinished Story." (1994)

Beyond Good and Evil

Friedrich Nietzsche   Philosophy

In these 296 aphorisms, grouped thematically and ranging in length from a few sentences to a few pages, Nietzsche attacks the long-held assumptions and prejudices of philosophy and advocates the "free spirit." He finds "modern scholarship" dull and mediocre, attacks anti-Semitism, and criticizes the English by proposing the "good European", who rises above nationalist sentiment. (1886)

Bhagavad Gita, The

See *Drama, Mythology, Poetry, and Sacred Writing*

Birth of Tragedy, The

Friedrich Nietzsche   Philosophy

See *Nonfiction*

Black Dahlia, The

James Ellroy   Novel / U.S.

This crime novel gives a fictional solution to a real murder. It is part of Ellroy's *L.A. Quartet*, which includes *L.A. Confidential*. (1996)

Black Like Me

John Griffin   Autobiography

See *Nonfiction*

Black Sheep, The

Honoré de Balzac   Novel / France

Balzac's depth of understanding of human relationships gives us the lives of two brothers in post-Napoleonic France, one a popular and handsome soldier, the other a sensitive artist. (1839)

Bluebeard's Egg: Stories

Margaret Atwood   Short Stories / Canada

Atwood's stories are about relationships between men and women, women and women, parents and children, and people and pets. As always, her depth of insight and acerbic style make for rewarding reading. (1983)

Book of the Dun Cow, The

Walter Wangerin   Novel / U.S.

This spiritual fable takes place on an animal farm ruled by the rooster Chanticleer. The animals of the farm are entrusted to keep an evil serpent underground. When the serpent changes its wiles, Chanticleer comes to rely more and more on God through His Servant, the Dun Cow. (1978)

Breakfast of Champions

Kurt Vonnegut, Jr.   Novel / U.S.

Vonnegut's savage satire was written as a 50th birthday present to himself; it tells of the meeting between Dwayne Hoover, a fabulously well-to-do Pontiac Dealer, and Kilgore Trout, an unknown and unsuccessful science fiction writer. The result of the meeting is Vonnegut at his best. (1972)

Bridge to Terabithia

Katherine Patterson   Novel / Children's Literature / U.S.

Although written for children, this inspiring Newbery award-winning novel can be read by anyone. A young boy and girl form an unexpected friendship and invent a magic kingdom until tragedy strikes. How that tragedy is overcome is a lesson for us all. (1978)

Bridget Jones' Diary

Helen Fielding   Novel / Britain

Fielding's wildly successful novel is actually a subtle treatment of Jane Austen's *Pride and Prejudice*. The intimate details of Bridget's diary introduce us also to a delightful cast of characters. Her story is continued in *Bridget Jones: The Edge of Reason*, modeled on Austen's *Persuasion*. (1997)

Brief History of Time: From the Big Bang to Black Holes

Stephen Hawking   Physics

See *Nonfiction*

Calcutta Chromosome: A Novel of Fevers, Delirium and Discovery

Amitar Ghosh   Novel / India

Part history, part science, part science fiction, this intriguing novel moves backwards and forwards in history as the protagonist investigates the mysterious disappearance of a fellow worker and finds himself discovering world-shaking secrets. (1997)

Calvin & Hobbes

Bill Watterson   Humor / U.S.

Bill Watterson is the creator, writer, and illustrator of this remarkably popular, witty, and often-profound comic strip that ran in over 2,300 newspapers from Nov. 18, 1985–Dec. 31, 1995. Calvin is a mischievous six-year-old and Hobbes is a tiger whom most people think is stuffed but who is very alive to Calvin. The strip is collected in 16 volumes.

Cambridge Lectures, The: Life Works

Stephen Hawking   Physics

This series of seven lectures, given at Cambridge University, includes the origin and history of the universe, the Big Bang, Black Holes, and quantum mechanics. (1996)

Canto General

Pablo Neruda   Poetry / Chile

See *Drama, Mythology, Poetry, and Sacred Writing*

Captain Trips: The Life and Fast Times of Jerry Garcia

Sandy Troy   Biography

Garcia (1942–1995) was the leader of the musical group, The Grateful Dead, and a respected musician who shaped much of 20th-century rock music. This biography is an excellent introduction to his life and the growth of the band. (1995)

Case for Vegetarianism, The: Philosophy for a Small Planet

John L. Hill   Health

Hill, a professor of law, presents a clearly articulated argument for a revolution in eating based on animal rights, health, global ecology, and world hunger. (1996)

Case of Wagner, The

Friedrich Nietzsche   Philosophy

Although he began as an admirer of Wagner, Nietzsche came to consider the musician's Christian and nationalist outlook decadent. (1888)

Cat's Eye

Margaret Atwood   Novel / Canada

See *Drama, Mythology, Poetry, and Sacred Writing*

Celestine Prophecy: An Adventure

James Redfield   Novel / U.S.

A manuscript found in Peru shows a blueprint for world harmony and individual spiritual growth through nine insights. However, those in power find it threatening and seek to destroy it. Redfield's book has gained a wide audience for its ideas rather than for its plot. (1994)

Centaur, The

John Updike   Novel / U.S.

Updike uses an ancient myth to unravel the relationship between a schoolteacher father and his teenage son. (1963)

Chaos: Making A New Science

James Gleik   Science

See *Nonfiction*

Charlie and the Chocolate Factory

Roald Dahl   Novel / Children's Literature / Britain

Young Charlie Bucket's dreams come true when he wins a chance to visit Willy Wonka's chocolate factory. What he discovers is beyond his wildest imaginings. Although written for children, Dahl's book has won the hearts of many adults as well. Quentin Blake's quirky drawings add immeasurably to the pleasure that this book brings. (1964)

Chef Paul Prudhomme's Louisiana Kitchens

Paul Prudhomme   Cooking

Prudhomme and his wife, K opened the 62-seat K-Paul's Louisiana Kitchen in 1979. It became an overnight sensation featuring the Cajun and Creole cooking of South Louisiana that has roots going back over 200 years. This is a collection of favorite recipes from the restaurant. (1984)

Chronicles of Narnia, The

C. S. Lewis   Novel / Children's Literature / Britain

Four children are sent to live in a country mansion during World War II; they discover another world called Narnia where they ultimately become kings and queens. The seven Narnia stories beginning with *The Lion, The Witch, and The Wardrobe* have become classics among young and old alike. (1950–1960)

Cider House Rules, The

John Irving   Novel / U.S.

This is Irving at his best. Wilbur Larch is a physician, philosopher, obstetrician, and abortionist at St. Cloud's orphanage in Maine in the 1930s and 40s. He and Homer Wells, his ward, apprentice, and surrogate son, are inextricably linked as each discovers the complexities of life and death. (1985)

Clan of the Cave Bear, The

Jean M. Auel   Novel / U.S.

The first book in the series *Earth's Children* introduces Ayla, one of the "others," who is adopted by a clan of Neanderthal cave people. Despite her struggles to conform, her advanced human traits cannot remain hidden. (1981) The other books in the series are The *Valley of Horses*, The *Mammoth Hunters*, and *The Plains of Passage*.

Collected Works of Edgar Allen Poe

Edgar Allen Poe   Fiction / U.S.

See *Drama, Mythology, Poetry, and Sacred Writing*

Color Purple, The

Alice Walker   Novel / U.S.

See *Drama, Mythology, Poetry, and Sacred Writing*

Communist Manifesto, The

Karl Marx and Frederich Engels   Political Theory

With Engels, Marx put forward the theory that human society, having passed through successive stages of slavery, feudalism, and capitalism, must advance to communism. Marx believed that capitalism had become a barrier to human progress and must be replaced by common ownership of the means of production and a planned economy where each would work according to ability and receive according to need. (1848)

Complete Works of Shakespeare

William Shakespeare   Drama / Britain

See *Drama, Mythology, Poetry, and Sacred Writing*

Compulsory Dancing

Da Free John   Philosophy

Avatar Adi Da Samraj, known publicly from 1979–1986 as Da Free John, subtitles this book *Talks and Essays on the Spiritual and Evolutionary Necessity of Emotional Surrender to the Life-Principle.* (1980)

Congo
Michael Chrichton   Novel / U.S.

A team of research scientists disappears in the jungle. A second team, attempting to find them, meets strangely aggressive gorillas. Crichton brings his command of adventure fiction together with his thorough research. (1980)

Cosmic Dawn: The Origins of Matter and Life
Eric Chaisson   Physics

Chaisson covers billions of years of cosmic history through astronomy, physics, chemistry, biology, geology, and anthropology in an attempt to come to an understanding of the origin of matter and of life. (1980)

Couples
John Updike   Novel / U.S.

Life is anything but settled among a group of young suburban married couples in a Massachusetts town in the 1960s. (1968)

Crystal Cave, The
Mary Stewart   Novel / Britain

The first book of Mary Stewart's Arthurian saga begins with the tale of Merlin, long before he became a magician and a Druid. (1970) See *The Hollow Hills* and *The Last Enchantment*.

Curious George
H. A. and Margret Rey   Novel / Children's Literature / France

Hans and Margret Rey came to the U.S. from France after fleeing the Nazi invasion in 1940. They brought with them the idea and preliminary drawings for this first book of over two dozen adventures of a curious little monkey and his companion, the man in the yellow hat. (1941)

Danny, The Champion of the World
Roald Dahl   Novel / Children's Literature / Britain

In this timeless story, Danny lives happily with his father, the best in the world, in a gypsy caravan until his father admits to the secret vice of poaching and introduces Danny to its dangers. (1975)

Dark is Rising, The

Susan Cooper   Novel / Britain

The Dark is Rising is the opening novel in a much-loved series after which it is named. The other books are *Over Sea, Under Stone, Greenwitch, The Grey King,* and *Silver on the Tree.* Four young people find themselves entering the world of magic as the legends of King Arthur come alive. (1973–1978)

Declaration of Independence

Thomas Jefferson, et al.   History / U.S.

The document balances freedom of the individual and government regulation. It can be found in many collections. Among the most accessible sources are *The Declaration of Independence and Other Great Documents of American History, 1775–1864* (Grafton, J, Ed.) and *The Declaration of Independence With Short Biographies of Its Signers* (Benson John Lossing)

Devil's Dictionary, The

Ambrose Bierce   Humor

Bierce published his humorous collection of satirical definitions in *The Wasp,* a weekly journal he edited in San Francisco from 1881–1886, and later collected them into this dictionary. His exquisite wit and skill with language have made this book a much loved source ever since. An example: "NOVEL, n. A short story padded." (1911)

Dharma Bums, The

Jack Kerouac   Novel / U.S.

Kerouac's thinly disguised autobiographical novel takes place in California as the narrator Raymond Smith meets Japhy Ryder, a thinly disguised Gary Snyder, poet, Buddhist and naturalist. (1958)

Diary of a Wilderness Dweller
Chris Czajkowski   Exploration

Chris Czajkowski tells the story of her epic journey to build a home in the wilderness beside an unnamed lake, 5000 feet high in the Coast Range of British Columbia, through journal entries and watercolor paintings. (1996)

Divine Secrets of the Ya-Ya Sisterhood
Rebecca Wells   Novel / U.S.

Forty-year-old Sivi begins to understand her mother through reading diaries and letters of the "Ya-Ya Sisterhood," consisting of her mother and her three close friends, whose lives have been dedicated to the reality that "bad girls have all the fun." (1999)

Do Androids Dream of Electric Sheep
Phillip K. Dick   Science Fiction / U.S.

In this futuristic story, Rick Deckard, also known as Blade Runner, is a special police officer. He is assigned to terminate human replicates that have lived unnoticed in the San Francisco of 2021 before beginning a murderous spree. (1968)

Doors of Perception and Heaven and Hell, The   922
Aldous Huxley   Philosophy

Huxley's title for the first part of this book is taken from William Blake: "If the doors of perception were cleansed, everything would appear to man as it is, infinite". Huxley gives an account of his experiences with mescalin. In *Heaven and Hell*, he explores how people in various cultures cleanse perception and the positive and negative results that follow. (1954)

Dracula
Bram Stoker   Novel / Ireland

The first and still the most famous of vampire tales is told through the diaries of the central characters: a young lawyer, Jeremy Harker, his fiancée Mina, her friend Lucy, and Dr. Seward, the superintendent of a mental hospital in Essex, England. Count Dracula comes out of deepest Transylvania to live on the estate next door to Dr. Seward. (1897)

Dragon Revenant, The: Dragonspell
Katherine Kerr   Novel / U.S.

This fourth book in *The Deverry Sequence* completes the fantasy set in Wales and tells of the truce between the humans and the world of fairies to oppose a greater evil. (1990) The other books are *Daggerspell*, *Darkspell*, and *The Bristling Wood: Dawnspell*.

Dreamwork
Mary Oliver   Poetry / U.S.

Mary Oliver is one of America's best-loved poets. Written in evocative, simple language, and steeped in nature imagery, her poetry is deeply spiritual and profoundly moving. (1986)

Dune
Frank Herbert   Science Fiction / U.S.

The first of the six-book series, *The Dune Chronicles*, is one of the most popular science fiction books ever published. It is a mixture of ecological awareness, spiritual insight, political understanding and gripping adventure. (1965)

Earth Gods, The
Kahlil Gibran   Poetry / Lebanon

Lebanese American Gibran's last work is a dialogue in free verse between three Titans on the subject of human destiny. (1931)

Eight, The
Catherine Neville   Novel / U.S.

In this thrilling novel, a young computer expert is sent on a mission to recover lost chess pieces; her story is linked to the fate of a novice during the French Revolution who discovers the secret behind Charlemagne's chess set. (1988)

Ender's Game

Orson Scott Card   Science Fiction / U.S.

Ender Wiggin is so promising that the government takes him from his family to train him to be commander-in-chief in the upcoming war with the insect-like creatures known as the Buggers. But Ender sees more than the people in power wish him to. (1985) Ender's story continues in *Speaker for the Dead, Xenocide, Children of the Mind,* and *Ender's Shadow.*

Equus

Peter Shaffer   Drama / Britain

See *Drama, Mythology, Poetry, and Sacred Writing*

Esau

Philip Kerr   Novel / Britain

Mountain climber Jack Furness is almost at the summit of a sacred Himalayan mountain when an avalanche wipes out his party; he escapes into a cave where he finds a skull. The adventure that follows leads him into the world of the Yeti, the Abominable Snowman. (1998)

Essays

Ralph Waldo Emerson   Philosophy

See *Nonfiction*

Essential Rumi, The

Maulana Jalal al-Din Rumi   Poetry / Persia

Thirteenth-century Persian Sufi mystic, Rumi, has been highly influential in the past two centuries, inspiring such diverse figures as Goethe and Gandhi. This translation by Coleman Barks, with John Moyne, has met with wide acclaim. (1994)

Eva Luna

Isabel Allende   Margaret Sayers Peden, trans.   Novel / Chile

Allende has been called a 20th-century Scherherazade, spinning one mesmerizing story after another. Eva Luna's story is filled with miraculous occurrences from her conception onward. Her adventures are interwoven with those of the European destined to become her lover. (1988)

Existentialism and Human Emotions

Jean Paul Sartre   Philosophy

Sartre argues that our lives are not predetermined but created through our choices. We, therefore, must accept responsibility for those choices. This is reputed to be the most accessible entry into the philosophy of Existentialism. (1957)

Eye of the Needle

Ken Follett   Novel / Britain

In this gripping spy novel, a World War II German agent has obtained secret information about the Allied D-Day landing. As he waits for his submarine at an English lighthouse, he finds himself involved in a love affair with a lonely woman. (1985)

Fahrenheit 451

Ray Bradbury   Novel / U.S

See *Fiction*

Fall on Your Knees

Anne Marie MacDonald   Novel / Canada

Set on the island of Cape Breton, Nova Scotia, this is the haunted story of five generations of the Piper family whose tragic secrets are finally revealed. (1997)

Far Off Place, A

Laurens van der Post   Novel / South Africa

See *Fiction*

Faust

Johann Wolfgang von Goethe   Drama / Germany

See *Drama, Mythology, Poetry, and Sacred Writing*

Favourite Game, The

Leonard Cohen   Novel / Canada

Cohen's protagonist, Brahman, "comes of age" realizing that the clearest path through life lies in myth and art. (1963)

Fifth Business

Robertson Davies   Novel / Canada

See *Fiction*

Fifth Sacred Thing, The

Starhawk   Novel / U.S.

This futuristic novel tells of a clash of societies, one based on co-operation, diversity, and art, the other on war and domination, as seen through the eyes of a family of witches and healers. (1993)

Fifty (50) Short Science Fiction Tales

Isaac Asimov   Short Stories / U.S.

This is a highly readable collection of short fiction by one of the sci-fi greats. Some stories are only a page long. (1997) See *Isaac Asimov: The Complete Stories*.

Firebrand, The

Marion Zimmer Bradley   Novel / U.S.

Bradley brings ancient Troy to life from the perspective of women caught in war, particularly Cassandra who predicts, and then experiences, the invasion of the Greeks against the walled city. (1987)

Forest House, The

Marion Zimmer Bradley   Novel / U.S.

In this prequel to *The Lady of Avalon*, the last remaining Druid priestesses attempt to keep peace between their people and the Roman invaders with whom they begin to fall in love. (1994)

Forrest Gump

Winston Groom   Novel / U.S.

Forrest is the mentally challenged and tenderhearted narrator of this delightful novel. He grows up in Alabama in the 1950s and '60s, achieves fame through playing football, goes to Vietnam where he is a hero, meets the President of the United States, and operates a highly successful shrimp business, all without thinking that any of it is in any way unusual. (1986)

Fountainhead, The

Ayn Rand   Novel / U.S.

Russian-born Rand fled the Soviet Union in 1926, came to New York and founded Objectivism. In this influential novel, her philosophy is embodied in Howard Roark, an architect whose fierce integrity defends his creative vision and sense of justice as individualism is pitted against collectivism. (1943)

Fried Green Tomatoes at the Whistle-Stop Café

Fannie Flagg   Novel / U.S.

Old Mrs. Threadgoode tells her life story to middle-aged Evelyn, whose not-very-happy life is transformed by the tale. She hears of tomboy Idgie and her friend Ruth in Whistle Stop, Alabama, in the 1930s. (1987)

Frogs Into Princes: Neuro Linguistic Programming

Richard Bandler and John Grinder   Psychology

Neuro-Linguistic Programming, first developed in the 1970s at the University of California by mathematician Richard Bandler and professor of linguistics John Grinder, has gained a wide following. Through understanding the ways in which we have been programmed to think, to feel and to act, we can learn how to free ourselves from these often limiting responses. (1979)

Galileo's Daughter: A Historical Memoir of Science, Faith, and Love

Dava Sobel   Biography

See *Autobiography, Biography, and History*

Game, The

Ken Dryden   Sports / Hockey

Widely acknowledged as the best hockey book ever written, *The Game* is a reflective look at the life of a professional athlete by the former Canadiens goalie who later became president of the Toronto Maple Leafs. (1989)

Gay Science, The

Friedrich Nietzsche   Philosophy

Nietzsche considered this "the most personal of all my books." In it he declares the death of God and claims that "we have killed him." (1887)

Geek Love

Katherine Dunn   Novel / U.S.

Described as a modern shocker, this is the story of a family of carnival "freak show" artists, their loves and revenge. (1989)

Giving Tree, The

Shel Silverstein   Novel / Children's Literature / U.S.

Silverstein's book about the give and take between a tree and a boy has become such a classic that it is the subject of academic symposia where there is much debate about the nature of giving and unconditional love. (1963)

Gödel, Escher, Bach: An External Golden Braid

Douglas R. Hofstadter   Philosophy

This extraordinary thought-provoking book became a best seller on its publication. The author combines the lives and works of Goedel (a German mathematical philosopher), Escher (a 20th-century artist of haunting images) and Bach (the famous German composer) to question the possibility of Artificial Intelligence. (1979)

Godfather, The

Mario Puzo   Novel / U.S.

Puzo's dramatic inside view of the Mafia and its gang wars is the unforgettable story of Vito Corleone and his power over friends and family. (1969)

Gone With the Wind

Margaret Mitchell   Novel / U.S.

Mitchell's famous novel is set in Georgia before and during the Civil War and is the story of Scarlett O'Hara, her three marriages, and her dedication to the preservation of her father's land. (1936)

Good Soldier Schweik

Jaroslav Hasek   Novel / Czechoslovakia

Schweik is the little man fighting against the bureaucratic military machine in this satirical condemnation of war and nationalism. (1930)

Goodbye Bafana: Nelson Mandela, My Prisoner, My Friend

James Gregory   Autobiography

Gregory was the prison warden for Nelson Mandela for 18 years. Raised as a disciple of apartheid, Gregory had ingrained beliefs that were shaken by the humility and wisdom of the man he guarded. From jailer, he was transformed into admirer and friend. (1995)

Grand Inquisitor, The

Fyodor Dostoevsky   Novel / Russia

In this famous Book V of *The Brothers Karamazov*, Ivan attempts to undermine Alyosha's faith by telling him a story of Christ being questioned by the Grand Inquisitor. (1956)

Great Fool: Zen Master Ryokan: Poems, Letters, and Other Writings

Abe Ryuichi Ryokan   Peter Haskel, trans.   Spirituality

Japanese poet Ryokan (1758–1831) was nicknamed "Great Fool." Ordained as a Soto Zen priest and certified as a master, Ryokan chose to practice the Way through living as a hermit in the countryside, begging for his food as was done by the Buddha, and writing of his humble life. (1996)

Green Mile, The

Stephen King   Novel / U.S.

Set in the American South in the 1930s, this is the strange tale of John Coffey, convicted of rape and murder, who awaits his death in prison. Coffey, however, has powers unknown to ordinary humans. (1996)

Grizzly Years: In Search of the American Wilderness

Doug Peacock   Exploration

After his second tour as a Green Beret medic in Vietnam, Peacock needs a quiet place to recover his soul. In the mountains of Montana he finds a sense of kinship with the grizzly bear as he directly observes their majestic animal behavior. (1996)

Guns, Germs and Steel: The Fates of Human Societies

Jared Diamond   History / Technology

Diamond, a biologist, investigates the large question of why some cultures, from the Ice Age onward, conquer, destroy, or out-breed other cultures. (1997)

Gunslinger, The

Stephen King   Novel / U.S.

Roland, the last gunslinger, must fight the man in black on his quest for the Dark Tower in this King fantasy. The other two titles of *The Dark Tower* series are *The Drawing of the Three* and *The Waste Lands*. (1982)

Half Asleep in Frog Pajamas

Tom Robbins   Novel / U.S.

Gwen Mati, a 29-year-old Filipino broker for a small firm in Seattle, is just about to make it into big money and the easy life when the stock market tumbles on a Black Thursday. Over the long weekend, Gwen has one bizarre adventure after another with a wild assortment of characters including a born-again monkey. (1994)

Haroun and the Sea of Stories

Salman Rushdie   Novel / India

Rushdie's wonderful parable about the nature of creativity follows a storyteller who loses his skill through a mysterious force that blocks the sea of inspiration. He must find a way to regain it. (1991)

Harry Potter

J. K. Rowling   Novel / Children's Literature / Britain

The series about the young wizard, Harry Potter, and his fight against the evil Voldemort have had phenomenal success among children and adults alike. While the imaginative world of Wizardry, Hogwarts, Muggles, invisibility cloaks and more bring readers into a fantasy world, a strength of the books lies in their truths about choices, loyalty, courage, and love. *Harry Potter and the Sorcerer's Stone* (1997), *Harry Potter and the Chamber of Secrets* (1998), *Harry Potter and the Prisoner of Azkaban* (1999), *Harry Potter and the Goblet of Fire* (2000), and *Harry Potter at the Order of the Phoenix* (2003).

Hatchet

Gary Paulsen   Novel / U.S.

After a plane crash, 13-year-old Brian Robeson survives alone in the Canadian wilderness for two and a half months, armed with his hatchet and astounding resourcefulness. Three further books follow Brian's survival adventures: *Brian's Return*, *Brian's Winter*, and *The River*. (1987)

Hearts in Atlantis

Stephen King   Short Stories / U.S.

King's collection of five stories about growing up in the 1960s is not in any way typical of coming-of-age tales. His intriguing blend of horror and fantasy meets with the very real horror of the Vietnam War to make this one of his best. (1999)

Hiroshima

John Hersey   History

See *Autobiography, Biography, and History*

Hitchhikers Guide to the Galaxy, The

Douglas Adams   Science Fiction / Britain

This is prolific writer Douglas Adams' cult classic. After a cosmic construction team making way for a freeway obliterates Earth, Arthur Dent and his pal Ford Prefect are forced to travel the galaxy, with hilarious results. (1979)

Hole in the Sky: A Memoir

William Kittredge   Autobiography

Kittredge's autobiography begins in the wilderness around the foothills of southeastern Oregon where his family owned a vast spread and held onto the myth of the western cowboy. He recalls the events of his childhood leading up to his time in the Air Force, his many marriages, and his emergence as a writer with a deep sense of the sacred and the interconnectedness of all life. (1992)

Hollow Hills, The

Mary Stewart   Novel / Britain

The second of Mary Stewart's trilogy based on the Arthurian Saga tells of the boyhood and coming-of-age of Merlin. (1973) See *The Crystal Cave* and *The Last Enchantment*.

Hollow Men, The

T. S. Eliot   Poetry / Britain

First published in *Poems 1909–1925*, Eliot's poem was immediately hailed as a masterpiece in its evocation of the spiritual desolation and emptiness of purpose in Europe following World War I. Its conclusion, "This is the way the world ends / Not with a bang but a whimper" has become a modern epigram.

Horse Whisperer, The

Nicholas Evans   Novel / U.S.

In a tragic riding accident, a teenaged girl loses a leg and her horse is traumatized. The girl's mother discovers a man who might be able to help the horse and that she, too, is in need of healing. (1995)

Hotel New Hampshire

John Irving   Novel / U.S.

John Berry's descriptions of his family, hotelkeepers, and bear-trainers, are both hilarious and profoundly moving. (1981)

Hundreth Monkey and Other Paradigms of the Paranormal, The

Kendrick Frazire, ed.   Science

Carl Sagan, Isaac Asimov, and Paul Kurtz are among the contributors to this compilation of articles about rational investigation of paranormal phenomena. (1991)

Hyperspace: A Scientific Odyssey Through Parallel Universes, Time Warps and the Tenth Dimension

Michio Kaku   Physics

Popular science writer and theoretical physicist Kaku teaches at the City University of New York. This book for the general reader introduces the theory of hyperspace (higher dimensional space) including parallel universes, superstrings, wormholes, black holes, time machines, and the fate of the universe. (1994)

I Had Seen Castles

Cynthia Rylant　Novel / U.S.

John Donde is 18, living in Pittsburgh with his family, and happy with his dreams of the future, when Pearl Harbor throws him into enlisting in World War II. The novel is a vivid account of his war experience, which turns out to be radically different from what he had imagined. (1993)

Iceman Cometh, The

Eugene O'Neill　Drama / U.S.

See *Drama, Mythology, Poetry, and Sacred Writing*

In Search of the Miraculous

P. D. Ouspensky　Philosophy

Ouspensky (1878–1947) studied intensively with G. I. Gurdjieff between 1915–1918, and throughout the rest of his life continued to promote Gurdjieff's system for developing consciousness. This book is considered by many to be the clearest written account of Gurdjieff's teaching. (1949)

Into The Wild

Jon Krakauer　Adventure / Wilderness

In April 1992, 24-year-old Chris McCandless attempted to survive alone in the Alaskan wilderness. His body was found four months later. Krakauer, a writer for *Outside Magazine,* was sent to cover the story and found enough material to write a book. (1996)

Into Thin Air: A Personal Account of the Mount Everest Disaster

Jon Krakauer　Adventure / Mountaineering

See *Nonfiction*

Isaac Asimov: The Complete Stories

Isaac Asimov   Short Stories / U.S.

This is part of a multi-volume collection by one of the most prolific and respected of science fiction writers. Asimov's strengths were his ability to visualize the future in terms of technology as well as its impact on humanity. (1990) See *Fifty Short Science Fiction Tales*.

Ishmael

Daniel Quinn   Novel / U.S.

This novel was the winner of the Turner Tomorrow Fellowship, a prize honoring fiction that produces creative and positive solutions to global problems. Ishmael is both a gorilla and a teacher who communicates with humans telepathically. His ideas for the future of the Earth lie in his outsider's view of human civilization. (1990)

Island

Aldous Huxley   Novel / Britain

Huxley's final novel takes the reader to a Pacific island, Pala, which has enjoyed an ideal society for 120 years. The modern world catches up with Pala when a newspaperman named Faranby is shipwrecked there. Too late, Faranby realized what is being lost. (1962)

It

Stephen King   Novel / U.S.

"It" is a child-killing monster that takes the shape of a child's worst fears. Seven adults return to Maine where each had met "It" when they were 11 years old. (1986)

James and the Giant Peach

Roald Dahl   Novel / Children's Literature / Britain

The orphan James escapes from his wicked aunts by boarding a peach with a crew of fabulous insects. This popular and delightful story lives on in the hearts of all who have read it. Quentin Blake's original illustrations add to its charm. (1961)

Jews and Blacks: Let the Healing Begin

Cornel West and Michael Lerner   Social Issues

African American Harvard Professor Cornel West and Jewish intellectual Michael Lerner have published their conversations, hoping for reconciliation between their respective groups. (1995)

Jitterbug Perfume

Tom Robbins   Fiction U.S.

This wildly funny novel brings together ancient Bohemia and New Orleans, a cast of weird and loveable characters, and a page-turning plot that involves secret formulae and beets. It is Robbins at his wacky best. (1984)

Joan of Arc

Mark Twain   Biography

Mark Twain said of this biography: "I like *Joan of Arc* best of all my books." Twelve years of research makes this a remarkably accurate biography of the life and mission of the Maid of Orleans. (1895)

John Carter of Mars Series

Edgar Rice Burroughs   Science Fiction / U.S.

Burroughs is perhaps best known for his *Tarzan* series. He was also a science fiction writer and began the eleven-book *John Carter of Mars* series in 1917 with *A Princess of Mars*. Carter is transported from the Civil War era to Mars where he encounters a fantastic world of green barbarians and maidens in distress.

Jurassic Park

Michael Crichton   Science Fiction / U.S.

With his usual excellent research, Crichton turns to paleontology in this thriller about dinosaurs brought back to life. (1990)

Keep the Aspidistra Flying

George Orwell   Novel / Britain

See *Fiction*

Key to Rebecca, The

Ken Follett   Novel / Britain

See *Fiction*

Killer Angels, The

Michael Shaara   Novel / U.S.

See *Fiction*

Kin of Ata Are Waiting for You, The

Dorothy Bryant   Novel / U.S.

This Utopian fantasy and symbolic journey of the soul was born out of the writer's deep spiritual hunger in our secular, mechanized, violent age. (1971)

Koran, The

Muhammad   Sacred Writing

See *Drama, Mythology, Poetry, and Sacred Writing*

La Religieuse

Denis Diderot   Novel / France

Diderot (1713–1784), French philosopher and man of letters, was the chief editor of the *L'Encyclopédie*, one of the great achievements of the Age of Enlightenment. He also published *La Religieuse*, considered then to be a shocking piece of fiction, written in the first person by a young girl who enters a nunnery and is harassed by the lesbian abbess. (1796)

Lady of Avalon, The

Marion Zimmer Bradley   Novel / U.S.

Bradley's Avalon, seat of the Goddess Mother religion, holds artifacts and memories of the Old Ones from Atlantis. The High Priestesses rely on visions of the incarnations of the Sacred King who will save Brittania in this prequel to *The Mists of Avalon* and sequel to *The Forest House*. (1997)

Last Days of Pompeii, The

Sir Edward George Bulwer-Lytton   Novel / Britain

Bulwer-Lytton offers a plausible and vivid story of the experience of the inhabitants of Pompeii in 79 C.E. from the first trembling of Mount Vesuvius until its final eruption in the last terrifying hours. (1834)

Last Enchantment, The

Mary Stewart   Novel / Britain

In the third of the *Merlin Trilogy*, Morgause, Arthur's half-sister, ensnares him into an incestuous liaison—and bears his son, Mordred, to use to her own evil ends. (1979) See *The Crystal Cave* and *The Hollow Hills*.

Last of the Breed

Louis L'Amour   Novel / U.S.

A part-Native American pilot is shot down over Siberia and must rely on his Indian skills to live off the frozen tundra. (1986)

Last Temptation of Christ, The

Nikos Kazantzakis   Novel / Greece

The fictional account of the daily sufferings of Jesus of Nazareth as he is plagued by visions and tormented by desires of the flesh caused a storm of protest when filmed as a movie. Jesus' last temptation is to marry, have children, and enjoy life as an ordinary human being. (1955)

Law of Love, The

Laura Esquivel   Novel / Mexico

In a blend of myth and magic realism, Esquival moves back and forth between the 16th and 23rd centuries in Mexico. The central characters are familiar with past incarnations and actively work through karmic debts. (1996)

Leaves of Grass

Walt Whitman   Poetry / U.S.

See *Drama, Mythology, Poetry, and Sacred Writing*

Letters At 3 a.m.: Reports on Endarkenment

Michael Ventura   Social Issues / U.S.

Ventura's columns collected from the *L. A. Weekly* in the 1990s are vivid, honest, provocative, and often funny. (1997)

Letters to a Young Poet

Rainer Maria Rilke   Philosophy

In a series of remarkable responses from 1903–1908, Rilke advises a young would-be poet on survival as a sensitive observer in a harsh world.

Leviathan

Paul Auster   Novel / U.S.

When the protagonist of this novel is killed early in the book, the story shifts to his best friend who tries to make sense of a seemingly lost life. (1992)

Liar's Club: A Memoir

Mary Karr   Autobiography

Karr, a prize-winning poet and critic, grew up in the refinery town of Port Arthur, Texas, with a mentally unstable artist mother and a hot-tempered, hard-drinking father who spent endless hours with his cronies in the Liars' Club. Her own story-telling gift has allowed her to look back on childhood pain with a remarkable sense of perspective. (1996)

Light in August

William Faulkner   Novel / U.S.

This critically acclaimed novel is about the tragedy of Joe Christmas, an orphan of ambiguous ancestry who believes he is part black in the American South in the early 20th century. (1932)

Like Water for Chocolate
Laura Esquivel   Novel / Mexico

In this delightful novel brilliantly interwoven with traditional Mexican recipes, Tita, raised in the kitchen with the cook, is denied her true love because she is the youngest daughter and must take care of her mother. Her lover's solution is to marry her sister so that he and Tita can be close to each other every day. (1992)

Lonesome Dove
Larry McMurtry   Novel / U.S.

Two retired Texas Rangers decide to experience a cattle drive of 2500 miles from the banks of the Rio Grande to Montana. This much-praised novel was a Pulitzer Prize-winner in 1985. *Dead Man's Walk* (1995) and *Comanche Moon* (1997) are prequels. The sequel is *Streets of Laredo.* (1993)

Long Walk, The
Stephen King   Novel / U.S.

Set in the near future, a boy is chosen to enter a walking competition with 99 others; contestants are shot as they begin to slow down to less than four miles an hour and the contest is over when one person remains. (1979)

Lost in Place: Growing Up Absurd in Suburbia
Mark Salzman   Autobiography

This coming-of-age autobiography is a humorous account of Saltzman's eccentric adolescence and his attempts to live like a Zen monk in suburban Connecticut. (1995)

Manticore, The
Robertson Davies   Novel / Canada
See *Fiction*

Marjorie Morningstar

Herman Wouk   Novel / U.S.

Stage-struck 19-year-old Marjorie Morgenstern leaves her Jewish family in New York for a summer stock theatre job where she falls in love with the director. The story of the next two decades of her life is tender and heart breaking, yet ultimately redeeming. (1955)

Mary Queen of Scots

Antonia Fraser   Biography

Mary, Queen of Scots was the cousin of Elizabeth I and the mother of James I. Queen of Scotland when she was one year of age, Mary was raised in France, married three times, and was beheaded by her own cousin. This is a definitive biography of a complex and still-loved personality. (2001)

Mastering the Art of French Cooking

Julia Child   Cooking

Child began a revolution in American cookery when this book was first published. It has since sold over 700,000 copies. French cuisine began with the Florentines, themselves heirs to the Romans. Child's techniques and recipes make exquisite food accessible to all. (1961)

Maximum Bob

Elmore Leonard   Novel / U.S.

This crime novel packed with quirky characters pits Kathy Baker of the Florida Department of Corrections against Judge Bob Gibbs, called Maximum Bob for his prison sentences. A plot to kill Gibbs keeps everyone busy in this fast-paced adventure. (1991)

Memoirs of a Geisha

Arthur Golden   Novel / U.S.

The beautiful daughter of an impoverished fishing family in pre-World War II Japan is sold into slavery at the age of nine to become a geisha, an entertainer trained in conversation, tea ceremony, dance, and song. She soothes careworn men in evening gatherings at teahouses and gains power through subtlety. (1997)

Midsummer Night's Dream, A

William Shakespeare   Drama / England

See *Drama, Mythology, Poetry, and Sacred Writing*

Midwives: A Novel

Chris Bohjalian   Novel / U.S.

A competent Vermont midwife delivers a baby by Caesarian section during an ice storm after she thinks the mother has died, and is then arrested for murder. (1997)

Miles: The Autobiography

Miles Davis   Autobiography

Trumpeter Miles Davis (1926–1991) is a legend as a pioneer in jazz. He overcame drug addiction and racism on his way to success. (1989)

Mists of Avalon, The

Marion Zimmer Bradley   Novel / U.S.

Bradley's retelling of the Arthurian legends from the viewpoint of the women central to the story begins as Christianity is taking over Britain, and the fairy world of Avalon is retreating. Morgaine (Morgan Le Fay) and Gwenhwyfar (Guinevere) struggle for power as they hold Arthur between them. (1983)

Modiglianni Scandal, The

Ken Follett   Novel / Britain

Follett turns to the world of art in this fast-paced crime novel about the discovery of a famous painting and the fight for its possession. (1976)

Momo

Michael Ende   Novel / Germany

Part fairy tale, part satire of our fast-paced, business-controlled society, this is the story of the orphan Momo and her quest to discover how time is being stolen and where it is hidden. (1984)

Monkey Wrench Gang, The

Edward Abbey   Novel / U.S.

This fictional account of environmentalists attempting to liberate parts of Utah and Arizona from evil road-builders has become an ecology classic. (1975)

Moon is a Harsh Mistress, The

Robert A. Heinlein   Science Fiction / U.S.

An unlikely band of dissidents mount a revolution on the moon in 2076, where "Loonies" are kept poor and oppressed by an Earth Authority. (1966)

Moonchild

Aleister Crowley   Novel / Britain

Two societies of rival magicians quarrel over an experiment to incarnate a supernatural being. (1929)

Moonshadow

Penelope Neri   Novel / U.S.

Neri's novel has all the features of a modern Gothic Romance: a young bride, a somber country estate, a distant husband, ghostly voices, and a surprise ending. (2001)

Moor's Last Sigh, The

Salman Rushdie   Novel / India

This story set in 20th-century India tells of Moraes "Moor" Zogoiby, whose mother has made him the subject of a famous series of paintings known as "The Moor Sequence," only to banish him from her sight. (1995)

Mutant Messenger Down Under

Marlo Morgan   Novel / U.S.

Partly autobiographical, an American doctor sheds her previous life when she joins a group of Australian aborigines, the telepathic and spiritually advanced descendants of a 50,000-year-old tradition. (1990)

Name of the Rose, The

Umberto Eco   Novel / Italy

This complex murder mystery is set in a medieval monastery and revolves around the discovery of lost books from classical times. (1981)

Narcissus and Goldmund

Hermann Hesse   Novel / Germany

Two medieval men, one content with monastic life, and the other very
much part of the world represent Hesse's theme of tension between flesh
and spirit, and emotion and reason. (1930)

Nausea

Jean Paul Sartre   Novel / France

A diary full of the thoughts, emotions, and everyday experiences of a
lonely and nihilistic outsider, Sartre's novel has become a classic of 20th-
century Existentialism. (1938)

Net Force

Tom Clancy   Novel / U.S.

The year is 2010 and computers are the new superpowers; those who
control the computers control the world. The U.S. Congress decrees the
Net Laws and puts together a computer security agency within the FBI:
Net Force. (1998)

Neverwhere

Neil Gaiman   Novel / Britain

Gaiman is the originator of the popular *Sandman* comic book series. In
this novel, an ordinary London businessman stops to help a girl bleed-
ing on the sidewalk, and his life as he has known it disappears; instead
he finds himself in a strange underground London with the girl, Lady
Door. (1997)

Of Water and the Spirit: Ritual, Magic, and Initiation in the Life of an African Shaman

Malidorma Patrice Some   Biography

See *Autobiography, Biography, and History*

One Hundred Love Sonnets

Pablo Neruda   Poetry / Chile

Nobel Prize-winner and communist political activist Neruda (the pen name of Ricard Eliecer Neftali Reyes) has become internationally famous as a profound poet. These poems are set against the backdrop of Isla Negra and dedicated to his beloved wife, Matilde Urrutia de Neruda. (1960)

One Hundred Years of Solitude

Gabriel Garcia Marquez   Novel / Columbia

See *Fiction*

One Thousand Chestnut Trees

Myra Stout   Novel / U.S.

A young New York writer journeys to Korea in an attempt to understand the birth country of her mother; as the story of her search for her heritage unfolds, the reader gets a vivid picture of Korean history. (1998)

Outer Dark

Cormac McCarthy   Novel / U.S.

An orphaned brother and sister in Appalachia have a child. The brother leaves it to die in the woods and lies to his sister about the cause of the baby's death. She sets out to find her son, and her brother follows. (1968)

Pale Blue Dot: A Vision of the Human Future in Space

Carl Sagan   Astronomy

Science writer Sagan, who taught Astronomy and Space Sciences at Cornell, uses the picture of the Earth taken by Voyager 1 in 1990 from a distance of 3.7 billion miles to remind us of our place in the vast expanse of space. This book encompasses interplanetary exploration, from the Apollo moon landings to the discoveries of the Voyager spacecraft. (1994)

Paradise

Toni Morrison   Novel / U.S.

In an all-black rural township in Oklahoma, nine men decide to wipe out a group of unconventional women who live in what is called the "Convent." Moving back and forth through time and the stories of the characters, Morrison gives an intricate understanding of fear, power, and the possibility of redemption. (1988)

Parsival

Wolfram Von Eschenbach   Poetry / Germany

See *Drama, Mythology, Poetry, and Sacred Writing*

Partner, The

John Grisham   Novel / U.S.

Grisham's mysteries always make exciting reading. In this one, a young partner in a Mississippi law firm steals 90 million dollars, is caught on the edge of the Brazilian jungle, and is brought home for trial. (1996)

People's History of the United States, 1492–Present

Howard Zinn   History / U.S.

Zinn considers the arrival of Columbus and the genocide that followed to be the beginning of a history of suppression and violence that has lasted to the present. Through quoting the voices of African Americans, women, American Indians, war resisters, and poor laborers of all nationalities, he is able to give alternative descriptions of events that are usually brushed aside or ignored.. (1995)

Perfect Storm: A True Story of Men Against the Sea

Sebastian Junger   Adventure

In October 1991, three weather systems collided off the coast of Nova Scotia to create the "storm of the century," with waves over 100 feet high. Among its victims was the Gloucester, Massachusetts sword fishing boat, the *Andrea Gail,* that vanished with all six crew-members aboard. (1997)

Perfume

Patrick Suskind   Novel / Germany

An intriguing novel about an illegitimate boy who grows up among fishmongers in 18th-century France and goes on to become the most famous perfume maker of all time, letting nothing stand in his way, including murder. (1987)

Philosophy of Andy Warhol, The: From A to B and Back Again

Andy Warhol   Philosophy

These eleven short chapters give a tiny glimpse into the mind of artist Andy Warhol and the Pop-art culture of the 1960s and '70s. (1975)

Philosophy of Spiritual Activity, The

Rudolf Steiner   Philosophy

Steiner based this book on the results of observing the human soul according to the methods of natural science. In it, he gives practical advice for developing the ability to think clearly by applying the exactitude of scientific observation to inner thought. It has also been translated as *Intuitive Thinking as a Spiritual Path* and *The Philosophy of Freedom.* (1894)

Pictor's Metamorphoses and Other Fantasies

Hermann Hesse   Novel / Germany

This collection of nineteen of Hesse's short stories ranges from fairy tale to satire and covers 50 years of the author's writings. (1972)

Picture of Dorian Gray, The

Oscar Wilde   Novel / Britain

Vain desires and personal power drive Dorian's moral dissolution, as he trades his soul for eternal youth while his portrait reflects his true age and the ugliness of his sins. (1890)

Pigs in Heaven

Barbara Kingsolver   Novel / U.S.

In the sequel to *The Bean Trees*, richly drawn characters deal with the past in order to face the present and struggle with issues of love, family, and truth. (1993)

Play It As It Lays

Joan Didion   Novel / U.S.

Set in the 1960s, this sharp-witted story describes the life of Maria, destroyed by her stint as a celebrity in Hollywood, who has cut herself off from any meaningful relationships. (1970)

Postcards From The Edge

Carrie Fisher   Novel / U.S.

The central character in this somewhat autobiographical novel is a young actress. She is drifting her way through Hollywood surrounded by characters highly adept at lying to themselves. (1987)

Power of the Myth, The

Joseph Campbell   Spirituality

During the last two years of Campbell's life, journalist Bill Moyers interviewed him for a television series for the Public Broadcasting Service (PBS). This fully illustrated book is the companion volume to that series and encompasses Campbell's lifelong study of history, art, philosophy, religion, and the relevance of mythology to modern life. (1988)

Prayer for Owen Meany, A

John Irving   Novel / U.S.

Owen Meaney kills the mother of his best friend when he hits a foul ball; from that point on, he thinks of himself as an instrument of God's will. The story of his life is filled with quintessential Irving humor and wisdom. (1989)

Pride and Prejudice
Jane Austen　Novel / Britain

See *Fiction*

Prince and the Pauper, The
Mark Twain　Novel / U.S.

Set in the mid-16th century, this is the delightful account of two boys, one an urchin from London's filthy lanes, the other a prince born in a lavish palace, who unwittingly trade identities. (1881)

Principles of Psychology
William James　Philosophy

James (1842–1910) transformed psychology from its traditional place as a branch of philosophy to a science based on experimental method. In his exploration of how we think and experience the world, he proposed that our thoughts are a continuous and active stream-of-consciousness. (1890)

Promiscuities: The Secret Struggle for Womanhood
Naomi Wolf　Social Issues

Wolf uses her own story and those of her friends to analyze the mixed messages that young women get about sexuality and the confusing path to self-understanding. (1997)

Prophet, The
Kahlil Gibran　Philosophy

This volume of 26 poetic essays has been translated into over 20 languages. The Prophet, who has lived in a foreign city for 12 years, is about to leave for home aboard a ship and addresses his followers on life's great questions. (1923)

Ramona

Helen Hunt Jackson   Novel / U.S.

Jackson's efforts to help the Ponca Indians of Nebraska resulted in this novel about a beautiful, illegitimate Scots-Indian orphan raised in privilege and the handsome and courageous Indian Alessandro. (1884)

Rapture of Canaan, The

Sheri Reynolds   Novel / U.S.

Ninah Huff is a member of the Church of Fire and Brimstone and God's Almighty Baptizing Wind; like the others, she spends her days and nights serving the Lord and waiting for the Rapture, the Second Coming of Christ. Her troubles begin with sinful thoughts about a boy, her prayer partner. (1996)

Reader, The

Bernhard Schlink   Novel / Germany

A 15-year-old boy is drawn into an affair with an older woman. Years later, they meet again when she is on trial for Nazi war crimes and he is a young law student. (1995)

Reason for Hope: A Spiritual Journey

Jane Goodall   Autobiography

Goodall's work with chimpanzees in Tanzania has been widely recognized as essential in understanding animal behavior. This is her story of her private life before, during, and after her time in Africa. (1999)

Rebecca

Daphne du Maurier   Novel / Britain

One of the best mysteries of the 20th century, this story is set in the West Country of England. Rebecca, the first wife of Maxim de Winter, has died. The second wife, who tells the story, becomes increasingly suspicious of Rebecca's death. (1938)

Red Storm Rising

Tom Clancy   Novel / U.S.

When Muslim terrorists destroy Russia's largest oil refinery, Russia invades the Persian Gulf with Operation Red Storm. Land, sea, and air battles erupt as N.A.T.O. and the U.S. rush to protect their interests. (1991)

Red Tent, The

Anita Diamant   Novel / U.S.

Jacob's daughter Dinah is mentioned briefly in *Genesis*. Diamant gives Dinah, her mother, and aunts— all wives of Jacob— full lives in this extraordinary novel of Biblical times. (1998)

Redwall Series

Brian Jacques   Novel / Children's Literature / Britain

This imaginative series published from 1986–present was written ostensibly for young people, but has gained a wide following among adults as well. In medieval Redwall Abbey, peace-loving mice, moles, shrews, and squirrels battle the dark side of the animal world.

Replay

Ken Grimwood   Science Fiction / U.S.

Jeff Winston suffers a mid-life heart attack and finds himself thrown back 25 years into his past; he is given the opportunity to replay his life many times over. (1996)

Requiem for a Dream

Hubert Selby, Jr.   Novel / U.S.

This is a very dark novel. Three young heroin addicts in Coney Island, Brooklyn, deceive themselves into believing that illicit drugs are the fastest way to wealth and happiness. (1978)

Return to Tomorrow (Star Trek Files)

John Peel   Science Fiction / U.S.

The original *Star Trek Files* magazines were compiled into 16 volumes and averaged 50 pages each. *Return to Tomorrow* is File Eight. (1985–86)

Ring of Endless Light, A

Madeleine L'Engle   Novel / U.S.

Vicky Austin is deeply saddened by her grandfather's death, but her sorrow is relieved when her friend Adam asks for her help with his dolphin experiment. (1989) Other books about the Austins are *Meet the Austins* and *Troubling a Star.*

Ringworld Series

Larry Niven   Science Fiction / U.S.

Ringworld is the first of three novels set in the far future that follow Louis Wu from the beginning of his investigation of an alien artifact, through his encounters with the Puppeteer Hindmost, to his lonely entrapment in Ringworld. (1970) *Ringworld* is followed by *The Ringworld Engineers* (1980) and *The Ringworld Throne.* (1996).

River Ki, The

Sawako Ariyoshi   Novel / Japan

Set in the late 19th and early 20th centuries, this is the story of Kimoto Hana, and her relationship with her grandmother, daughter, and granddaughter as they cope with life beside the River Ki. (1959)

Robber Bride

Margaret Atwood   Novel / Canada

The Grimm's fairy tale, *The Robber Bridegroom,* is the inspiration for Atwood's novel about three women who are variously involved with the charismatic Zenia whom they think is dead. When she suddenly returns, each woman is forced to face herself. (1993)

Rocking Horse Winner, The

D. H. Lawrence   Novel / Britain

See *Fiction* under the title *Complete Short Stories of D. H. Lawrence*

Rule of the Bone

Russell Banks   Novel / U.S.

In this novel of betrayal and redemption, Banks gives an authentic voice to the narrator, a homeless, drug-addicted teenager living on the streets of New York who seeks his father in the Rastafarian culture of Jamaica. (1995)

Rush Limbaugh is a Big Fat Idiot and Other Observations

Al Franken   Social Issues

This is a collection of 45 short pieces of biting satire and social commentary on the American political scene of the 1990s by a *Saturday Night Live* writer. (1995)

Sackett

Louis L'Amour   Novel / U.S.

From 1965–1980, L'Amour wrote 18 novels describing several generations of a family who flee 17th-century England and come to America. In this second of the series, the family, joins the westward push in their commitment to freedom. (1961)

Sacred Buffalo: The Lakota Way for a New Beginning

James G. Durham   Spirituality

See *Nonfiction*

Sahara

Clive Cussler   Novel / U.S.

Cussler's hero, Dirk Pitt, unlocks a mystery that involves the assassination of President Lincoln, the disappearance of a pilot over the desert, and a deadly red tide that could threaten the world's oxygen supply. (1992)

Sand and Foam

Kahlil Gibran   Philosophy

This compilation of short maxims and aphorisms contains Gibran's essential philosophy. (1926)

Sandman (series)

Neil Gaiman   Novel / Britain

Gaiman's 75-part graphic novel (comic book) series was launched in 1989 and bound into ten volumes. The series tells the story of Dream, captured by an occult group in 1916 and held prisoner until his escape in 1988. (1989)

Secrets of the Yellow Brick Road: A Map for the Modern Spiritual Journey

Jesse Stewart   Spirituality

Stewart sees spiritual truths in *The Wizard of Oz*, written by Theosophist L. Frank Baum. Although Stewart intended this as a resource for young people, there is much to help any questing souls integrate their own Lion, Tinman, and Scarecrow in. He interweaves insights with the original story and scenes from the film. (1997)

Selected Letters of the Marquis de Sade

Margaret Crosland, ed.   Letters / France

This is a series of letters written by de Sade from 1777–1794; although sexually non-explicit, the letters are a good starting point in understanding the original sadist's complex mind. (1963)

Selected Poetry of Robinson Jeffers, The

Robinson Jeffers   Poetry / U.S.

See *Drama, Mythology, Poetry, and Sacred Writing*

Selections from Ralph Waldo Emerson

Stephen Whicher, ed.   Philosophy

See *Nonfiction*

Sense of Freedom, A

Jimmy Boyle   Autobiography

Boyle grew up in the slums of Glasgow into a world of violent crime and was imprisoned at the age of 23. There, he turned his life around, met his therapist wife and discovered art. He is now a famous sculptor who writes and lectures on the need for prison reform. (1985) The second volume of autobiography is *The Pain of Confinement*.

Separate Reality, A: Further Conversations with Don Juan

Carlos Castaneda   Reflections

In *The Teachings of Don Juan*, Castaneda published the account of his five-year apprenticeship to a Yaqui Indian sorcerer. *A Separate Reality* tells of his return to Mexico for more teaching and visions. (1972)

Shannara Series, The

Terry Brooks   Novel / U.S.

Brooks' series of ten novels are epic fantasy at its best, full of druids, trolls, and skull-bearers. (1977–2001)

She Would Draw Flowers

Kirsten Savitri Bergh   Poetry / U.S.

Kirsten was 17 when she and her friend Nina died suddenly in an auto accident. Her mother, Linda Bergh, published her daughter's legacy of paintings, drawings and poetry and now works with teens in many schools, inspiring them to tap into their creativity and remain true to their ideals. (1997)

She's Come Undone

Wally Lamb   Novel / U.S.

Delores, the protagonist and narrator of this testament to the human spirit, experiences what might seem overwhelming odds: her parents' divorce, her mother's mental illness, her rape at 13, and obesity as a young woman. Nevertheless, she retains her quirky warm humor and extraordinary perspective. (1992)

Shibumi

Trevanian   Novel / U.S.

An espionage thriller with a philosophical twist, this novel follows an American who survived the bombing of Hiroshima and went on to become an assassin dedicated to destroying "The Mother Company," an oil and nuclear power conglomerate. (1979)

Shogun

James Clavell   Novel / U.S.

A European sea captain comes to understand the Japanese in the 17th century as they move from feudalism to unity under one ruler. (1989)

Signal to Noise

Neil Gaiman   Novel / Britain

This "comic book," or graphic novel, with illustrator Dave McKean, tells the story of a screenwriter racing against time to complete his play, interwoven with the story of peasants in the 2nd millennium. The book has been adapted for the stage. (1992)

Silence of the Lambs

Thomas Harris   Novel / U.S.

A young FBI trainee interviews the imprisoned psychopathic killer Hannibal Lecter in an attempt to get into the mind of another psychopathic killer on the loose. (1991)

Sister Water

Nancy Willard   Novel / U.S.

A fish museum in Michigan is the setting for this poetically written magic-realist family drama about an aging woman and her two daughters as they struggle to find a way into the future. (1993)

Six Stories of the Jazz Age and Other Stories

F. Scott Fitzerald   Short Stories / U.S.

This collection of nine stories written in the 1920s and '30s contains most of Fitzgerald's best short fiction. (1960)

Skinny Legs and All

Tom Robbins   Novel / U.S.

A can of beans, a conch shell, a painted stick, a spoon, and a dirty sock make their way across the sprawling geography of the U.S., sharing their philosophies and insights as they go. The human characters are no less fascinating in this hilarious satire that tackles lust, materialism, the nature of time, and war in the Middle East. (1990)

Slave, The

Isaac Bashevis Singer   Novel / U.S.

Set in 18th-century Poland, this is the story of a Jewish man who marries a Gentile and, in trying to live with her in an outwardly devout Jewish community, is met with hypocrisy. (1962)

Snow Crash

Neal Stephensen   Science Fiction / U.S.

Hiro Protagonist, the hero of this entertaining read, lives in the not-too-distant future in a world of cybernetic technology and corporate franchise city-states. (1992)

Snow Falling on Cedars

David Guterson   Novel / U.S.

When Carl Heine's body is found in the ocean off the coast of Washington, suspicion turns to Kabuo Miyamoto, a member of the island's Japanese American community. During the trial many memories surface, but the most insistent is the imprisonment and loss of land that the Japanese in North America suffered during World War II. (1995)

Something Happened

Joseph Heller   Novel / U.S.

A middle-aged New Yorker is tired of his executive job in New York. He cannot understand how he went from being an enthusiastic young man to a drone-like suburbanite. (1974)

Sons and Lovers

D. H. Lawrence   Novel / Britain

This classic novel is about Paul Morel's growth to manhood, his relationship with his mother and the two women who vie for his affection. (1913)

Sophie's Choice

William Styron   Novel / U.S.

A young Southern writer moves to Brooklyn in the aftermath of World War II and meets Sophie, a non-Jewish Polish woman who has survived internment in a concentration camp. Sophie's lover is a Jewish American obsessed with the struggle he feels he has been denied. (1976)

Sphere

Michael Crichton   Science Fiction / U.S.

A team of top scientists is sent to investigate what is assumed to be the wreckage of an alien space ship on the ocean floor. What they find is stranger than they could have imagined. (1987)

Stand, The

Stephen King   Novel / U.S.

In this end-of-the-world scenario, a rapidly mutating flu virus is accidentally released through a U.S. military error and quickly kills almost all of Earth's human population. (1978)

Starship Troopers

Robert A. Heinlein   Science Fiction / U.S.

Earth is at war with insect-like aliens and one young man decides to join the military. Heinlein uses this basic plot to bring to life his controversial philosophical ideas of the tension between the individual and the collective. (1959)

Stones From the River

Ursula Hegi   Novel / U.S.

This is a powerful story of Hitler and the Nazi's rise to power in Germany in the 1930s through the eyes of Trudi Montag, a dwarf who uses her ability to tell stories to save herself from the fate to which her otherness would have doomed her. (1994)

Stranger in a Strange Land

Robert A. Heinlein   Science Fiction / U.S.

In an enormously popular story in the 1960s, a young earthling raised on Mars returns as a total innocent to Earth where human beings and society are new to him. He inherits an enormous fortune and is able to spread a message of free love and "groking," a form of telepathic communication. (1962)

Stuart Little

E. B. White   Novel / Children's Literature / U.S.

E. B. White (1899–1985), essayist, editor, illustrator, is perhaps most famous for his children's books. Stuart Little's lonely quest for the "perfect and unattainable" remains a lifetime favorite of anyone who has read it, as do White's other children's classics *Charlotte's Web* and *The Trumpet of the Swan*. (1945)

Sula

Toni Morrison   Novel / U.S.

Nel Wright and Sula Peace grow up together in a small Ohio town. Nell chooses to remain, marry, and raise a family. Sula Peace rejects all that Nel has embraced. (1973)

Summer Tree, The

Guy Gabriel Kay   Novel / Canada

This is the first novel in *The Fionavar Tapestry* trilogy, followed by *The Wandering Fire* (1986) and *The Darkest Road* (1986). Inspired by Tolkein and based on Celtic and Norse mythology, it relays the adventures of five students who find themselves in a world where all myth begins. (1985)

Sunshine Sketches of a Little Town

Stephen Leacock   Novel / Canada

Set in a fictitious small town in Southern Ontario early in the 20th century, these humorous stories are filled with eccentric characters and delightful satire. (1912)

Swimming with the Giants: My Encounters with Whales, Dolphins, and Seals

Anne Collet   Biology

Through her 20 years of studying sea mammals from Antarctica to the Azores to the Arctic, Collet, an impassioned marine biologist, has brought together her depth of understanding and her scientific concern for their future. (2000)

Symbols of Transformation

Carl Gustav Jung   Philosophy

Through comparative mythology and case analysis, Jung forms his theory of the process of symbol formation from archetypes that come from the collective unconscious and play an important role in the life of each individual. (1912)

Tales from the Shawangunk Mountains

Marc B. Fried   Exploration

Subtitled *A Naturalist's Musings—A Bushwhacker's Guide*, this is a collection of adventures, reflections, and remembrances from over 20 years of living in the New York Shawangunk region. (1982)

Tales of the City

Armistead Maupin   Novel / U.S.

Tales of the City is the first of six books of stories written for the *San Francisco Chronicle*. Maupin compellingly describes the comings and goings of the straight and gay boarding house residents at 29 Barbary Lane as they move between heartbreak and happiness. (1978-1989)

Tao of Pooh, The

Benjamin Hoff   Spirituality

While Eeyore frets and Piglet hesitates and Rabbit calculates and Owl pontificates,Pooh just is. This delightful book explains Taoism through A. A. Milne's classic, *Winnie the Pooh*, which he claimed he didn't write for children in the first place. *The Te of Piglet* is a companion volume. (1982)

Tao Te Ching

Lao-Tzu   Sacred Writing

See *Drama, Mythology, Poetry, and Sacred Writing*

Ten Principal Upanishads, The

Sri Purohit and W. B. Yeats, eds. and trans.   Sacred Writing

See *Drama, Mythology, Poetry, and Sacred Writing*

Thin Red Line, The

James Jones   Novel / U.S.

A fictional account of the battle between American and Japanese troops on the island of Guadalcanal in World War II enters the minds of men under the stress of war. (1962)

Things They Carried, The

Tim O'Brien   Novel / U.S.

This collection of short stories is loosely based on experiences of the author and other young men he came to know in the Vietnam War. (1999)

Thorn Birds, The

Colleen McCullough   Novel / Australia

McCullough weaves a story of three generations working and living in the Australian outback. Meggie and a Catholic priest whom she cannot marry share love and sorrow. (1977)

Through the Mickle Woods
Valiska Gregory   Novel / Children's Literature / U.S

In this modern fairy tale, a king whose wife has died comes to an old cave in the Mickle Woods where he hears three stories that give him comfort in his grieving. (1992)

Thus Spake Zarathustra
Friedrich Wilhelm Nietzsche   Philosophy

Nietzsche's Zarathustra is a prophet-figure distantly based on the ancient Persian mystic philosopher Zoroaster. In this book, Nietzsche introduces the Übermensch, or superman, who transcends the limitations of conventional morality and perfects himself during his earthly existence rather than looking forward to an after-life. (1883–1892)

Tibetan Book of Living & Dying
Sogyal Rimpoche   Spirituality

This sourcebook of sacred inspiration from Tibetan tradition includes songs and poetry from Buddhist sages as well as Sogyal Rinpoche's lucid introduction to the practice of meditation, to karma and rebirth, to care and love for the dying, and to the trials and rewards of the spiritual path. (1992)

To the Hilt
Dick Francis   Novel / Britain

Dick Francis' mystery thriller is about a solitary painter, heir to a fortune, who lives alone in Scotland until he is attacked because he is unknowingly hiding a secret. (1996)

Trainspotting
Irvine Welsh   Novel / Scotland

Popular, funny, compassionate, and troubling, this is a compelling series of loosely connected tales about young heroin addicts in an Edinburgh housing development. (1993)

Trinity

Leon Uris   Novel / U.S.

This novel is in part a chronicle of a Northern Irish farm family from the 1840s–1916 and in part a love story about a young Catholic rebel and a Protestant girl who struggle to find peace in war-torn Ireland. (1976) The story is continued in *The Redemption* (1995).

Tuesdays with Morrie: An Old Man, a Young Man, and The Last Great Lesson

Mitch Albom   Philosophy

After 20 years, Mitch Albom, a sports columnist for the *Detroit Free Press*, rediscovers his former mentor and professor Morrie Schwartz. In the last months of the older man's life, Albom visits him every Tuesday, just as he had done back in college, until Schwartz dies. Their rekindled relationship is the basis for this bestseller. (1997)

Twits, The

Roald Dahl   Novel / Children's Literature / Britain

The nasty and nastier Mr. and Mrs. Twit are given their comeuppance in this timeless story. (1980)

Two Thousand One (2001): A Space Odyssey

Arthur C. Clarke   Science Fiction / Britain

Clarke combines technical expertise and remarkable imagination in this best known of his science fiction works from which he wrote the screenplay for Stanley Kubrick's film. A discovery on the moon leads to a manned space adventure assisted by a computer named HAL 9000. (1968)

V for Vendetta

Alan Moore   Novel / Britain

The scene is set in 1992 Britain in an alternate future in which Germany has won World War II. Britian is a Fascist state. A vigilante named V roams London fighting for freedom against the structures of power that keep people fearful and pacified. (1990)

Velveteen Rabbit, The

Margery Williams Bianco   Novel / Children's Literature / Britain

This classic children's book about a toy rabbit's quest to become a real rabbit with all its dangers and excitement is an allegory about how each of us can become real. Set in comic book format. (1922)

Venetian's Wife, The

Nick Bantock   Novel / Canada

A young woman becomes involved in the search for a famous Vedic art collection belonging to a 15th-century Italian adventurer when a man, who will only communicate through e-mail, hires her. The story is told through richly illustrated diaries. (1996)

Virgin and the Gypsy, The

D. H. Lawrence   Novel / Britain

A sensitive rector's daughter in a small English town meets a wild gypsy and finds her world overturned. (1930)

Walking Drum, The

Louis L'Amour   Novel / U.S.

Kerbouchard is a 12th-century hero who wanders through Europe, the steppes of Russia and Byzantium experiencing love, battles, and treachery. (1984)

Way of the Peaceful Warrior

Dan Millman   Autobiography

During his junior year at the University of California, Dan Millman, then training and hoping to become a world-champion gymnast, met his mentor, Socrates, at an all-night gas station. The unpredictable Socrates proceeded to change Millman's life by teaching him the "way of the peaceful warrior." (1985)

Way Past Cool

Jess Mowry   Novel / U.S.

Set in Oakland, California, this realistic novel tells of a truce between rival gangs and a threat by an outsider. (1993)

Weetzie Bat

Francesca Lia Block   Novel / U.S.

In Los Angeles, punk queen Weetzie Bat with Slinkster Dog and her best friend Dirk, drive around in a '55 Pontiac (named Jerry) looking for her "Secret-Agent-Lover-Man." (1989)

Welcome to the Monkey House

Kurt Vonnegut, Jr.   Short Stories/ U.S.

Contemporary author, Kurt Vonnegut, Jr., has a phenomenal appeal across generations with more than a dozen books . This collection of 25 short stories is the ideal introduction to his genius. (1968)

What They Fought for, 1861–1865

James M. McPherson   History / U.S.

A close study of thousands of personal letters and diaries written by soldiers during the Civil War has given McPherson an understanding of the attitudes and motives of ordinary soldiers. (1994)

Wheel of Time, The

Robert Jordan   Science Fiction / U.S.

This internationally popular fantasy series contains vivid descriptions of an imagined world populated with wizards and wise women fighting the Dark Force. (1990–1997)

White Oleander

Janet Fitch   Novel / U.S.

After her mother is sent to prison for committing a murder, young Astrid spends time in a series of foster homes. Her own search for identity is made more difficult by her need to make peace with her mother. (1994)

Whittaker Chambers: A Biography

Sam Tanenhaus   Biography

Chambers was a writer and student at Columbia University when he decided to become a Communist in 1925. This is the story of his career as a spy and his defection in 1938, and his naming of a group of high government officials as fellow spies. (1997)

Winter King, The

Bernard Cornwell   Novel / Britain

A mixture of history and fantasy, this book is about Derfel, a warrior in pre-Norman Britain, who has been trained by Merlin. (1995)

Winterdance: The Fine Madness of Running the Iditarod

Gary Paulsen   Exploration

The Iditarod is a 1150-mile winter sled-dog race between Anchorage and Nome. *Winterdance* is Paulson's account of this 17-day ordeal. (1994)

Wise Child

Monica Furlong   Novel / Children's Literature / U.S.

A young Scottish girl is born into luxury and abandoned by her parents. After her grandmother's death, she is taught by a white witch and learns the secrets of herbal healing, astronomy, mathematics, Latin, the value of hard work, and the reality that all things are interconnected. (1987) The prequel to this novel is *Juniper*.

Witch of Blackbird Pond, The

Elizabeth George Speare   Novel / U.S.

Young Kit Tyler comes from Barbados to colonial Connecticut. When she befriends a widow thought to be a witch, townspeople begin to suspect her a witch. A Newbery Prize-winning novel. (1959)

Woman in White, The

Wilkie Collins   Novel / Britain

An early novel of sensation, a precursor to the thriller and detective novels of the 20th century, this tale contains all of the elements of mystery: guilty secrets, lurid descriptions, and wild events. (1860)

Women's Room, The

Marilyn French   Novel / U.S.

French's highly successful novel about women's issues is seen as a landmark in feminist understanding. (1977)

World According to Garp, The

John Irving   Novel / U.S.

Hilarity and tragedy is indescribably mixed in the story of the illegitimate son of a feminist who develops, as we all do, his own system of survival. (1982)

World of Wonders

Robertson Davies   Novel / Canada

See *Fiction*

Youth in Revolt

C. D. Payne   Novel / U.S.

Nick Twisp, the central character in this exhilarating and very funny novel, has been called a modern Holden Caulfield (from *The Catcher in the Rye*). Through his adolescent diary, we learn about every aspect of his confusing life as we sympathetically enjoy his bewilderment. (1993)

ACKNOWLEDGMENTS

Ever since I published my first title, *Waldorf Student Reading List*, a small book for elementary school teachers and parents, I have looked forward to producing one for the high school level. This inspiring collection was created through the generosity and commitment of the faculty and staff from the many participating schools. Soliciting the summer and outside reading lists and the curriculum materials from each school was a monumental task. I am especially grateful to those dedicated people who collected the material from the teachers and staff. Even as the students moved through the grades, they kept us informed of changes in the lists and curricula.

My co-editor, John Wulsin, committed himself to this project with enthusiasm in spite of his own demanding schedule. He established the substantial network of school contacts and wrote the introductory article on reading. As the project progressed, he organized workshops and focus groups with colleagues at teacher conferences. I am especially indebted to him for his advice on the appropriate grade levels and subject categories for each book title. His patience and reliability were invaluable.

It's one thing to have a list of books, but each title really needs a description to entice the reader to explore further. Lynne Laffee, a former English teacher from Newburyport High School, wrote the annotations of the Native American titles.

My second co-editor, Anne Greer, joined us at the suggestion of David Mitchell. She assumed the enormous task of turning the salient points of each book's contents into brief annotations. She was undaunted as the list grew from 850 to almost 1500 titles. What an extraordinary woman! In addition to that challenge, she also wrote the *Reader's Road Map* introducing each section. Thanks to her talents, even the most reluctant readers will be inspired. I treasure our friendship.

Meg Gorman's *Foreword* is one of the jewels of this book. Her passion and energy is boundless whether she is working with her students, parents, or colleagues. Mention one title and three hours later she will still be telling you about "just one more." Attending one of her workshops makes one want to go right back to school or run to the library. Working with all these outstanding teachers has been "awesome" — to quote the youth! They are devoted to teaching young adults and are always interested in helping anyone find just the right book at the right time!

Past and present colleagues from the Association of Waldorf Schools of North America (AWSNA) together with the Waldorf Teacher Education Colleges offered support right from the beginning. I was especially grateful that Christy and Henry Barnes were eager to help by offering their personal favorites from their decades of teaching. Our peer reviewers included Marianne and David Alsop, Donald Bufano, Jeanne Elliot, Douglas Gerwin, Catherine Greenstreet, Ina Jaenig, René Querido, Howard Schrager, and Betty Staley. Each offered significant commentary. Betty's early work with high school curriculum development inspired me to launch this project. We appreciate her collegiality and her endorsement of our work.

Thank you to those in the focus groups: Kathy Burnetta, Joan Congdon, Susan Demanett, Alba Lucia Diaz, Mary Echlin, Meg Gorman, Andrew Levitt, Alix Lowethal, Robin Masciocchi, and Patricia Sexton. Their confidence and excitement in the project spurred us on. Other contributors included Ruth Pittman, Patricia Ryan, David Sloan, Jacqueline Stern, and Jon Wright. I welcomed the interest of publishers Michael Dobson and Claude Julian. Thank you to Books for the Journey in Victoria, Australia for permission to use their name in our title. My heartfelt thanks go to Katrina Kenison for her generous testimonial. She inspires many readers with her own endeavors as a parent, author, and editor.

Many reference librarians and bookstore staffs were invaluable. They made suggestions for categories, shared school reading lists, mentioned personal favorites, and directed us to a variety of resources. Thanks go to the staff at Widener Library of Harvard University, Boston Public Library, and the Merrimac Valley Library Consortium, especially in Amesbury and Newburyport, MA. Margie Shepherd offered her expertise as the Amesbury's Young-Adult Librarian. And what would we have done without the World Wide Web!

Even editors sometimes need an editor, especially as the project nears completion. My friend Nancy Parson assumed this role with equanimity and considerable interest and skill. She also deserves full credit for creating the concept of the *Reader's Road Map*. She and Bob Lathe also keep my website running smoothly.

The day-to-day support is always critical. My assistant, Zahava Fisch ably handled so many details that I'm sure I'll forget a few: entering data, researching titles and authors, endless proofing, together with tracking my other publishing projects. I am grateful that she knows this book backwards and forwards. Tuck Moss, my friend and Macintosh wizard, patiently offered his long distance technical support. I could not have produced this book without copyeditor Susan Conger and three design consultants. Thanks go to Dale Hushbeck for the original cover concept; Mary Coburn of Z de Zigns for her graphic expertise; and Mayapriya Long of Bookwrights for putting it all together to create our book. Mayapriya's professional expertise transformed our complex digital files and graphics into an outstanding product. In addition, I am personally grateful for the patience, style, and grace that she brings to her artistry.

And of course there's my marvelous family: two of my daughters, Gillian and Francesca, as well as my twin sister, Penelope, stepped in during critical editing periods to review and offer fresh perspectives. And to my unendingly patient husband, Paul, who never questioned why I was buried in my office so many weekends and evenings this past year, I give my love. I am blessed that he instinctively knew when to take me for a walk or out for dinner. We're both looking forward to gardening and going to the beach.

Happy reading —

Pamela Johnson Fenner

The Waldorf High Schools who participated in this project included schools in the following cities: Austin (TX), Chicago (IL), Denver (CO), Honolulu (HI), Kimberton (PA), Lake Champlain (NY), Lexington (MA), Portland (OR), Sacramento (CA), San Francisco (CA), Saratoga Springs (NY), Vancouver (BC, Canada), Toronto (ONT, Canada), and Washington (DC).

Additional Waldorf Schools include: East Bay (CA), Emerson (NC), Green Meadow (NY), Garden City (NY), Hartsbrook (MA), Hawthorne Valley (NY), Hazel Wolf (WA), High Mowing School (NH), Highland Hall (CA), Rudolf Steiner School (MI), Rudolf Steiner School (NY), Shining Mountain (CO) Summerfield School and Farm (CA), Tara Performing Arts High School (CO). Watershed High School (Waldorf Methods Charter) (MN), and Youth Initiative High School (WI). Information about these and other Waldorf schools can be found on these websites: *www.awsna.org* and *www.bobnancy.com*.

THE EDITORS

PAMELA J. FENNER

Pam grew up in a large family in a small New England town. After receiving a B.S. in Biology from Chatham College, Pittsburgh, PA, she completed a Master of Arts in Teaching Science (MAT) from Harvard University, Cambridge, MA. She taught science in two public schools.

During 21 years in northern California, Pam worked as a childbirth educator; marketing assistant for an arts organization; and as a grade 1–3 assistant. While her youngest child attended Marin Waldorf, Pam completed her Waldorf Teacher Education. She worked at two Waldorf schools in community development. Returning to her hometown in Massachusetts, she published three books and helped start a Waldorf school in Eliot, ME. She occasionally consults to schools. *Books for the Journey* is her fourth book.

ANNE J. GREER

Anne has taught adolescents and young adults for 36 years, 18 of which at the Toronto Waldorf School in Canada. Her two daughters attended Waldorf schools from Kindergarten through Grade 12. Anne's education includes a B.A. from Mount Allison University, Sackville, New Brunswick; B.Ed. from Dalhousie University, Halifax, Nova Scotia; and an M.A. from Acadia University, Wolfville, Nova Scotia.

Desmond Gross

In 1998, Anne retired from full-time teaching to live with her husband beside the ocean in Nova Scotia. She consults to Waldorf High Schools, writes articles about working with adolescents, and occasionally teaches.

JOHN H. WULSIN, JR.

Maureen Hayslip

John grew up in Cincinnati, Ohio and completed his Waldorf Teacher Education at Emerson College, England. He completed a B.A. in English at Harvard College, Cambridge, MA and taught for four years in two non-Waldorf independent high schools.

John has been teaching English and Drama for 22 years at Green Meadow Waldorf School, from which his children have graduated. With an M.A. in English and American Literature from Columbia University, NY, he has also taught Poetics to adults of the Eurythmy School of Spring Valley, NY. He teaches at the Waldorf High School Teacher Education program at Rudolf Steiner College in Fair Oaks, CA. He has authored three books and many articles for educational journals.

INDEX

OTHER PUBLICATIONS FROM MICHAELMAS PRESS

• *Waldorf Education: A Family Guide*

P. J. Fenner, ed. $24.95   ISBN: 0-9647832-1-5

#1 introduction to Waldorf Education available. This comprehensive book is a collection of articles describing Waldorf Education—the curriculum, philosophy, history, celebrations and traditions. Perfect book for teachers, parents, libraries, and college classes.

• *Beyond the Rainbow Bridge: Nurturing our children from birth to seven*

Barbara J. Patterson and Pamela Bradley $17.95   ISBN: 0-9647832-3-1

Based on a successful Parent Enrichment class led by an experienced early child-hood teacher who offers us her deep understanding of children, along with seasoned practical wisdom. Readers will learn about healthy rhythms in home and school; what kind of play stimulates imagination; how to protect the child's developing 12 senses; sensible ideas for creative discipline; how to create birthday stories, knot dolls and puppets.

• *Waldorf Student Reading List*

Fenner and River, eds. $8.95   ISBN: 0-9647832-0-7

Includes books appropriate for each grade level, stories to read aloud from pre-school through Grade 8, and specialized lists for science and American history. Used by parents, teachers, and students in Waldorf schools, public and private schools, home schools, bookstores, and libraries.

AMESBURY, MA 01913-0016 USA

Add $4.50 for shipping for each U.S. order
VOLUME DISCOUNTS AVAILABLE

PHONE: 978-388-7066   EMAIL: orders@michaelmaspress.com

FAX: 978-388-6031   URL: www.michaelmaspress.com